Beneath the striking differences between George Eliot and Flaubert, the two great mid-nineteenth-century novelists possess a surprising amount in common. Both writers in their prime works, *Madame Bovary* (1857), and *Middlemarch* (1872), occupy themselves with the inner life and the patterns of illusion of their protagonists to a degree that takes them markedly beyond their contemporaries. Both place much stress on the "drama of incommunicability," or alienation, in their novels, enacting it in the lives of their characters in ways that look significantly toward the twentieth-century novel. Each novelist is profoundly aware of the novelist's own plight and that of the characters as living citizens of a dead universe. The private patterns of illusion cherished by their characters become a subject for absorbed examination—freshly attractive for their warmth and color seen against the chilly, colorless background insisted upon by mid century science. Each has a twofold consciousness, of inner illusion and outer bleakness, so that the lives of their characters are presented in a kind of "binocular vision," a double perspective which views their private experience and aspirations against a running counterpoint of ironic realism. This double vision makes both Flaubert and Eliot pioneers of the modern novel. Both anticipate the art of Henry James, especially *The Portrait of a Lady* (1881), a milestone in the history of psychological narrative.

Professor Smalley's study opens with the temperament, style and outlook of these two pioneers, then proves the psychological affinities of *Madame Bovary* and *Middlemarch*. Her comparison carries on to Flaubert's *A Simple Heart* and Eliot's *Daniel Deronda*.

GEORGE ELIOT AND FLAUBERT

PIONEERS OF THE MODERN NOVEL

BY BARBARA SMALLEY

OHIO UNIVERSITY PRESS : ATHENS

FOREWORD

IT IS UNLIKELY THAT ANY SERIOUS CRITIC WOULD TODAY QUESTION THE importance of George Eliot's place in the development of the modern English novel, still less that of Flaubert in the progress of the French; but no one to my knowledge has thought it worth giving much attention to the similarities that exist between the two authors. The two may seem a pair with little in common. The respects in which they differ are, to be sure, large; but in their separate ways—and with a perhaps surprising amount of similarity beneath the surface—both were pioneers in modern psychological narrative, the process (to paraphrase D. H. Lawrence in regard to Eliot) of putting all the significant action inside the minds of the characters. Both novelists in their prime masterpieces, *Madame Bovary* (1857) and *Middlemarch* (1872), occupy themselves with the inner life of their protagonists to a degree that takes them markedly beyond their predecessors. Both lay much stress on what Victor Brombert, for Flaubert, calls the "drama of incommunicability," enacting it in the lives of their characters (each character beholding the outer world from his unique point of sight) in ways that look significantly toward the twentieth-century novel. Both authors are, at the same time, intellectual children of the mid-nineteenth century, registering in memorable forms and with a poignancy blunted for later novelists their acute awareness of their plight as living citizens of a dead universe, a universe

v

devoid of personality or sensation outside man himself. Such a view is borne in upon them inescapably by mid-century science. Both writers deal with it in the lives of their characters by means of profound correlatives. Human illusions, in a darkened universe, become both freshly attractive for their warmth and color (since warmth and color have finally and totally withdrawn from tenable conceptions of the ultimate outer reality) and freshly ironic, since they stand out against a chilly impersonal background. For both Flaubert and Eliot this twofold consciousness leads to treating the lives of their characters in forms of "binocular vision" (the term is Thibaudet's for Flaubert), a double perspective presenting the private experience and aspirations of their protagonists with a running counterpoint of ironic realism. In both authors this double vision constitutes a factor essential to their narrative art and an important link between them as pioneers of the modern novel. In this, and in other respects that go deep, both anticipate the art of Henry James, particularly James in his first masterpiece, *The Portrait of a Lady* (1881), a further milestone in the history of psychological narrative and another searching study of the forms of human illusion.

A word concerning method: Especially in the separate chapters devoted to *Madame Bovary* and to *Middlemarch* it may on occasion seem that I am keeping to the narrative line of Flaubert and George Eliot unduly—to a degree that involves mere storytelling. A careful reader will, I think, absolve me from the charge. The only way I have found for following Flaubert's and Eliot's particular ways of handling psychological narrative is by tracing their narrative sequences, focusing intensively upon passages that present the interior life of their characters but providing enough of the story to effect a coherent context. My efforts to abstract beyond that point have invariably taken me into what seemed arid and desert territories. Emma Bovary seeking spiritual guidance through the Abbé Bournisien or creating fantasies of elopement journeys with Rodolphe Boulanger needs to be followed intimately for the point to be clear that Flaubert is achieving something new to fiction. So also with Dorothea Brooke, "a child dancing into a quick sand on a sunny morning" (to quote Eliot's friend Barbara Bodichon), a significantly fresh psychological study both in her period of passionate self-drama and in her subsequent period of disillusion and adjustment, finding her bright upper world become a place of baffling walls and airless corridors (as Isabel Archer was in turn to find her reality in James's novel). With Lydgate equally and with Casaubon, Rosamond, and Bulstrode to a lesser extent, the psychological narrative is a central thread but woven inextricably with other strands of the story. I have tried to be stringent with simply narrative links, giving the emphasis to the sort of action that goes on inside the characters.

Both Eliot and Flaubert are pioneers in the art of psychological narrative, but there is, it probably goes without saying, nothing tentative or incomplete about their achievements in the field. Whether Joyce or Proust, representing a far more advanced state of the art, also represents a more satisfying state of it is a question without an answer, though there has been assuredly no dearth of widely differing opinions. They seem in recent years to suggest that, on the whole, pursuing the journey too far inward may take one beyond the best scenery.

Since this book is intended primarily for English-speaking readers, I have presented quotations from the French in translation. My aim as a translator has been somewhat special and differs often from the aim of translators of complete novels of Flaubert's into English. Even when the result is a slightly awkward English phrasing, I have kept as close as I could to Flaubert's own diction and rhythms, providing a freer translation only at places where an attempt at literalness would seriously distort the original rather than render it in English. (Where I have had to resort to phrases that are only roughly equivalent, I have ordinarily supplied Flaubert's French either in brackets or in the notes.) An instance in point where fidelity to the original has seemed more important than grace is my translation of Flaubert's description of Emma's epochal waltz with the Viscount at Vaubyessard, where I have preferred to keep as close as I could to Flaubert's rhythms, which capture something of the incremental effect of the waltz on Emma's consciousness even in the process of the dancing.

My indebtednesses are many, but special thanks are due Professors François Jost, Bruce Mainous, and Harris Wilson for their wise counsel and to the Librarians of the University of Illinois for innumerable services. Above all there is my great debt to Professor Donald Smalley. It is no exaggeration to say that George Eliot, Flaubert, and the modern novel have shaped a large part of our daily conversation for five years. Without his unfailing tolerance and inestimably generous aid at all stages this book could never have attained its present form.

March 19, 1973   Barbara Smalley

CONTENTS

I

THE DUAL WORLDS OF GUSTAVE
FLAUBERT AND GEORGE ELIOT

LOOKING FOR RESEMBLANCES BETWEEN FLAUBERT AND GEORGE ELIOT may strike a reader offhand as likely to be an exercise in misdirected ingenuity. The two are in some ways nearly diametrical opposites. It is true that George Eliot, as V. S. Pritchett observes,[1] has as little of lyrical "madness" in her temperament as any major English novelist; and it is also true that Flaubert, even under the restraints he imposed on himself in *Madame Bovary*, is full of that commodity. There are, however, similarities of importance between these two giants of the nineteenth-century novel. The differences are great, and some of them are illuminating; but at least from the perspective of this book, the similarities go deeper and matter more. Flaubert and George Eliot focus on the intimate patterns of the inner life of their characters with an emphasis unknown in the novelists that preceded them. Though Emma Bovary dominates Flaubert's novel to a greater degree than Dorothea Brooke or the other protagonists of *Middlemarch* dominate that novel, Eliot makes the private worlds of Dorothea Brooke, Edward Casaubon, Tertius Lydgate—even the less intricate experience of Rosamond Vincy-Lydgate—a subject for absorbed inspection. The two novelists are in their separate ways influences of great interest and value for the work of the eminent novelist who was to carry the psychological novel a stage further toward the twentieth century.

1

i. FLAUBERT, GEORGE ELIOT, AND THE CRITIQUES OF HENRY JAMES

The close kinship of Flaubert and James as the progenitors of the modern novel has been a byword (some there are who would say a cliché) of criticism for at least as far back as the appearance of Percy Lubbock's widely influential analyses of *Madame Bovary* and *The Ambassadors* in his *The Craft of Fiction* in 1921. The meaning of George Eliot for James has been less remarked upon, but in the years since F. R. Leavis's emphatic pronouncements in his *The Great Tradition* (1948), it has received considerable attention. Its particular nature figures as a subject of importance in the pages that follow. James, like Flaubert and (to a lesser extent) George Eliot, was a critic as well as a creative artist. His analyses of the work of his two forerunners are, like so much else in the body of his critical writings, valuably suggestive. I am not sure that it would have occurred to him that Flaubert and George Eliot had much in common; it was as supreme exemplars of very nearly opposite qualities that they meant most for him. What he has to say about them as individual creative artists serves helpfully to point up significant differences between them—differences that are large in implication regarding their two special talents, and what James himself learned from them. Making clearer the nature and extent of such differences and drawing heavily on James's own critiques in the process seems a desirable step before going farther into what Flaubert and Eliot may be considered to have in common. Both are pioneers of modern narrative emphases, but they explored this relatively uncharted region as authors of widely and significantly divergent genius.

Flaubert's *Madame Bovary* concentrates with an intensity new to fiction upon the inner life of a single protagonist. Flaubert proceeds in theory (though somewhat less, to be sure, in fact) to compress his materials and to cultivate a meticulously "impersonal" method. His struggle to keep his own personality aloof from the life of his action exacted from him the celebrated "agonies of art" of which he complains so often and so eloquently to Louise Colet, poetess, confidant, at times his mistress, in letters that have become in the history of criticism nearly as well-known as the novel itself. In contrast, George Eliot's masterpiece, *Middlemarch*, is an expansive novel bearing the outward form of the Victorian three-decker (*Middlemarch* actually ran to four slender volumes) so popular in the middle decades of the nineteenth century in England. It is nearly three times the length of *Madame Bovary*, and it carries not only two major movements but three additional plots as well,[2] including, for example, Eliot's substantial study of the inner life of the evangelical banker Nicholas Bulstrode with its intricate but absorbing record of internal debate and rationalization, piety and avarice, devious dealing with himself and with the Lord. Far from attempting to hold herself to an "impersonal" relationship to her dramatis personae, Eliot enters into the intimacies of their lives by way of running commentary. Eliot's method of narration is far more complex, far more given to brilliant irony and second meaning, than all save a few among her earlier critics allowed for; but the narrator provides for her audience *on theory* authorial commentary designed to encourage in her reader sympathetic insight into the private worlds of her characters. The unity of *Middlemarch* is predominantly, as Mark Schorer observes, a "unity of moral scene." More specifically, as another critic has ably though briefly illustrated, *Middlemarch* is a novel of "regeneration through successive disenchantments."[3] *Madame Bovary* is at least equally a novel in which successive disenchantments are intimately viewed as they are experienced by the protagonist; but "regeneration" in the context of *Madame Bovary* would imply ideas as alien to Flaubert's vision of life in a provincial town (*moeurs de province* is Flaubert's subtitle) as they are inherent in Eliot's "Study of Provincial Life" (to quote the subtitle of *Middlemarch*) across the Channel in the county of Warwickshire. The lived moment and its sense impressions attain in Flaubert's novel a sensuous immediacy that Eliot, in her habitual concern for the larger meaning of the moment, rarely achieves or would be likely to wish to achieve. This is not intended to imply that George Eliot for her part fails to see things graphically or to see them as they register themselves in the intimate experience of her individual characters. A fact of importance for this study is that Eliot effected in the English novel an advance in psychological realism comparable, though less widespread in its impact at the time of first appearance, to that Flaubert effected in France or that Henry James was to effect in succeeding decades. "Specificity," "body of particularized life," "freshness of particularity"—phrases that read like variations on James's own famous criterion of "solidity of specification" as the supreme virtue of the novel—are words of a kind figuring with frequency and importance in later twentieth-century criticism of Eliot,[4] even as their counterparts have for a longer period figured large in criticism of Flaubert. Whereas Eliot's powers are often at their best in the extended portrayal of her characters' moral dilemmas, however, Flaubert's powers are often happiest in the sensuous poetry of the isolated moment. The difference in overall effect is very large. From the point of view of a novelist in the English tradition, Elizabeth Bowen remarks (with conscious hyperbole), Emma Bovary is not really a character at all: "She consists in sentiments and sensations, in moments for their own sake."[5] Henry James had much earlier observed the distinction. "It is not in the temper of English vision to see things as M. Flaubert sees them," James wrote in 1876, "and it is not in the genius of the English language to present them as he presents them." But *Madame Bovary* provided for James, writing at the outset of his own career, in the year of the publication of his first novel, *Roderick Hudson*, the sense of lived experience more than any other novel he could remember: "The accumulation of detail is so immense, the vividness of portraiture of people, of places, of times and hours, is so poignant and convincing, that one is dragged into the very current and tissue of the story; the reader himself seems to have lived in it all, more than in any novel we can recall." The intensity of the experience became at last too great to bear and left the reader "overwhelmed with disgust and pity."[6] The critique is curiously divided against itself, as James seems to be in his reactions to the novel. The artist in him relives vividly a major experience at the same time that James the moralist, firmly grounded in the tradition and outlook of the English novel, cannot help feeling that it had been an experience of art of a sort that did not entail moral value sufficient to justify the impact it had had on him. Much later in his own career, in the same year as his *The Wings of the Dove* (1902), James was to assess *Madame Bovary* once more. In his preface for an English translation, James confesses himself an old admirer who dates his devotion to the novel from the time when as a very young person in Paris he had encountered it as it was making an initial appearance in the pages of the *Revue de Paris*. Though he must still complain that Emma Bovary's experience is too small an affair for the immense amount of art expended on her, and judge the moral purpose of the tale inadequate, viewed from the perspective of James's own English-speaking consciousness, James by now is much more intent than he had been a quarter century earlier upon recording the inestimable significance of Flaubert as the "novelist of the novelist" for himself and for other practitioners of the craft of fiction. It is a significance so great, indeed, that James and other novelists who have succeeded Flaubert must acknowledge him as having been indispensable for them: "May it not in truth be said that we practice our industry, so many of us, at relatively little cost just *because* poor Flaubert, producing the most expensive fictions ever written, so handsomely paid for it?" And so James proclaims *Madame Bovary* "absolutely the most literary of novels, so literary that it covers us [later novelists] with its mantle." Flaubert in his masterpiece bears the flag for all writers of fiction intent upon practicing the novel as art. Emma Bovary's inadequacy to the role she plays in the art of the novel notwithstanding, in Flaubert and what he makes by his agonies of art from the experience of a heroine unworthy of him—this commonplace "embodiment of helpless romanticism"—there is still, James avers, "endlessly much to be learned."[7]

In serving as critic for the novels of George Eliot, James encountered no such inadequacy of subject. *Middlemarch*, he had written shortly after its publication in 1872, offered "that supreme sense of the vastness and variety of human life" that only the greatest novels could produce. Nothing for him in all previous English fiction surpassed the reality of the scenes between the physician Lydgate and his wife Rosamond. (Others have experienced this reaction—T. S. Eliot was later to declare that Rosamond in her admixture of weakness and terrible tenacity frightened him more than Goneril or Regan).[8] Such power for realism was the more remarkable in James's eyes because George Eliot's mind was in his judgment predominantly contemplative and analytic. Her natural tendency was toward the abstract, but she had consciously "commissioned herself to be real," and James found the resultant tension between the two impulses in her a fertilizing process that had produced a manner rich and flexible.[9] Some months later James was to express again his admiration for "the magnificent vehicle of the style of *Middlemarch*."[10] It is clear that what James found most to admire in Eliot's style was her genius for rendering fine distinctions in the analysis of human experience and human

5

motive—a field in which James was in turn to achieve such memorable successes. "Of all our English prose-writers of the present day," he had earlier declared on the basis of novels that had preceded *Middlemarch*, "I think I may say, that, as a writer simply, a mistress of style, I have been very near preferring the author of *Silas Marner* and of *Romola*,—the author, too, of *Felix Holt*. The motive of my great regard for her style I take to have been that I fancied it such perfect solid prose. Brilliant and lax as it was in tissue, it seemed to contain very few of the silken threads of poetry; it lay on the ground like a carpet, instead of floating in the air like a banner."[11] Eliot's achievement, as he was to continue to feel, lay in presenting with a remarkable fullness the impression of the vastness and variety of human life. Her works, and especially *Middlemarch*, were to continue to impress him as products of a "magnificent mind, vigorous, luminous, and *eminently sane*."[12] The last word serves as a key. *Middlemarch*, more than any other of Eliot's novels with the possible exception of parts of *Daniel Deronda*, carries "sanity" approximately as far as genius can carry that attribute with it into the territories of art that portrays minds in turmoil. V. S. Pritchett was to recognize a half century later Eliot's special gift for bringing to bear upon the complexities of human experience "the clarifying force of a powerful mind." No other Victorian writer, he concluded, had as much to teach the modern novelist. She was the first of the simplifiers, and her greatest gift was for cutting "moral paths through the picturesque maze of human motive." She was a forerunner of the psychologists, a pioneer investigator into the world of will, a novelist of the "idolatries of the superego." Her imagination was, however, essentially prosaic. What she lacked for rising to still higher levels of art, as Pritchett saw it, was "madness."[13]

The sort of madness that Pritchett had in mind was so much at work in Flaubert that his problem was to keep it under anything like control. He had vowed to do so in *Madame Bovary*, yet even there it is an essential quality of the novel's greatness. Flaubert's prose at its best has learned, as Edmund Wilson says, "to hear, see and feel with the delicate senses of Romanticism at the same time that Flaubert is disciplining and criticizing the Romantic temperament."[14] Moreover Flaubert, in a variety of remarkable images such as that of the organ grinder of Tostes, the fantastic many-tiered wedding cake, the waltz at Vaubyessard, the blind beggar who sings at the moment of

Emma's death, writes in a way that does not have much to do with the medium of rational discursive prose but has a great deal to do with a special province of the poetic imagination—a "peculiar phantasmagoric quality," to quote Wilson[15]—to be cultivated more consistently by the Symbolists in a later generation, as it was already by Flaubert's friend Baudelaire. *Madame Bovary* differs greatly from *Middlemarch* in this respect—perhaps more markedly than in any other.

Henry James the critic, writing in the years before the creation of his own novels, seems to a large extent unaware that in dealing with Flaubert and Eliot he is going to school to them as well. *Madame Bovary* could strike him as something amazingly powerful in its effect on the reader, but he dismissed it in his early critique as ultimately a vulgar tale and fortunately a unique achievement that not even Flaubert himself could reproduce. Yet Flaubert had been so strong an influence on the novel in France that James could write in the same critique: "Gustave Flaubert is of the school of Balzac; the brothers De Goncourt and Emile Zola are of the school of Flaubert."[16] There is not much to suggest that he was aware he had himself in subtler ways and primarily under the influence of Flaubert's first great novel sat under the same master. James as critic, as we have seen, had much more to say about the novels of George Eliot. On the one hand he is more unreservedly enthusiastic about them, and on the other he is less willing to see in them a fresh departure in the art of the novel. *Middlemarch* with its multiple plots he pronounced an "indifferent whole," even though it was splendid in style and a veritable "treasure house of detail."[17] The phrase is suggestive, for if Henry James among critics of George Eliot shows, as F. R. Leavis maintains, a "finer intelligence than anyone else,"[18] the dictum requires qualifying as W. J. Harvey qualifies it at some length to show the degree to which James read the novels creatively, revealing the "frustrated artist" in his formative years often showing through the judgments of the critic, making the "criticized thing his own." Harvey maintains it is no accident that James in the period 1880–1890, the years of *The Portrait of a Lady*, *The Bostonians*, *The Tragic Muse*, and *The Princess Casamassima*, is "much more like George Eliot than like any modern novelist."[19] James hailed Dorothea Brooke as the "great achievement" of *Middlemarch*, but he was not satisfied with what

George Eliot had managed to do with her. Dorothea was more memorable than the part she was allowed to play and "altogether too superb a heroine to be wasted."[20] Some eight years after this critique, in *The Portrait of a Lady* (1881), James paid George Eliot the ultimate acknowledgment of modeling his own heroine Isabel Archer to a remarkable degree according to the patterns of Eliot's own heroines and especially Dorothea Brooke—so much so that Leon Edel, James's eminent biographer and critic, suggests that this early masterpiece of James's can be called "a 'George Eliot novel' written by James in the way he believed she *should* have written."[21] (It is also a 'Flaubert' novel, though Edel does not say so, in the way it concentrates upon and builds itself around the dilemmas of a single central intelligence and in its tendency toward "impersonality" in tone and method.)

ii. George Eliot in the Twentieth Century

Not only James but most other early critics seem to have been unaware of, or unwilling to comment on, the part George Eliot had played in moving toward modern psychological narrative. A notable exception was Edith Simcox, later a friend and sometime confidant of the author, who proclaimed at once the revolutionary qualities of *Middlemarch* underlying its conventional aspects. Eliot's new novel, she announced unequivocally in the *Academy* (1 January 1873), marked an "epoch in the history of fiction." It drew its incidents as no novel before it had done from the internal life of its characters and presented in the form of fictional narrative what amounted to a "profoundly imaginative psychological study."[22] Leslie Stephen (father of Virginia Woolf) a few years later commented appreciatively on the singular power of Eliot's analysis of Lydgate's nature and the power with which she traced his engulfment in the tentacles of his awesomely ego-centered wife, "like a swimmer sucked down by an octopus."[23] At the turn of the century W. C. Brownell could declare George Eliot the chief of the "psychological novelists" and likely to hold that position in the face of the claims of Henry James, for all his intricate subtleties and delicate nuances. *Middlemarch*, Brownell believed, was still the favorite novel among intellectual readers,[24] though he offers his comment tentatively.

It was the novelists themselves rather than the critics who, in the first decades of the twentieth century, were most aware of the part George Eliot had played in the development of psychological fiction. Early in his career D. H. Lawrence singled out George Eliot as the first English novelist to start "putting all the action inside," and declared the decided value of her work for his own.[25] Marcel Proust's enthusiasm for Eliot began apparently even in his boyhood.[26] *The Mill on the Floss*, with its extended and sensitive exploring of childhood, was a book that Proust read over and over; and if André Maurois is right, Proust learned much from the opening chapter of *The Mill on the Floss* in shaping his early plans for *Remembrance of Things Past*.[27] There is evidence that Proust was familiar with other of Eliot's novels, and especially *Middlemarch*. Edmond Jaloux maintains that Eliot's memorable analysis, unparalleled in earlier literature, of the gradual disintegration of Tertius Lydgate was especially valuable for Proust in his forming his own concept of time, and sees the meaning of Eliot for Proust as important in both extent and depth.[28] Virginia Woolf in a sympathetic essay of 1919 praised the special qualities of *Middlemarch*, George Eliot's "magnificent" masterpiece, at a time when critics as well as readers were still generally blind to its particular claims to excellence. It was, Miss Woolf affirmed, "one of the few English novels written for grown-up people."[29]

David Cecil, writing in 1935, was possibly the earliest of critics to present at some length George Eliot's qualifications for being considered (in England) "our first modern novelist." Cecil concedes that Eliot follows in part traditional practices (James had six decades earlier decided that *Middlemarch* had taken the development of the "old-fashioned English novel" as far as it could go[30]). Eliot employs the traditional formulas that the novel had borrowed from the drama—conflicts in love, marriage, inheritance, and the like—but she employs them with a crucial difference. Her approach to her characters represents a revolutionary advance in the conception of what constitutes significant action suitable for narrative. Her overriding concern is not as with earlier novelists personality as it performs its drama in the outer world but the "psychological elements underlying that personality." Her memorable portrayals are all studies of action that goes on inside the minds of her characters.[31] It is only in more recent years, however, and mainly since the appearance of F. R. Leavis's widely influential *The Great Tradition* in 1948—a book that insists on considering George Eliot a major English novelist, a forerunner of Henry James but a writer of greater stature than James—that *Middlemarch* has been generally accepted as a novel in which the patterns of motive and vision challenge the critic's full alertness. A few months later, and presumably quite independent of Leavis's study, Mark Schorer published an essay that demonstrated the sort of probing analysis of Eliot's subtleties of style and form that has gone on flourishing in more recent years. Schorer demonstrates to what a remarkable extent metaphorical language in *Middlemarch*, much of it implicit rather than self-declaring in its metaphorical qualities, is concerned with the psychological or moral states of the characters.[32] *Middlemarch* is today considered a prime landmark looking toward the modern emphasis in fiction upon the inner life, the private realities, of the characters, a work in which profundity and subtlety of treatment of the inner experience of the characters may be considered with the intensity that has for much longer been accorded to *Madame Bovary*. Donald Fanger can without hesitation pair George Eliot with Flaubert as one of the two major exponents of the " 'normative' ironic realism" that was to establish itself in the fiction of Western Europe in the second half of the nineteenth century—a realism that consciously breaks through the traditional formulas of the novel to concentrate upon human experience in its often anti-romantic reality.[33] Few critics would today question the conclusion of Walter Allen (both novelist and critic) that *Middlemarch* and the Gwendolen Harleth portions of *Daniel Deronda* represent pioneer studies in psychological narrative that for nearly a century have been "part of the climate in which every English novelist has been brought up."[34]

iii. Dividing Realities: The Unshared World

In both *Madame Bovary* and *Middlemarch* the main focus of interest has shifted from traditional scenes of overt action and dialogue as in the theater to exploration of individual patterns of thought and feeling at deeper levels than novelists of an earlier time had considered necessary or perhaps conceivable. "To Don Quixote," J. Hillis Miller observes, "the windmills are giants, to Emma Bovary Rodolphe is the fulfillment of her romantic dreams, and for Henry James the novel presents not facts but someone's interpretation of them." The movement has been from "once objective worlds of myth and romance into the subjective consciousness of man." The romantic vision continues to exist, but it has become a reality only as a fact of someone's particular form of consciousness. "The drama has all been moved within the minds of the characters, and the world as it is in itself is by implication unattainable or of no significance. Love, honor, God himself exist, but only because someone believes in them."[35] Both Flaubert and Eliot are in an important sense intellectual artists of the mid-nineteenth century with a profound and profoundly disturbed underlying awareness of a world in which customs and channels of thought once considered aspects of a shared and relatively stable world view are no longer possible. It was one thing for an author of the Enlightenment, or even of succeeding decades through the early part of the nineteenth century, to write of a society that was still made up of people living more or less in the manner of their forefathers and holding common assumptions based on a long tradition. *Middlemarch* is in theory set in 1830–32, and the dramatis personae would in the main have felt little impact from the revelations of science or the invasions of the Industrial Revolution into the nature of their lives in a provincial town. In actuality, however, with George Eliot as with Flaubert, the writer's exploration of human personality is eminently and distinctively from a mid-century perspective. Emma Bovary in her successive frustrations, blindly searching for fulfillment in the outer world that will verify her romantic visions, is in important ways a correlative for her creator's own sense of futility and frustration. Dorothea Brooke (or Hetty Sorrel nearly two decades earlier) finds herself suddenly faced with dilemmas without apparent solutions in a world that has without warning become alien and impersonal. George Eliot had undergone a more gradual but equally painful discovery of dark labyrinths where she had once confidently assumed there were sunlit pathways. Both Flaubert and George Eliot counterpoint inner vision and discordant outer reality in a distinctive manner that becomes a major fact in their novels, a fact that dominates to a marked degree the way in which both writers anticipate later developments in psychological narrative.

Gustave Flaubert, the product of a household in which the mother was a traditional French Catholic and the surgeon father was an intellectual and free-thinker, was even in his youth subject to dramatic contrasts in attitude. He was baptized in the Church, but there is no record of his having taken his First Communion.[36] By 1840, at the age of eighteen, he was recording in his intimate notebook sentiments that seem curiously divided in the sort of world view they imply: "Never will man know the Cause, for the Cause is God; he knows only successions of phantom Forms; a Phantom himself, he runs among them, tries to catch them, they flee; he runs after them, back and forth, stops only when he falls into the absolute void, then he rests." And immediately below this with only a paragraph indentation: "Miracle, in religion, is an absurdity—it has importance only in the brains of philosophers." And on the page following: "I want Jesus Christ to have existed, I am sure that he did—why? Because I find the mystery of the passion the most beautiful thing in the world."

George Eliot's change from the faith of her youth to the painful acceptance of agnosticism in her maturity was something less visceral and more concerned with the movement of western thought than was Flaubert's; but for the better understanding of the reactions of both it may be well to recall briefly what had happened to the world view of writers and many other intellectuals by the middle of the nineteenth century.

Even in the eighteenth century, the idea of a deity in the theistic sense, an answering presence in the universe, had been rejected by the Encyclopedists in France and by the empirical philosophers of England. The potential poignancy of such a view and its implications did not, however, seem to impress either philosophers or poets by any means as much as did an exhilaration over the new freedom from the untidiness of outmoded superstitions and the splendors of the fresh new vision of universal order. Isaac Newton in 1713 could write feelingly of "this most beautiful system of the sun, planets and comets" which "could only proceed from the counsel and dominion of an intelligent and powerful being." Such a being ought not "to be worshipped under the representation of any corporeal thing," but Newton apparently did not feel that such sentiments were inconsistent with his being a devout Christian.[37] Pope could celebrate a deistic view of the universe in his *Essay on Man* (1733-34) without assuming that he was in any serious way endangering his position as a Roman Catholic author. Later in the century Gibbon, Tom Paine, and many other English intellectuals could treat theism as an absurdity, and in

France Holbach could wax enthusiastic about a universe that was capable of being accounted for in terms of matter and motion, offering for man's contemplation "nothing but an immense, an uninterrupted succession of causes and effects."[38]

With the early years of the nineteenth century the Romantic authors of England generally assumed the existence of a spirit that pervaded all nature. Shelley, to be sure, was fascinated with electricity as a branch of science but saw in it mainly a magnificent and many-faceted symbol for his sense of a universe governed by a Platonic or Neo-Platonic oversoul. In France, novelists and poets wrote without any strong sense that science was progressively revealing data with sinister implications about personality, human or divine, or the validity of a romantic view of man. Writers appear largely to have accepted as still valid the assumption that the human consciousness was in one way or another a microcosm of a master consciousness that ruled the universe and gave it its laws. The romantic conception of man as essentially heroic, the compelling protagonist in the middle of a universe that was his stage, is seen at its extreme expression in such a drama as Byron's *Manfred,* where the protagonist through the sheer effort of his human will defies the spirits of air and earth and masters all the powers of the elements. In the end Manfred, indeed, very nearly proves a match for Satan himself; for the impression is that the Arch Devil in person—no minor official of the netherworld—has arrived to claim him. Significantly, Manfred dismisses the Abbot of St. Maurice who comes in the final scenes to plead with him to accept traditional religion and look to the Church for his defense as simply irrelevant for the lonely confrontation he must soon experience. Only somewhat less ebullient in their romantic egoism are such heroes as Goethe's Werther, Hölderlin's Hyperion, Chateaubriand's René, Shelley's hero in *Alastor,* or, to be sure, Shelley's Prometheus, who, though in some ways a self-denying personage, is seen at the very center of the forces of a universe alive with personality.[39]

But scientists, and especially astronomers, geologists, and biologists, were beginning, even while the majority of the poets and novelists more or less ignored them, to accumulate a devastating array of data for lowering the artist's estimate of his own or his protagonist's importance in the universe. As early as 1833, Thomas Carlyle in *Sartor Resartus,* his veiled spiritual autobiography, had expressed under the guise of his German protagonist, Professor Teufelsdröckh, the terrible sense of man's isolation that had come over him under the influence of the mechanists. The universe, it had struck him with overwhelming force, "was all void of Life, of Purpose, of Volition, even of Hostility." Outside himself, the one sentient point in all its waste places, the universe had become "one huge, dead, immeasurable Steam-engine, rolling on, in its dead indifference, to grind me limb from limb." Loneliness was at the heart of his terror: "Why was the Living banished thither companionless, conscious?" So appalling was his feeling of alienation that he would have preferred a universe inhabited by an evil force rather than by no personality at all: ". . . nay, I often felt as if it might be solacing, could the Arch-Devil himself, though in Tartarean terrors, but rise to me, that I might tell him a little of my mind."[40] By the mid-nineteenth century, writers of poetry and fiction were more and more feeling the impact of such a vision of a blind universe running of its own inertia. Tennyson in *In Memoriam* (1850), like Carlyle, was to record his impressions of a universe devoid of personality other than his own; and, like Carlyle, who provided in *Sartor* an eventual "Everlasting Yea" to succeed his "Everlasting No," was to portray the period of his agonized doubt more graphically than the period of tentative faith that was to follow. Early in *In Memoriam*, Sorrow, "Priestess in the vaults of Death," whispers to the persona of the poem that there is no personality directing the course of the stars:

> 'The stars,' she whispers, 'blindly run;
> A web is wov'n across the sky;
> From our waste places comes a cry,
> And murmurs from the dying sun: . . .'

But, Sorrow continues, all the speaker hears is actually the echo of his own voice ricocheting from dead planets in the vast sepulchre of the universe, the vaults of Death. Along with such experience of isolation in a sepulchral cosmos went an awareness of the origin of human life as animal rather than spiritual, a portion of nature "red in tooth and claw" in a world that had always been and would continue to be a stage for battles of one species against another for survival in a pitiless struggle for existence.[41] Flaubert's description of man as a creature

14

who "bleated for the infinite" in vain and could no longer escape from his own wretchedness[42] was a familiar one by the middle of the nineteenth century.

The essential theory of evolution was familiar to the thinking public well before mid-century; but Darwin's *Origin of Species* (1859) gave added authority to the scientists' view through its careful documentation of the war for survival in a world where only the fittest survived, even for the brief moment possible to the individual life. The impact of this vision upon the minds and nerves of literary artists of the next decades often figures graphically in their works. Scientists and philosophers could record their observations in objective terms, but poets and serious writers of fiction must feel their facts upon their pulses. James Thomson in *The City of Dreadful Night* (1874) depicts his narrator looking on as the massive statue of an angel with a sword crumbles bit by bit before his eyes. At the same time the simulacrum of a couchant sphinx, looking blankly toward the future, apparently beholding "nothing in the vast abyss of air," remains intact: "I pondered long that cold majestic face/ Whose vision seemed of infinite void space."[43] A more discursive rendering of the same theme appears earlier in the poem:

> There is no God; no Fiend with names divine
> Made us and tortures us; if we must pine,
> It is to satiate no Being's gall. . . .
> I find no hint throughout the Universe
> Of good or ill, of blessing or of curse;
> I find alone Necessity Supreme. . . .
> A few short years must bring us all relief:
> But if you would not this poor life fulfill,
> Lo, you are free to end it when you will,
> Without the fear of waking after death.

Such reactions to the darkened universe were not confined to the intellectuals of western Europe. Turgenev in *Fathers and Sons* (1862) had through his character Bazarov rendered a prose equivalent. Though arrogant in his knowledge of science and proud of his commitment to the perspective upon human life that he has adopted through its teachings, Bazarov can find reflection upon human destiny a disturbing matter: " 'The tiny space I occupy is so infinitely small

15

in comparison with the rest of space, in which I am not, and which has nothing to do with me; and the period of time in which it is my lot to live is so petty beside the eternity in which I have not been, and shall not be. . . . And in this atom, this mathematical point, the blood circulates, the brain works and wants something. . . . Isn't it hideous? Isn't it petty?' "[44] Tolstoy's Levin in *Anna Karenina* (1878) "had been stricken with horror, not so much at death, as at life, without the least conception of its origin, its purpose, its reason, its nature. The organism, its decay, the indestructibility of matter, the law of the conservation of energy, evolution, were the terms that had superseded those of his early faith." The riddle of his own identity and the fragile hold that the individual human being possesses upon consciousness in a world that is indifferent to either his life or his death in it becomes for him a terrifying obsession: " 'I cannot live without knowing what I am and why I am here. And that I can't know, so therefore I can't live' Levin would say to himself." The thought drives him to the edge of self-destruction: "And Levin, a happy father and husband, in perfect health, was several times so near suicide that he had to hide a rope lest he be tempted to hang himself, and would not go out with a gun for fear of shooting himself."[45]

iv. Flaubert: Visions in Counterpoint

Authors and many other intellectuals sought various ways—ranging from the way of the Church to the exotic escapism of Gautier—of coping with the chill picture of life and matter that science had documented and insisted upon. The French Symbolists were to solve the problem for themselves by simply rejecting the scientists' cosmos and creating an arbitrary world of their own in art.[46] This was in part Flaubert's own resort—a turning aside from trying to find order in the total universe to find a fierce absorption in creating order as a sort of demigod or God-substitute in a microcosm of his own making. "Yes," he wrote Louise Colet while he was composing *Madame Bovary*, "I maintain (and this should be a dogma in the life of an artist) one must carry on his existence in two parts: to live like a bourgeois and to think like a demi-god. Physical and intellectual pleasures have nothing in common. . . . If you seek happiness and beauty at the same time, you will obtain neither the one nor the other, because beauty comes only after sacrifice. Art, like the Jewish God, feeds on burnt offerings. . . . Art is vast enough to demand possession of the entire man" (C, III, 305–306).

But Flaubert was too much a realist to find such escape effective. The consciousness of outer darkness on the other side of his studio window would penetrate his world of art. It is this awareness of two worlds, the world of private experience and the world of scientific reality, and of the fact that his characters like himself must for better or for worse live in both, that goes far to determine both the subject and the manner of *Madame Bovary*.

Flaubert's correspondence abounds in passages suggesting his frequent gloomy consciousness that for mid-nineteenth-century man, the universe no longer held its former benign aspect:[47] "I find that man is more of a fanatic than he ever was," he writes Louise Colet in May, 1852, "but now he is fanatical about himself. He sings only of himself, and his thoughts, which once leaped beyond the suns, devoured space . . . now find nothing larger [to focus on] than this misery of his real life, which they formerly tried incessantly to escape" (C, II, 414). Flaubert was probably already aware of scientific theories that allowed the life-giving sun itself only the status of a deteriorating or "dying" star—an awesome symbol, as Tennyson had employed it, for the futility of man's hopes for immortality. "The monks hope in vain," Flaubert was later to write; "the sun is not on their side, because nothing is eternal, not the sun itself. And we, poor little particles of dust, [are] tiny vibrations of an immense movement, lost atoms!" (C, V, 260). "Do not rebel against the idea of total oblivion," Flaubert wrote in another letter. "Invoke it rather! Those who are like us must have a religion of despair. One must be on a level with destiny, which is to be impassive like itself. By force of repeating to oneself 'It is so, it is so' and by contemplating the black emptiness one becomes calm" (C, IV, 341).

Flaubert is not, on the other hand, so regularly given to pessimism and resignation as such passages might imply. For Flaubert also experienced, perhaps especially at the time of *Madame Bovary*, whether they were directly connected to brief periods of creative triumph or not, moments of an almost Shelleyan sense of the glory of existence. "Sometimes (in my best days in the sun [*dans mes grands jours de soleil*])," he wrote Colet, "in a glow of enthusiasm that made my skin

17

tingle from my heel to the roots of my hair, I have had glimpses of a state of mind so superior to ordinary life that compared to it fame would be nothing and happiness itself of no consequence" (C, II, 395). That Flaubert continued to feel the attractions of such moments, regardless of what his reasoning processes told him of the absurdities of believing in them, is suggested by the ending of the final version of his *The Temptation of Saint Anthony*.[48] Here he presents, as the closing scene of his drama, the cruel dialectic between the two irreconcilable visions that obsess his protagonist—and certainly to an extent (as Flaubert was to confide to Louise Colet) the author as well.[49] Overcome by his spiritual laborings, Saint Anthony falls to the ground with a despairing cry that after all there is "Matter, nothing but matter." But even as he says this, the sun rises with a great glory. Facing the risen sun at this crisis of his life, Saint Anthony experiences a moment of beatific vision:

> Day appears at last, and, like the lifting of
> curtains within a tabernacle, clouds of gold,
> unrolling in great folds, reveal the sky.
> In the midst, in the very disk of the sun,
> shines forth the face of Jesus Christ.
> Anthony makes the sign of the cross and once
> more takes up his prayers.
>
> (The End)[50]

Conflicts of impulse and attitude continued to be part of Flaubert's experience as he worked on *Madame Bovary*. "I am turning toward a kind of aesthetic mysticism (if the two words can be used together)," he wrote Colet in September, 1852, "and I wish it were stronger." Sensitive people, disgusted with the age, might well, he felt, return to cultivating mysticism, as in other dark ages. "But, lacking any theological foundation, what will be the basis of this enthusiasm, which is so ignorant of its own self?" (C, III, 16–17). As for Flaubert himself, he could inform Colet some months later that even in the moment in which he was writing the sound of church bells was sending him into "Catholic raptures" and inciting in him the urge to go to confession! (C, III, 156). In *Salammbô*, the novel that was to follow *Madame Bovary*, intensely lyrical passages are interspersed with passages of the most brutal realism—scenes of battle, catalogues of objects extolling in a sort of autohypnotic prose poetry their sensuous appeal, pagan religious rites performed with extremes of orgasmic fury and sadism. In many ways *Salammbô*, as critics have so often observed, seems to celebrate the exuberant unleashing of Flaubert's romantic self after its years of bondage to the discipline he had imposed upon it in creating *Madame Bovary*. There is not much in *Salammbô* to parallel the ironic counterplay of inner romantic vision with realistic detail of village life that forms so prominent a feature of the novel that preceded it. "*Moeurs de province*," the second title of *Madame Bovary*, would sound alien indeed in the world of the Carthaginian priestess of the goddess Tanit, Salammbô, who, after the death by torture of the magnificent Libyan giant Mathô, dies of grief for the demise of this former enemy who had become her passionate lover. The dingy affairs of Emma Bovary carried on by stealth in rural retreats or in second-class hotel rooms, are in another world, a world much closer to the one Flaubert must himself inhabit whether he managed to escape it temporarily in moments of creative triumph or Catholic rapture, or whether he resolved to contemplate calmly the black emptiness, repeating to himself, "It is so, it is so."

In *Madame Bovary*, as Edmund Wilson suggests, Flaubert anticipates both Symbolism and Naturalism, and authors as diverse as Valéry and Zola could both claim relationship.[51] A part of Flaubert's nature urged him toward transcendental vision and such gorgeous phantasmagoria as were to figure so uninhibitedly in *Salammbô*, while another part of him restrained such effusions and drove him in the direction of analysis and realism. Even at the outset, Flaubert found that such double vision involved him in "terrifying difficulties of style," so that he suffered greatly. There were in him, he wrote Louise Colet, "two distinct persons: One who is infatuated with bombast, lyricism, great flights of eagles, sonorities of phrase and lofty ideas," while the other "digs and burrows into the truth as deeply as he can, who likes to bring out a little fact as effectively as a big one, who would like to make you feel almost *physically* the things he reproduces . . ." (C, II, 343–344). Suppression of his lyrical self continued to give him much trouble. "A bad week," he wrote a few weeks later (in February, 1852). "In my other books I was slovenly; in this one I am trying to be precise. . . . No lyricism, no comments, the author's personality absent. It will make sad reading; there will be much that is wretched and sordid" (C, II, 361). In a few more weeks, however, he has made progress and now envisions a workable adjustment of his two selves in his writing: "The total value of my book," he writes Colet in March, 1852, "if it has one, will be in my having known how to walk straight forward on a hair, suspended between the twin abysses of lyricism and of vulgarity (which I want to fuse into an analytical narrative). When I think of the possibilities of this, I am dazzled" (C, II, 372).

"Lyricism" led to the splendid prose poetry that characterizes *Madame Bovary*, to the eloquent passages, mainly concerned with Emma's romantic fantasies, that critics have often been inclined to attribute not simply to Flaubert but to the artist soul of Emma Bovary, though the distinction is frequently crucial if one is to see clearly the relation of author and protagonist in this novel. "Vulgarity" figures with almost equal prominence as Flaubert, from his self-enforced perspective, suspended above his twin abysses, balances his portrayal of Emma's romantic fantasy life with his portrayal of the Hogarthian detail of the outer reality of Yonville-l'Abbaye that his realistic (and ironic) self perceives. This double vision, or "binocular vision," to employ a term of Albert Thibaudet's,[52] is an essential fact in the art of *Madame Bovary*. It leads to the major paradox of the novel—Flaubert's (and in turn the reader's) delighted fascination in exploring the intricacies of an undistinguished mind—a mentality that is agile but devoted to small luxuries, self-flattery, idolatrous and uncomprehending worship of what it conceives to be the life of the *haute monde*, a faith, passionate and undiscriminating, in the clichés of sentimental romantic literature. Flaubert is capable of rendering the most banal of his heroine's intimate desires in prose that is often poetry, providing, so to speak, an inspired musical score for a tasteless libretto. Flaubert found that in working up his scenes for *Madame Bovary* he must concern himself with "attentive observation of the most vapid details." His characters had to be "absolutely commonplace" though they must inevitably lose part of their picturesqueness by his necessity of making them speak "in a literary style." It was, he continued in his letter on the subject to Colet, a problem of *interpreting* in language of his own the commonplace thought by means of an artist's resources—of having to write "of ordinary life as one writes history or epic (but without misrepresenting the subject). Sometimes I wonder. *But it is perhaps a great experiment, and very original.*"[53] Flaubert's awareness of the novelty of his subject matter and his special manner of presenting it, balancing inner vision with exterior vulgarity, and of the dazzling possibilities of his experiment, surface in such passages of his correspondence as these, but are present as an undertone to a great many more.

Often in the earlier parts of *Madame Bovary*, Flaubert's ironic counterpointing, even in its juxtapositions of scene with scene, is comic in overtones, as when Emma, staring vacantly out the window of her home in Tostes, sighs for the perfumed life she fancies goes on uninterruptedly in the aristocratic precincts of Vaubyessard, while the barber at the window of his shop across the street sighs for the waste of his talents and dreams of owning a busy shop in the best district of Rouen. Even in the most famous instance of such counterpointing, the *locus classicus* for the technique, in which Rodolphe's practiced clichés for promoting the illusions appropriate to romantic love are interrupted from time to time by earthy phrases from the master of ceremonies at the Agricultural Fair being conducted just below, the overtones are still broadly comic. As the novel progresses, Emma's romantic egoism leads to more and more sinister coloring. Her fantasy of Charles's transforming himself into a famous surgeon terminates in the screams that penetrate the Bovary parlor while the Surgeon Canivet amputates Hippolyte's gangrened leg. The monotonous whining of Monsieur Binet's lathe becomes more and more cosmic in its commentary, unvarying and impersonal, upon the fate of human aspirations. In the end it is Emma herself who offers the ironic commentary when, in her death scene, the blind beggar sings outside her window about a summer day and a young girl's dream of flirtation and love, and Emma sees as her last illusion the hideous face of the blind beggar standing out against the eternal blackness and utters a final "atrocious, frantic, desperate laugh."

v. George Eliot: Correlatives for Outer Darkness

The fascination of tracing the patterns of an intricate but in significant ways a commonplace mind figures with prominence in *Middlemarch* as well, though the differences between the temperaments of

Tertius Lydgate and Emma Bovary are indeed large. The particular sort of "vulgarity" that colors the illusions of Lydgate and impels him into a disastrous marriage with a monolithically commonplace provincial beauty is finely traced, and the ironic juxtapositions of Lydgate's patterns of vision and his exterior reality provide scenes of great interest. Lydgate's "spots of commonness"—as George Eliot was to call them in an extended and important authorial intrusion that shows she is nearly as aware of the fresh possibilities of her particular subject and manner as Flaubert had been of his—are made much of in *Middlemarch*. The subject has added paradox in that Lydgate is not the product of a farm and a provincial town but a gentleman by birth and breeding, the nephew of a baronet, a man who has finished his schooling in Paris. Lydgate's spots of commonness have at least as much to do with arrogance as with hedonism, and his disaster is a death of noble ambition that precedes by a long interval his physical death. One self in the divided spirit of Eliot's scientist-physician reflects Eliot's intense preoccupation with the moral self or, to return to Pritchett's term, the idolatries of the super-ego. George Eliot's study in character closest to the temperament and situation of Emma Bovary does not appear in *Middlemarch* but in *Adam Bede*, her first novel, published in 1859 only two years after *Madame Bovary*.

The absolute self-absorption and hedonism of Emma and Hetty Sorrel of *Adam Bede* render them, despite a number of obvious differences, curiously alike, especially in their fantasy life. Hetty has not had Emma's advantages in schooling and cannot share the excitements of sentimental literature. Without this resource, Hetty pursues a life of romantic illusion by studying her reflection with the aid of two candles placed in brass sockets at the sides of an antique mirror— a mirror blotched with age but possessed of a mahogany base and a frame still showing spots of its original gilding. The implications of narcissism and altar-worship are explored—indeed, they are insisted on. Before the mirror Hetty escapes for the time her life of dairy chores and tendance upon the children of the farm (she is an orphan, motherless like Emma and like her without maternal affection in her own nature). Her fantasies are encouraged by the attentions of the young squire Arthur Donnithorne, a bucolic English equivalent of Emma's Vicomte of Vaubyessard and her Rodolphe Boulanger in one. At her makeshift altar Hetty adds cheap finery to her person and dreams (in a manner not at all unlike Emma's as she turns the pages of the Keepsakes with their engravings of elegant leisure) of transformation into a grand lady, of riding in her own coach, dressing for dinner in brocaded silk and feathers and thin slippers, of being loved by a rich aristocratic gentleman and admired and envied by inferiors. The portrayal has its decided interest, but Eliot has not yet learned to manage such experience with an effective ironic distancing. The author loses part of the life of her material by hovering closely behind her character's shoulder, specifying for the reader the kind of attitude he is to assume—falling short of full effectiveness in the handling of her story, in other words, precisely in an area where Flaubert had already shown himself an innovator of major importance. It is the later part of Hetty's tale that has won the admiration of readers and critics—the episodes of her journey in despair. In these she wanders an outcast among strangers, sleeping in a sheepfold or in woodland, contemplating suicide beside dark pools but without resolution enough for the act itself, abandoning to die the child born during her confused travels, and finally resigning herself in prison to the sentence of death by hanging. Hetty is rescued in a brief episode somewhat out of tune with the realism that distinguishes other parts of this remarkable first novel; but Eliot's exploration of Hetty's experience of a world abruptly turned alien and indifferent to her sufferings is work of a high order. In the dozen years between *Adam Bede* and *Middlemarch* Eliot was to find means of rendering the inner life of more complex victims of romantic egoism. Dorothea Brooke, as George Levine has already pointed out, is in her experience of pathless darkness where she had once expected sunlit high roads very like James's Isabel Archer.[54] Both are portrayed with a quality of ironic double vision that was already possible to Flaubert by the eighteen-fifties but was not to become a fully developed aspect of Eliot's art for another decade.

A half year after the appearance of *Adam Bede*, George Eliot published anonymously in the July issue of *Blackwood's* a tale enacting the terrors of the human mind confronting its own destiny in terms strangely contrasting to the rich realism of her first novel. In this "frightening vision of cosmic evil and meaninglessness,"[55] horror becomes the dominant note. The protagonist, Latimer, is cursed with a gift of prevision which, even in his moment of writing, forces upon

23

him an accurate knowledge of his coming death by suffocation. Even from childhood he has felt an alienation from all persons, including his immediate family. With the discovery that he possesses a preternatural ability to see with precision and clarity places he has never visited in the body, he at first revels in his power; but the implications of such visions—the appalling brevity of the individual human life, the loveless and alienated condition in which men pass their lives—are soon frighteningly manifest to him, and excessive knowledge becomes an agonizing burden. Marriage to a beautiful wife whose contempt for him he cannot avoid knowing opens up new kinds of hostility that the human soul must confront. For Bertha is designed, to quote Knoepflmacher, to represent George Eliot's own "deep fears of the natural world's hostility to ideals, to all conscious striving toward goodness and perfection." Latimer's recurring nightmare of "strange cities, of sandy plains, of gigantic ruins, of midnight skies with strange bright constellations" represents the author's own starkest allegory of the human mind deprived of the veil of illusion, published appropriately in the year of Darwin's *Origin of Species.*

Flaubert in his maturity could still find escape at times into something like the Catholic raptures of his youth—ecstatic reveries that continued to be a part of his experience.[56] For George Eliot's less mercurial temperament, the poetry of her youthful religious experience had to be relinquished once she could no longer find valid grounds for assuming the existence of a spirit in the universe outside her own. The great charm of her humor, and especially the brilliant play of wit that figures as such an important factor in the art of her fiction, pervasive rather than self-declaring, continued with her; but coming to accept unalterable scientific law as the total chill reality of the universe outside herself was for her a process felt along the heart and in the pulses. She was to relive it on intimate terms, providing memorable correlatives for her own deeply felt experience, in the lives of a succession of her characters, from Hetty Sorrel to Maggie Tulliver to Romola to Dorothea Brooke and onward to Gwendolen Harleth. Eliot's most graphic correlatives for confrontation with a darkened universe occur in the record of the last of these, for in the story of Gwendolen, Eliot's balancing ironic vision of *Middlemarch* gives place in crucial scenes to the depiction of hysterical terror induced by exposure to calculated brutality. The portrayal is of great force and memorable; but Gwendolen is a markedly less complex study of the inward life than Dorothea Brooke. Eliot is exploring fresh ways of rendering the clash of inner vision with the reality of a cruelly impersonal world, a reality that in Gwendolen's experience encompasses marriage to a sadist and an all but overwhelming obsession to terminate the relationship by murdering him. James found her a fascinating rendition of the "universe, forcing itself with a slow, inexorable pressure into a narrow, complacent, and yet after all extremely sensitive mind, and making it ache with the pain of the process."[57] This is, with a significant adjustment, an outline for the story of James's own Isabel Archer (Isabel is by no means so "narrow" a nature). It works still better as an outline for *Madame Bovary*. It represents, with the same necessary and important adjustment as for Isabel, the story of Dorothea Brooke, where the incidents as in James's handling have less to do with hysteria or fantasies of overt violence, but portray eloquently the inexorable pressure of an impersonal universe manifesting itself painfully in the consciousness of the young heroine. The author had herself undergone the experience.

vi. George Eliot's Journey into Unbelief

George Eliot was through her teens not only a practising Anglican Christian but an exceedingly pious one. In her early twenties, friendships with the Brays and the Hennells, intellectual families living not far from her in the English Midlands, opened new vistas to her, and she was soon reading widely in books that would have shocked her earlier mentors. She began to question the dogmas in which she had been reared and then to reject them. The first effect of denying her specifically Christian faith was to free her imagination of inhibitions without destroying her strong religious impulses. For a number of years she adopted a pantheistic view of nature not unlike that of Wordsworth's poetry, and if her description is more prosaic than his, her vision in this period seems to have been a joyous one. "There are externals (at least, they are such in common thought)," she wrote in 1842, in the first months of her liberation, "that I could ill part with— the deep blue, glorious heavens, bending as they do over all, presenting the same arch, emblem of a truer omnipresence, wherever we may be chased, and all the sweet, peace-breathing sights and sounds of this lovely earth. These, and the thoughts of the good and great, are an inexhaustible world of delight; and the felt desire to be one in will and design with the great mind that has laid open to us these treasures is the sun that warms and fructifies us."[58] She was apparently still within the period of this world view when, in 1846 in her twenty-seventh year, she completed her translation of *Das Leben Jesu*, David Friedrich Strauss's epochal higher critical life of Jesus. Her real break with her religious view of nature and her adoption of the secular humanism of her mature years seems to have taken place some time shortly before 1852.[59] By then she was an active and influential editor of the *Westminster Review* and closely associated with some of the most important figures in English freethinking circles. She enjoyed close friendships with two of the leading exponents of Comte's Positivism, Frederic Harrison and George Henry Lewes; and in 1854 she became the common-law wife of Lewes.[60]

Rejecting the specific theology of the religion in which she had grown up had been a liberating, even an exuberant, experience. Forsaking the poetry of her belief, her vision of a universe endowed with personality, was to prove, as Matthew Arnold would have warned her a quarter-century later,[61] a more painful step. "The ocean and the sky and the everlasting hills are spirit to me," she could write reassuringly to a friend of her childhood, an evangelical minister, in early 1848, "and they will never be robbed of their sublimity."[62] But that another view of the world was already claiming her at times is suggested by her letter to Sara Hennell a few months later: "Alas for the fate of poor mortals, which condemns them to wake up some fine morning and find all the poetry in which their world was bathed only the evening before utterly gone!" Even the poetry of duty might forsake one for a season, "and we see ourselves, and all about us, as nothing more than miserable agglomerations of atoms—poor tentative efforts of the Natur Princip to mould a personality." Whenever the decisive moment came (if, indeed, there was one), her turn from pantheism to the austere outlook that succeeded was a step that, granted her associates on the *Westminster* and the intellectual climate in which she lived and moved, she could hardly refuse to take. The "highest and best thing," she declared as her settled view later, "is rather to suffer with real suffering than to be happy in the imagination of an unreal good."[63] If we judge from the imagery she chooses in a letter of 1860, her own suffering was genuine and profound. The person endowed with strength of intellect as well as strength of feeling, she writes her friend Barbara Bodichon, must reject the comfort offered by the churches; for the "highest 'calling and election' " is not to look for relief at the expense of clarity of intellect, but rather to "*do without opium* and live through all our pain with conscious, clear-eyed endurance."[64]

Despite all the acclaim awarded Eliot's successive novels, the 1860's, Miriam Allott concludes in an essay devoted to the subject, were her period of deepest gloom and greatest religious travail—a period in which she was exploring for the first time the bleaker aspects of her own lot and that of her fellow inhabitants of a darkened planet in a mechanistic universe.[65] Her works of the 1860's reveal her personal anguish as it passes obliquely into the experience of her protagonists— the loss of childhood faith in Maggie Tulliver, for example, and Romola's struggle to regain her spiritual equilibrium. With *Middlemarch*, Mrs. Allott maintains, George Eliot regains her own balance and rediscovers values in the busy life around her that help to countervail her sense of the grimness of the human destiny, the many frustrations of the present and its ultimate nothingness. Agreeing with nearly everything else in Mrs. Allott's essay, I would nevertheless suggest that it is specifically in *Middlemarch* that George Eliot's own vision of a darkened universe becomes for the first time fully realized in her art. It is in *Middlemarch* (and a major reason for that novel's claim to greatness) that the individual worlds of illusion of her protagonists become an ambitious subject for absorbed analysis. Henry James was not alone in finding in Dorothea Brooke something intensely meaningful beyond the part she occupied in the action. Eliot's artist friend, Barbara Bodichon, pronounced Dorothea the greatest thing Eliot had achieved, though the image it evoked was deeply disturbing. It was the picture of "a child dancing into a quick sand on a sunny morning."[66] Dorothea represents, as a more recent critic suggests, one of the truly memorable embodiments in literature of the collision between the world of inner experience and a dark outer world, anticipating as she does E. M. Forster's Mrs. Moore, and confronting her own version of the Caves of Marabar. She enacts on levels of profound meaning humanity's baffled confrontation with the "mocking rhythm of a wider, but impersonal and alien, natural order."[67] Tertius Lydgate, Edward Casaubon, Nicholas Bulstrode also reveal, each in his individual way, a remarkable new depth in George Eliot's portrayal through correlatives of her own experience of transition from a warmly lighted private world to a crisis of loss and bafflement. It was on the basis of his reading of *Middlemarch* that Frederic Myers, a Fellow of Trinity College, Cambridge, wrote George Eliot thanking her as one who had come to terms with the world of fact but who could, despite having been forced to surrender her faith, still make life seem noble in its potentialities.[68] Eliot's visit to Cambridge in May, 1873, provided the material for Myers's well-known description of his conversation with her in the Fellows' Garden. Gordon Haight warns against taking this account with its heightened tone overseriously. With allowances made, however, it seems worth quoting in part as suggestive of Eliot's darker view in the period of *Middlemarch*. Eliot as they walked spoke with great earnestness about "*God, Immortality, Duty* . . . how inconceivable was the *first*, how unbelievable the *second*, and yet how peremptory and absolute the *third*." Myers underwent, he tells us, a moment of stark epiphany. It seemed to him that he was gazing in a final twilight of the world on "vacant seats and empty halls,—on a sanctuary with no Presence to hallow it, and heaven left lonely of a God." *Middlemarch* is indeed in the experience of its protagonists a kind of hybrid, though a great one. It is in its way eminently a religious novel but, as Mark Schorer has observed, it is a "novel of religious yearning" deprived of "a religious object."[69]

vii. *Madame Bovary* AND *Middlemarch*: TWO VERSIONS OF ROMANTIC EGOISM

George Eliot's idiom is not Flaubert's, and discursive wit plays a much greater part in it. There is nothing in Eliot's manner quite like Flaubert's juxtaposition of scene with scene for implicit and "impersonal" commentary,[70] as in his playing in parallel with our vision of Emma, sighing at the window of her home for the gilt and perfume of Vaubyessard, a vignette devoted to the barber across the way sighing for a fashionable shop in Rouen; nor is there anything in Eliot quite like Flaubert's fantastic prose lyric detailing the absurd non sequiturs of ornament that make the monstrous wedding cake of Charles and Emma into a masterpiece of ironic commentary. Eliot is,

however, with Flaubert, a psychological realist possessed of a remarkable gift for "binocular vision," an aspect of her genius that
though it for long went all but unrecognized is one that must figure
with prominence if we are to enter far into the particular nature of
her handling of illusion in her novels. Both writers have a compelling
sense of the dialectic going on, in their own experience and in the
experience of other human beings, between two worlds—the world
of warmly personal vision and the world of cheerless objectivity—
that each individual must perforce inhabit. In both *Madame Bovary*
and *Middlemarch* the romantic egoism of the main characters becomes a motif of major importance. In *Middlemarch*, George Eliot
employs for the individual ego and its unique perspective on the
world a particular symbol, the abraded mirror and the candle, that
appears in numerous and often oblique variations throughout the
novel. It is most directly (and perhaps most prosaically) presented in
application to the commonplace but tenacious egoism of Rosamond
Vincy. A pierglass or a polished steel surface, Eliot tells us, will when
subjected to frequent rubbing, as by a housemaid, become multitudi-
nously scratched, so that the little scarcely perceptible lines run in all
directions without a pattern of their own; "but place now against it a
lighted candle of illumination, and lo! the scratches will seem to arrange themselves in a fine series of concentric circles round that little
sun." Flaubert would have ended there and let the image do its own
work; but it is not Eliot's manner to do so: "These things are a
parable. The scratches are events, and the candle is the egoism of any
person now absent—of Miss Vincy, for example."[71] "We are all of us
born in moral stupidity," George Eliot says elsewhere in the novel,
with an uninsistent allusion in passing drawn from her familiarity
with Quarles' *Emblems*, "taking the world as an udder to feed our
supreme selves." Dorothea, absorbed in her own self-drama, has
been unable to see that her pompous and reticent husband Edward
Casaubon "had an equivalent centre of self, whence the lights and
shadows must always fall with a certain difference" (xxi.156–157).

For what *romantic* means if we apply it to the egoism of Emma
Bovary or the protagonists of *Middlemarch*, a standard dictionary
definition serves fairly well—"not practical; visionary or quixotic;
as a *romantic scheme*." For Emma, however, the phrase to stress is
"not practical," whereas for Dorothea Brooke, Tertius Lydgate, or

even Edward Casaubon, the emphasis needs to be placed on "visionary or quixotic." Dorothea Brooke's ardent self-drama is built around her desire to view herself as a latter-day Saint Theresa in the service of humanity. She is eminently altruistic, but she is looking, like Don Quixote, for heroic challenges rather than homely service in modest causes. It is not random whimsy that makes George Eliot quote *Don Quixote* for six lines as her motto for her second chapter of *Middlemarch*, preluding Dorothea's vision of Edward Casaubon as a scholarhero, and herself as his companion in giving the world a key to all mythologies, with Don Quixote's transforming, in accordance with his particular angle of perception, a barber approaching with a brass basin atop his head into a cavalier wearing the golden helmet of Mambrino. Casaubon is himself confident in all but his darker moments that he is destined to transform his labyrinthine accumulations of notes into a synthesis that will effect a new step forward in the world's knowledge. Tertius Lydgate in the parallel plot views himself as a scientist-physician heroically engaged in solving nothing less than the secrets of living tissue. They are all three romantic egoists, though even in the instance of Lydgate, the "emotional elephant" who has oriental fantasies, patent and direct self-indulgence, unabashed hedonism, is not an important part of their experience.[72] They are in the tradition of such heroes as Shelley's Prometheus or Keats's Hyperion or Browning's Paracelsus; and James's Isabel Archer will show her close kinship with them. As *Madame Bovary* progresses, Emma becomes more and more a romantic egoist in another tradition, the Satanic, with its preoccupation with exotic vision and varieties of orgiastic hedonism. Flaubert's natural inclination, as Mario Praz illustrates at some length in *The Romantic Agony*, was toward romanticism of the school of de Sade and (later) Huysmans and one aspect of Byron's complex inclinations (Praz does not allow at all sufficiently for the Quixotic element in Byron and his protagonists). Praz sees Flaubert in prose and Baudelaire in verse as falling exactly at the midpoint between "Romanticism and the Decadence, between the Fatal Man and . . . the Fatal Woman, between the period of Delacroix and that of Moreau."[73] In any event, George Eliot and Flaubert are perhaps in no other respect so widely dissimilar as they are in the particular kind of romanticism that colors the illusions of Emma Bovary and the illusions of the main characters of *Middlemarch*.

viii. Two Versions of Ironic Realism

Eliot's confidant was her husband, George Henry Lewes, who was almost constantly at her side, so that there is no equivalent in her correspondence to Flaubert's invaluable letters to Louise Colet. In *Adam Bede*, however, where she is at the start of her career and especially conscious of attempting a new sort of realism, George Eliot declares at some length her defiant resolve to dispense with the kind of scenes and characters that embellish popular novels—that "represent things as they never have been and never will be." She is determined, she says, to present men and events as she herself has seen them living and toiling in the actual world. She is going to give testimony as if she were at a trial and under oath. She will present people without any attempt to "straighten their noses, nor brighten their wit, nor rectify their dispositions."[74] Letting the imagination go its own way, she continues, is for the creative writer a perilous temptation. Falsehood is easy to create and truth is difficult to adhere to. It is only with much hard work and thought that a novelist can come close to portraying the actual life of his characters. And it is still harder for anyone, novelist or not, to tell anything like the truth about what goes on inside him: "Examine your words well, and you will find that even when you have no motive to be false, it is a very hard thing to say the exact truth, even about your own immediate feelings,—much harder than to say something fine about them which is *not* the exact truth" (xvii.180). One is reminded of the agonies Flaubert had been undergoing not much earlier on the other side of the Channel, suppressing his natural inclination to color his narrative more vividly than his new dedication to realism and impersonality would allow. He had given up, he wrote Louise Colet, the "mythological and theological fireworks" of his *The Temptation of Saint Anthony* (without publishing the book) and had for five years devoted himself to "peering into the clammy and mildewed corners of the soul" (C, II, 365). He was determined to keep to commonplace characters. "Here are two mediocrities in the same milieu," he wrote Colet of Charles Bovary and Rodolphe Boulanger, "and I must differentiate between them. If I succeed, it will be a strong point, I think, for it will be like painting in two shades of the same color without sharp contrasts—some-

31

thing not easy to do. But I fear that all these subtleties will be boring, and that the reader will want to have more movement" (C, III, 86).

A major fact, it is true, separates the psychological realism of George Eliot from that of Gustave Flaubert; and it is linked with her insistence on authorial comment as an accompaniment to her faithful and unimproved picture of human beings. She is not willing to let her art justify itself simply on the grounds of truth-telling or as its own excuse for being. Her representations, like Flaubert's, are designed to paint characters as they really exist; but she is earnestly concerned, she tells us in *Adam Bede*, that such revelations should serve to instruct the reader. They are meant to impart to him a sense of deep human sympathy for his fellow creatures, who do rough work and have weatherbeaten complexions. "In this world there are so many of these common coarse people, who have no picturesque, sentimental wretchedness!" (xvii.181–182). This conviction of the artist's obligation to induce insight into the suffering of others runs through her statements even from the time of her *Westminster Review* critiques written before she herself had taken to composing fiction.[75] The attendant peril of sermonizing, entering the story as earnest novel commentator, insisting on and prescribing what the reader's response is to be, is a great one; and Eliot in the earlier novels of her career, as in her portrayal of Hetty Sorrel or Maggie Tulliver or Romola, is, as many readers and critics have complained, not entirely untouched by it. Though the young Henry James in the years of the appearance of these novels can admire Eliot's manner without much demur, later critics—even F. R. Leavis, for all his immense esteem for Eliot's seriousness of purpose—can feel in them a bent toward a direct presence of the author that "has to be stigmatized as weakness."[76] It is, one gathers, in these novels that Pritchett finds the yearning for self-improvement so heavily present in the tone as to dampen his enthusiasm, whereas he can call *Middlemarch*, despite its deficiency in lyrical madness, the English masterpiece of its age—a work offering us as does no other novel of its time the clarifying force of a powerful mind exploring the inner life and consciences of the dramatis personae.[77]

Flaubert, in contrast, even when he is dealing most intimately with Emma Bovary's self-drama, plays in parallel an ironic contrapuntal vision that heightens both the pathos and the comedy inherent in her illusions. George Eliot's practice in *Middlemarch* is not, however, so far from Flaubert's in effect as might at first thought seem at all likely, even though the realistic counter-vision is apt to be presented in the voice of the narrator herself, interposing unabashedly to offer sympathetic commentary upon the situation. It is a question whether any one compelled to make the choice would prefer to have his inner life offered to the public gaze as Flaubert presents the dreams of Madame Bovary or to have his experience sympathetically explained in the manner George Eliot employs when she traces the special forms illusion takes in the lives of Tertius Lydgate or Edward Casaubon or Rosamond Vincy. George Eliot's irony in *Middlemarch* is often more devastating than Flaubert's simply because, in point of fact, she shows herself to be more objective than the famous master of the "impersonal" method. Her authorial comments, though they seem shaped by a conscientious effort to render a truthful and unbiased testimony, often lay bare her character's faults all the more cruelly because we feel there is no possibility of making a case for the character that the author has not already weighed and considered.

It is in these terms, for example, that Eliot presents for our exercise of insight and sympathy the private world of Edward Casaubon, a man of about fifty, sickly, pompous, pedantic, who has recently become affianced to Dorothea Brooke, a full-blooded girl of nineteen who accepts at face value all his apparent claims to the role of scholar-hero and is eager to set about helping him in his great work of providing the world with a key to all mythologies, thus far existent in the form of a vast accumulation of notebooks. Some of the other characters of the novel have been quite hard upon him, believing that he has simply taken advantage of Dorothea's naïvely trusting nature. But George Eliot as narrator undertakes to defend Casaubon by showing how his situation looks as seen in the light of his private vision and not as it is viewed by alien minds in patterns divergent from his own, each according to the particular ego-centered mind that is doing the interpreting. It is one thing, Eliot tells us, for Dorothea to seize on Casaubon as the right tinder she has been awaiting to light up her own life; but it does not necessarily follow that Casaubon has found himself kindled in the same way. It is unfair of the neighbors to judge so: "If to Dorothea Mr. Casaubon had been the mere occasion which had set alight the fine inflammable material of her youthful illusions, does it follow that he was fairly represented in the minds of those less impassioned personages who have hitherto delivered their judgments concerning him?" The fact is Casaubon has found, even during his period of courtship, that romance makes demands that puzzle and demoralize. All he has read in the classical and later poets has led him to assume that the situations of courtship can be relied upon to produce raptures. But the poets have proved false guides; raptures have not come to him:

> For in truth, as the day fixed for his marriage came nearer, Mr. Casaubon did not find his spirits rising; nor did the contemplation of that matrimonial garden-scene, where, as all experience showed, the path was to be bordered with flowers, prove persistently more enchanting to him than the accustomed vaults where he walked taper in hand. He did not confess to himself, still less could he have breathed to another, his surprise that though he had won a lovely and noble-hearted girl he had not won delight,—which he had also regarded as an object to be found by search. (x.62–63)

The imagery of such passages is less insistent than Flaubert's, but it has its cumulative effect and implications. Casaubon in his years of bachelorhood has assumed that at some future time he can expect the enjoyments of love as one part of the payments due him by the world for his patient investment of his years in uninspired labor. "Poor Mr. Casaubon had imagined that his long studious bachelorhood had stored up for him a compound interest of enjoyment, and that large drafts on his affections would not fail to be honoured . . . ." For all of us, George Eliot pauses to generalize, "get our thoughts entangled in metaphors and act fatally on the strength of them." And apparently in metaphors, one must add, where even the limited area of supposed alikeness is itself an illusion. As for Casaubon: ". . . there was nothing external by which he could account for a certain blankness of sensibility which came over him just when his expectant gladness should have been most lively. . . . Here was a weary experience in which he was as utterly condemned to loneliness as in the despair which sometimes threatened him while toiling in the morass of authorship without seeming nearer to the goal. And his was that worst loneliness which would shrink from sympathy" (x.63). Thus Casaubon is the victim of his own success. He has become in middle age the accepted

suitor of a beautiful maiden, but only his sense of duty compels him
to go on acting the part of lover and future husband, a role in which
he has become imprisoned by a terrifying excess of good fortune.
George Eliot's irony, here as so often elsewhere in *Middlemarch*, is
by no means canceled by her theory of sympathetic insight.

Emma Bovary's pattern of illusion, channeled by her sentimental
reading but following inclinations for self-indulgence that were with
her even before she entered the convent school at Rouen, leads her by
degrees into a Satanic form of romanticism and to eventual suicide
by arsenic. In *Middlemarch* romantic egoism takes less sensational
turns, but it is scarcely less a fact in the private worlds of the protagonists. It is romantic egoism that leads Dorothea Brooke into a
disastrous marriage with Edward Casaubon; and it is Casaubon's
own brand of romantic egoism (so unusual as to be virtually without
precedent among suitors in earlier fiction) that makes him, an aging
and sickly pedant, assume there is nothing remarkable in a young
girl's finding him attractive. It is romantic egoism that blinds Lydgate
to the nature of Rosamond Vincy (though there is ample evidence to
warn him if he possessed the power to see) and her particular un-
suitability for becoming the wife of a scientist who intends to win
his niche in the annals of medicine beside Paracelsus and Vesalius.
Lydgate survives his many disillusionments; he continues to carry on
his routine medical practice for some years. The spirit has, however,
died before the man; his heroic vision of himself has left him, and he
goes willingly to his grave at fifty. Edward Casaubon dies of heart
disease that is, one assumes, hastened in its effect by his growing
sense of his inability ever to complete his "Key to all Mythologies"
and his painful awareness that Dorothea no longer has any faith in
his own illusion of greatness, an illusion that he himself has been able
to cherish in his private experience only by protecting it jealously
from collision with reality.

ix. The "Drama of Incommunicability"

Flaubert's portrayal of M. Homais, pharmacist, or M. Lheureux,
merchant, is strikingly different from Eliot's portrayal of Mr. Vincy,
ribbon manufacturer, or Nicholas Bulstrode, banker. Flaubert's outright hatred of the French bourgeoisie, a hatred shared in the main

35

by his first readers on the appearance of *Madame Bovary* in instalments in the *Revue de Paris*, differs widely from Eliot's sympathetic vision of the citizens of *Middlemarch*, however merciless such searching insight into the lives of her characters can at times become, and her assumption, on the whole, that she is addressing no elitist audience but a large portion of the English middle class. *Middlemarch* appeared originally in bi-monthly parts which were so widely popular that Mudie's Circulating Library found itself obliged to buy heavily for its solidly middle-class patrons. *Madame Bovary* took Flaubert into the French courts on a charge of outraging public morals and religion. *Middlemarch* established George Eliot more firmly than ever as a preceptor of morality, a "Great Teacher," paid homage in a multitude of letters and gifts of flowers, fruit, and books. Yet *Middlemarch* scarcely urges readers to flatter themselves with bright hopes or encourages them to look for simplistic solutions for their problems more than does *Madame Bovary*. Both novels anticipate later fiction in their presentation of human alienation in a dark universe. A dominant theme in the modern novel in general and the psychological novel in particular is the sense of isolation that has become increasingly a factor in human consciousness. W. H. Auden sums up the basic dilemma of modern man as the problem of living in a society where men are no longer sustained by tradition even while they are unaware of having lost it. The individual in such a world is "forced to do deliberately for himself what in previous ages had been done for him by family, custom, Church, and State." He is forced to work out in isolation what had once been supplied him as an inheritance— "the principles and presuppositions in terms of which he can make sense of his experience."[78]

With rare exceptions, writers in earlier centuries did not view man in this light. Even in the Victorian novel, David Daiches points out, plot patterns remained public, and "anything significant that occurred to a character was symbolized by change in fortune or status" as in earlier fiction. It is in the twentieth-century novel that the shift is generally assumed to come. From seeing the characters from a public view the emphasis changes to concentrating upon the individual character's inner world as it appears to him alone. "The modern novelist is born when that publicly shared principle of selection and significance is no longer felt to exist and can no longer be depended on."[79] As a generalization, the statement does well; but George Eliot in *Middlemarch* is already deeply engaged in dealing with her characters in terms of their own views and judgments as opposed to the public's interpretation, even as Flaubert at a somewhat earlier time was doing across the Channel in tracing the inner life of Emma Bovary. Seen by the public eye, Casaubon is a respected and well-to-do citizen, likely still to enjoy a deanship or even a bishop's palace. Seen within, he is a weary and uninspired laborer in darkened vaults, the victim of increasing periods of chill realization that the work to which he has devoted his life is fated to remain a congeries of unassorted notes. Dorothea, for her part, finds her problems complicated rather than solved by being freed from an incompatible husband and made the inheritor of a large fortune. Defying or rather ignoring the opinion of her social group, Dorothea elects a course Jane Austen could hardly have permitted her, relinquishing her fortune and marrying badly (to a "foreigner" of no status in the eyes of her relatives and neighbors). Lydgate represents even more clearly Eliot's tendency to allow her characters' inner state to work at odds with what the world sees of them. In the eyes of his wife and his society, Lydgate prospers as a doctor with a wealthy clientele. It is only in his own eyes and in terms of his interior life that he has been vanquished by circumstance and become a bitter failure.

Both Flaubert and Eliot notably anticipate the modern psychological narrative in their enactment of what Victor Brombert calls Flaubert's "drama of incommunicability."[80] Alienation, incommunicability, as a fact of the human condition is so pervasive an assumption in Joyce or Proust that it is less a particular theme to be pointed up in individual scenes than the very groundwork of the narrative as a whole. For Flaubert and Eliot, on the other hand, the theme is both fresh and urgent. It is material for presentation in particular scenes and situations designed to dramatize the barriers between person and person, and especially scenes that in the stock of sentimental fiction would be settings for shared intimacies and the very opposite of alienation. "If Conrad, in the light of later developments, seems modern," observes J. Isaacs, "how much more so is Flaubert."[81] And he cites the famous scene at the Agricultural Fair (*Comices agricoles*) as a particular instance. Certainly the scene is a high point in Flaubert's drama of Emma's life of illusion. Her dream of finding in

Rodolphe the answering spirit her nature is searching for is played here in brilliant fugal arrangement with Rodolphe's hollow language of sentiments he no longer has any faith in and the councillor's specious oratory about the dignity and honor of the farmer's daily life, a life the councillor would assuredly have no willingness to take part in, together with a grotesque ground bass of honest rural reality from the prizes being awarded for hogs, rams, manures, and the like. Equally effective as a rendering of isolation and incommunicability is the scene in which Emma and Charles, lying awake in bed, pursue their separate fantasies, Charles planning the future life of Berthe, their daughter, through various happy stages of her girlhood and on into a safe marriage to a worthy young bourgeois; while Emma at Charles's side fancies herself in Rodolphe's arms, carried away by galloping horses into exotic lands beyond the mountains where they will row in gondolas or swing in hammocks, robed in gowns of starry silk. Charles at last snores, Berthe coughs, but Emma pursues her fantasy till dawn. Or there is the scene at the village church where Emma has gone to share her spiritual yearnings with the Abbé Bournisien, who chatters about his parish chores, as oblivious to her world and preoccupations as she is to his. But the drama of incommunicability figures in many situations of the novel and is equally present in such scenes as Rodolphe's taking his souvenirs of former love affairs out of the cookie box in which he stores them, rummaging among dust and desiccated rose petals, finding old bouquets, garters, pins, masses of hair, some of it blonde and some dark, and saying to himself wearily, "What a lot of nonsense!"

If Eliot's enactments of human alienation are often less graphic, there is still more emphasis on the importance of incommunicability as a fresh theme for fiction. Lydgate's experience as a medical student in France with the actress Laure prepares us for his disastrous failure of insight into Rosamond's real nature beneath her own version of playing a character not her own. When Laure is charged with the murder of her husband on stage, the scene of the drama having led to an actual rather than a pretended stabbing, Lydgate rises from the audience to her defense. On her acquittal he follows her into the provinces to propose marriage. He has no knowledge of her beyond the simulacrum of innocence he himself creates from the beauty of her person and voice, and he is totally unprepared for her calm revelation that she had intended to kill her husband because he bored her and refused to play in theaters outside Paris. Lydgate's dialogue with Rosamond before their marriage is a brilliant example in miniature of the incommunicability which is to become so predominant and sinister a fact of their life together. When Rosamond tells Lydgate she will defy her father's command to break their engagement, Lydgate blesses her for her display of constancy. But Rosamond, in assuring him that she never gives up anything she has once set her mind on, means more than Lydgate is aware of. Her terrible, calm tenacity, her refusal either to enter into passionate dialogue or to relinquish any line of conduct she has determined to follow, is to destroy all his own highest purposes. It is Lydgate, the man of science and familiarity with the outer world, who is forced to subordinate himself to this blonde, "infantine" provincial maiden whose blue eyes never quail before his angriest commands. As Eliot informs us at an early stage in their relation, each "lived in a world of which the other knew nothing" (xvi.123). For Lydgate, who speaks of once having learned all of Scott's poems by heart and who entertained visions of Rosamond's bringing him ideal happiness "of the kind known in the Arabian Nights" (xxxvi.257), marriage becomes a drama of appalling progressive insights into his state of absolute isolation utterly at odds with the promises of romantic literature. Dorothea Casaubon also finds marriage an awakening to a cruel reality of alienation. The honeymoon in Rome proves to be a time of bleak disenchantments in which, through a series of painful scenes, she comes to realize that her husband possesses a nature quite unlike her own—"an equivalent centre of self, whence the lights and shadows must always fall with a certain difference" (xxi.157). For Casaubon as well the honeymoon proves, instead of a time of drawing together and the discovering of shared tastes as literature and tradition would have it, a period of disturbing realizations announcing his wife's separateness. He had expected her to provide him with "a soft fence against the cold, shadowy, unapplausive audience of life," but she was already showing unmistakable signs of becoming instead an observer who stood apart and judged him, a representative of the unapplausive audience he feared, capable of "agitating him cruelly just where he most needed soothing" (xx.150).

Eliot's portrayal of Nicholas Bulstrode is in some ways her most complex embodiment of the theme of alienation in *Middlemarch*. It is not hard to guess what Dickens would have done with this evangelist banker who employs his wealth and his piety to secure power over others. Bulstrode would not have served him badly for a portrait to be placed somewhere between Mr. Pecksniff and the Reverend Mr. Honeythunder. Even in the hands of Charlotte Brontë, Bulstrode would have been likely to turn into another Brocklehurst, viewed without much notion of his carrying on a complex drama inside him. George Eliot alone among Victorian novelists could render with searching sympathy the inner experience of this sickly, sober financier, monolithic to the outer view, who must daily convince himself that his earnest wish to serve his god is not in conflict with his fierce concomitant passion for amassing this world's goods and bending others to his will. Tortuous rationalization is the only means of reconciling the demands of his nature into some sort of quiescence, and often this is not an easy process. "This was not what Mr. Bulstrode said to any man for the sake of deceiving him," George Eliot assures us; "it was what he said to himself—it was as genuinely his mode of explaining events as any theory of yours may be, if you happen to disagree with him. For the egoism which enters into our theories does not affect their sincerity. . ." (liii.382). Bulstrode for twenty years has kept all knowledge of his guilty past not only from other citizens of Middlemarch but from his wife. This is the drama of incommunicability in its extreme form. Yet in the end Bulstrode must face the partner of all his later life knowing that she has finally learned his secret.

The scene in which Harriet Bulstrode compassionately lets her husband know her willingness to accept full companionship in bearing the burden of his humiliation is an impressive one and a reminder that while Eliot enacts the drama of alienation powerfully in the lives of her characters, she also places great value in *Middlemarch* as elsewhere upon her conviction that the human lot can be alleviated through rare but precious moments of compassion and fellow feeling. Ian Milner protests that critics in general from the time of first publication onward have considered the dominant tone of *Middlemarch* one of disillusion and disenchantment. There is, he argues, much counterpointing of sad and gay in this vast novel, and essentially a "tragicomic contrasting of light and dark." There is, he insists, a peril in adopting a theory of this novel that is too rigid and schematized.[82] When one considers the canvas as an entirety, Milner has a substantial case. The modern reader, however, is apt to relive in his memory precisely those parts of the novel that are essentially enactments of disillusion and disenchantment. "All through his life," George Eliot tells us, "Mr. Casaubon had been trying not to admit even to himself the inward sores of self-doubt and jealousy" (xxxvii.277). His suffering as his death draws near is made poignant by his inability to communicate to anyone the genuine depth of his desire to rescue something from the welter of his notebooks for posterity. He attempts to impart his feeling to Lydgate, but the sing-song of his utterance and the pomposity of his language strike Lydgate as comic rather than tragic. Eliot reminds us that the situation is indeed "sublimely tragic" though it cannot impress Lydgate that way, full as he is of hope for his scientific experiments and more than usually complacent in his early period of delightful flirtation with Rosamond. "But there was nothing to strike others as sublime about Mr. Casaubon, and Lydgate, who had some contempt at hand for futile scholarship, felt a little amusement mingling with his pity."

There would come a time when Lydgate could bring deeper insight to such a confidence, but he "was at present too ill acquainted with disaster to enter into the pathos of a lot *where everything is below the level of tragedy except the passionate egoism of the sufferer*" (xlii.310, italics mine). Dorothea's self-doubt and distress faced with the enigma of helping a husband who rejects pity and cares for nothing outside his absorption with his studies offers something Lydgate can better understand. When she begs him for instruction, her agonized appeal strikes a responsive chord: "For years after Lydgate remembered the impression produced in him by this involuntary appeal—this cry from soul to soul, *without other consciousness than their moving with kindred natures in the same embroiled medium, the same troublous fitfully-illuminated life*" (xxx.214, italics mine). Three months had altered Dorothea's outlook from the rash romanticism of her period of courtship to a sense of dark enigmas for which there were no apparent solutions: "Her blooming full-pulsed youth stood there in a moral imprisonment which made itself one with the chill, colourless, narrowed landscape, the shrunken furniture . . . . All existence seemed to beat with a lower pulse than her

41

own, and her religious faith was a solitary cry, the struggle out of a nightmare in which every object was withering and shrinking away from her" (xxviii.202). Knoepflmacher is emphasizing a major theme in *Middlemarch* when he compares Dorothea to E. M. Forster's Mrs. Moore.[83] For Dorothea also is exploring in profound ways her Caves of Marabar, where, whatever the individual ego shouts into the blackness, the response out of the darkness is simply a meaningless "boum." Later Dorothea is to find ways of making life more bearable. She is to subordinate all her selfish concerns at one crisis to give her energies to an attempt to aid Rosamond. But her language, if it is to be considered consonant with the mode of tragi-comedy, requires placing heavy emphasis on the first element in the compound. "Trouble is so hard to bear, is it not?" she counsels Rosamond. "How can we live and think that any one has trouble—piercing trouble—and we could help them, and never try?" Dorothea's voice, Eliot tells us, had become "like a low cry from some suffering creature in the darkness." Lydgate knows, she assures Rosamond, that she, Dorothea, has had much distress during the period of her husband's illness and death— distress from unwittingly causing much pain to a mate whose inner life lies hidden and mysterious. Lydgate knows, she says, that she has "felt how hard it is to walk always in fear of hurting another who is tied to us" (lxxxi.583). Dorothea has come a long way from the time when her greatest cause for anxiety about her near-sightedness was fear of treading on Celia's puppy (iii.23). She has experienced deeply (as had Casaubon for his part) the paradox of the greatest isolation's coming from the relationship where romantic literature and tradition promised the greatest protection from isolation: There is something "even awful," she says, in the nearness that comes with marriage. It is such scenes as these, dramatizing the loneliness of the human ego even in the act of communicating something of its sense of isolation to another, that signalize *Middlemarch* as a novel looking beyond its time toward the twentieth century. Calvin Bedient would put the emphasis somewhat differently. It is the "feverish yearning for fame" on the part of the main characters, he maintains, that "makes George Eliot our contemporary." A post-Christian hunger for recognition by posterity has replaced the Christian yearning for personal immortality, and with George Eliot this hunger first forces its way into the English novel.[84] I would suggest, however, that Bedient is nearer the mark when he writes in a later paragraph that we, like the author of *Middlemarch*, are acutely aware of our plight "besieged by personal insignificance in an insignificant world, unconfirmed, unattended, yet anxious, withal, to prove ourselves equal to some unarticulated challenge." It is "egoistic disappointment," Bedient insists, that gives *Middlemarch* its powerful identity. Egoistic disappointment is indeed at the heart of the situation with each of Eliot's main protagonists in *Middlemarch*; for it is this that Dorothea and Lydgate must learn to live with and that Casaubon had lived with, secretly, with his pangs jealously concealed from the public eye, all his mature life. The theme figures very large in *Middlemarch*, but what we carry away from the novel is not the failure of Dorothea to become another St. Theresa or Lydgate to discover the secrets of living tissue. It is the way the theme is acted out powerfully on both narrative and symbolic levels in the intimate experience of the characters. "We read the story," as Gordon Haight says, "not to learn that [Dorothea] is disillusioned but to see how she will bear it."[85]

L. C. Knights pronounces Henry James the "first of the 'modern' novelists" on the basis of his early "apprehension of the isolation of the individual."[86] Knights gives special attention to *The Portrait of a Lady* "because it indicates so clearly what was, in various forms, one of James's main preoccupations—a preoccupation with the plight of the trapped creature." The strength of the novel, he feels, "comes largely from the evoked contrast of the heroine's 'fund of life'—'her delighted spirit'—and the 'cold obstruction' that thwarts it. This is a feeling that runs through James's work from first to last." It is also the feeling that pervades *Madame Bovary* and *Middlemarch*, though the delights of Emma's spirit are in good measure different from those of Isabel's. Like Flaubert, James had feared that his narrative would fail to hold its audience because it was "too exclusively psychological," too little occupied with exterior incident and too much with inner state. "The idea of the whole thing," James recorded in his Notebook, "is that the poor girl, who has dreamed of freedom and nobleness, who has done, as she believes, a generous, natural, clearsighted thing, finds herself in reality ground in the very mill of the conventional."[87] Looking back on his work a quarter-century later, James saw Isabel's long scene of internal monologue—"it all goes on without her being approached by another person and without her leaving her chair"—as "obviously the best thing in the book" though it was so because it epitomized the general plan.[88] *The Portrait of a Lady* puts the action inside the minds of the characters in ways that strongly invite comparison with *Madame Bovary* and *Middlemarch*. It is unlikely, as James was himself aware, that it could have been written without them.

George Eliot's view of the void that lies outside the human personality's illusion and is its inescapable destination is not Flaubert's; there is nothing in *Middlemarch* embodying the author's own disturbed sense of the cosmic Everlasting No so vividly, with such power of poetic "madness," as does Emma's final atrocious laughter or Charles Bovary's shriek of horror when he lifts the veil from her corpse's decomposing face. Such scenes imply a nihilism that differs significantly from George Eliot's more intricate view of human possibility, within sternly constraining limits, of finding meaning and fulfillment even in a world where egoistic illusions are likely to lead one into endless blind labyrinths or face to face with iron walls. But George Eliot in England, like Flaubert in France, introduced into the novel a new preoccupation with character as opposed to incident, and the inner vision as opposed to the shared social vision. Like Flaubert but in her own quite different idiom she presented the two worlds of her characters in ironic counterpoint, making the human tendency to romantic egoism and the pursuit of cherished fantasies a subject for absorbed examination. *Middlemarch* is a vast canvas, admirably structured in its way, but with a sort of unity that makes of Eliot's provincial community a microcosm with far broader social implications than Flaubert's relatively narrow though more fiercely concentrated focus permits. But Eliot's main protagonists resemble Emma Bovary in ways that matter deeply for the future of psychological fiction. They are all enveloped in their respective self-dramas, and they all struggle with varying degrees of success or failure to follow out patterns that are intensely real to them—patterns of illusion that represent sharply individualized visions of the outer world as seen through the distortions of a vividly particularized ego. As pioneers in the presentation of their characters' inner experience George Eliot and Flaubert have a revealing amount that they share. Where they differ, the difference is also illuminating.

44

NOTES

1. "George Eliot," *The Living Novel* (London, 1946), p. 94.

2. For an analysis of the complex yet brilliantly unified design of *Middlemarch*, see Mark Schorer, "The Structure of the Novel: Method, Metaphor and Mind," in *Middlemarch: Critical Approaches to the Novel*, ed. Barbara Hardy (New York, 1967), pp. 12–24.

3. David R. Carroll, "Unity through Analogy: An Interpretation of *Middlemarch*," *Victorian Studies*, II (1959), 307.

4. See, for example, F. R. Leavis, *The Great Tradition* (1948; New York, 1954), pp. 11, 110, 139, *et passim*; W. J. Harvey, *The Art of George Eliot* (New York, 1961), pp. 72, 73, *et passim*; Barbara Hardy, "Introduction," to *Middlemarch: Critical Approaches to the Novel* (as in my note 2), p. 10; David Daiches, *A Critical History of English Literature* (New York, 1960), II, 1068 ff. For James's criterion of "solidity of specification," see his "The Art of Fiction," in *Henry James: The Future of the Novel*, ed. Leon Edel (New York, 1956), p. 14 *et passim*.

5. "The Flaubert Omnibus," *Collected Impressions* (New York, 1950), p. 25.

6. "Charles de Bernard and Gustave Flaubert," *French Poets and Naturalists* (London, 1893), pp. 199, 206. James found the tale as a whole "rather a vulgar tragedy," and, despite his great admiration for its power, "fortunately" inimitable, even by Flaubert himself (pp. 199, 206). The essay had appeared originally in the American literary magazine *The Galaxy* in March, 1876. James considered the novels of even his beloved Balzac "morally and intellectually superficial" and "extraordinarily gross and turbid" and Balzac, for all his power to pour forth "flashes and volleys of [terrestrial] wisdom," often a charlatan. "It is probable that no equally vigorous mind was ever at pains to concoct such elaborate messes of folly." It was Balzac's superb "sense of this present terrestrial life which has never been surpassed, and which in his genius overshadowed everything else"—"Honoré de Balzac," *French Poets and Novelists* (London, 1893), pp. 88–89. The essay was first published in the late 1870's.

7. "Gustave Flaubert," in *Henry James: The Future of the Novel*, pp. 125–161.

8. *The Three Voices of Poetry* (New York, 1954), p. 18.

9. "George Eliot's *Middlemarch*," in *Henry James: The Future of the Novel*, pp. 86, 88. The critique first appeared in *The Galaxy* for March, 1873.

10. "George Eliot's *The Legend of Jubal*," in *A Century of George Eliot Criticism*, ed. Gordon S. Haight (Boston, 1965), p. 89. The critique had appeared originally in the *North American Review* for October, 1874.

11. "The Spanish Gypsy," in *A Century of George Eliot Criticism* (as in my note 10), p. 55. Originally published in the *North American Review* for October, 1868. James finds in Eliot's poetry much rhetorical energy and "neat things expressed with rhythmic felicity," but not much genuine poetic fire.

12. "The Life of George Eliot," *Partial Portraits* (London, 1888), pp. 56–57. Italics mine. Jerome Thale is especially challenging among later critics in his attempt to define the nature of Eliot's special employment of the "direct style," from which she exacts a full range of its possibilities in rendering judgments at the same time that she is constantly concerned as well with acknowledging the complexity of the situation in which the character is placed. Hers is a style, Thale says, that, without becoming

impressionistic or metaphoric, can "catch the vague and half-noticed states of consciousness, the realm of unformulated intention." Symbolic imagery, though often richly present in her pages—"extensive, subtle, and varied"—is employed mainly to reinforce and give emotional coloring to other kinds of meaning. "Nowhere in George Eliot is the imagery, important as it may be, the chief means of communicating or the secret key to the novel."—*The Novels of George Eliot* (New York, 1959), pp. 150–159.

13. "George Eliot," pp. 87–94. Except for *Wuthering Heights*, Pritchett decided, he found no adequate amalgam of madness in any English novel of the entire Victorian period.

14. *Axel's Castle: A Study in the Imaginative Literature of 1870–1930* (New York, 1931), p. 11.

15. *Ibid.*, p. 255. An excellent analysis of the essential mode of such scenes, "vibrating between realism and symbolism, [which] clearly point forward to the Joycean epiphany," is to be found in Peter K. Garrett's *Scene and Symbol from George Eliot to James Joyce: Studies in Changing Fictional Mode* (New Haven, Conn., 1969). My more elaborate treatment of them from a different perspective in Chapter II stems mainly from the parallel chapter in my doctoral dissertation "The Pattern of Illusion: A Correlative Study in the Novels of Flaubert and George Eliot," University of Illinois, 1968.

16. "Charles de Bernard and Gustave Flaubert," pp. 198–199.

17. "George Eliot's *Middlemarch*," pp. 81–83, 89.

18. *The Great Tradition*, p. 42.

19. Harvey, pp. 17–32, *passim*. The words quoted occur at p. 19.

20. "George Eliot's *Middlemarch*," p. 83.

21. *Henry James: The Conquest of London* (New York, 1962), p. 371. Professor Edel feels, nevertheless, that F. R. Leavis and other critics have made larger claims for the influence of George Eliot on James than are warranted. George Levine shows convincingly the remarkable resemblances between Dorothea Brooke and Isabel Archer in outlook and situation in "Isabel, Gwendolen, and Dorothea," *ELH*, 30 (1963), 244–257. See also Philip Leon Greene, "Henry James and George Eliot," Diss. New York University, 1962, especially pages 143–167.

22. "*Middlemarch*," *The Academy*, IV (1873), I.

23. "George Eliot," *Cornhill Magazine*, XLIII (1881), 167–168.

24. "George Eliot," from *Victorian Prose Masters* (1901), in *A Century of George Eliot Criticism*, pp. 171, 177.

25. Jessie Chambers, *D. H. Lawrence: A Personal Record* (London, 1935), p. 105. George Eliot was, Chambers says, an important part of Lawrence's early reading. See also F. R. Leavis, *D. H. Lawrence: Novelist* (New York, 1956), pp. 123–124, 157, and his *The Great Tradition*, pp. 37 ff.; Harry T. Moore, *D. H. Lawrence: His Life and Works* (New York, 1964), p. 26 (Moore sees a strong influence of George Eliot in Lawrence's first novel, *The White Peacock*).

26. John Philip Couch, *George Eliot in France: A French Appraisal of George Eliot's Writings, 1858–1960* (Chapel Hill, N.C., 1967), p. 149 ff. Professor Couch's book represents a thorough study of this aspect of George Eliot's influence, with special attention to her meaning for Marcel Proust.

27. *A la recherche de Marcel Proust* (Paris, 1949), p. 29.

28. "Sur la psychologie de Marcel Proust," *Hommage à Marcel Proust* (Paris, 1927), pp. 146–147.

29. "George Eliot," *The Common Reader* (New York, 1948), pp. 229–242. The essay originally appeared in the *Times Literary Supplement* in 1919.

30. "George Eliot's *Middlemarch*," p. 89.

31. *Victorian Novelists* (Chicago, 1958), pp. 262, 280. Cecil's volume was first published under the title *Early Victorian Novelists* in 1935.

32. "Fiction and the 'Matrix of Analogy,'" in *A Century of George Eliot Criticism*, pp. 270–278. Schorer's analysis appeared originally under the same title as part of his influential analysis dealing with Jane Austen and Emily Brontë as well (the *Kenyon Review* for Fall, 1949). For an especially noteworthy example of more recent studies along roughly similar lines, see Hilda M. Hulme's "The Language of the Novel," in *Middlemarch: Critical Approaches to the Novel*, pp. 87–124.

33. *Dostoevsky and Romantic Realism* (Chicago, 1967), p. 125.

34. *George Eliot* (London, 1964), pp. 180–181.

35. *The Disappearance of God: Five Nineteenth-Century Writers* (Cambridge, Mass., 1965), p. 12. For the five writers Miller concentrates upon—De Quincey, Browning, Emily Brontë, Arnold, and Hopkins—God still lived though for a time he had become fearfully remote. For Flaubert (except in his mystical moments) and for George Eliot, the total conceivable reality outside of man himself had become a lifeless void.

36. *Gustave Flaubert: Intimate Notebook 1840–1841*, introduction, translation and notes by Francis Steegmuller (New York, 1967), note on pp. 54–55.

37. "The Mathematical Principles of Natural Philosophy," in *Enlightened England*, ed. Wylie Sypher (New York, 1947), pp. 59–60. See also Sypher's headnote for the selection.

38. Quoted in John Herman Randall, *The Making of the Modern Mind* (Boston, 1940), p. 274.

39. See C. M. Bowra, *The Romantic Imagination* (New York, 1961) for an especially interesting elaboration of the great romantics' insistence on finding a transcendental order that gave meaning to existence. For the romantics the power that moves the universe "could not be but spiritual" (p. 22).

40. *Sartor Resartus*, ed. C. F. Harrold (New York, 1937), pp. 164, 166. In the terms of *Sartor* it is Professor Diogenes Teufelsdröckh who speaks; but the work is patently Carlyle's spiritual autobiography, and Carlyle is recounting his own experience of the "Everlasting No."

41. *In Memoriam*, ed. Jerome H. Buckley (Boston, 1958), Lyrics III, LVI, pp. 180, 208–209.

42. *Correspondance*, ed. Louis Conard (Paris, 1926), II, 414, in *Oeuvres complètes de Gustave Flaubert*. Subsequent quotations from Flaubert's letters will be followed by volume and page number of this edition unless otherwise indicated. To make it clear that the correspondence of Flaubert is being quoted, a *C* (for *Correspondance*) will precede volume and page number.

43. Passages of *The City of Dreadful Night* referred to here occur at lines 725–769; the lines quoted in the remainder of the paragraph occur at lines 1000–1039, *Victorian and Later English Poets*, eds. James Stephens, Edwin L. Beck, Royall H. Snow (New York, 1937), pp. 1101, 1104–1105.

44. *Fathers and Sons*, ed. and trans. Ralph E. Matlaw (New York, 1966), p. 102.

45. *Anna Karenin*, trans. Rosemary Edmonds (Penguin Books, 1954), pp. 820, 823. Miss Edmonds gives the family name as *Karenin*.

46. See especially C. M. Bowra, *The Heritage of Symbolism* (London, 1959), pp. 2–3, *et passim*.

47. For a more ambitious treatment of the subject, see Anthony Thorlby, *Gustave Flaubert and the Art of Realism* (New Haven, Conn., 1957), especially pages 1–24.

48. Flaubert wrote three versions of *La Tentation*, the first in 1849, the second in

1856, and the final version in 1872. See René Dumesnil, *Gustave Flaubert* (Paris, 1932), pp. 131, 338.

49. Flaubert to Louise Colet (July 6, 1852): ". . . passion does not make poetry, and the more personal you are, the more feeble. I have always sinned in that way myself. I have always put myself into what I wrote. Instead of Saint Anthony, for example, it is I who undergo this temptation . . ." (C, II, 461–462).

50. *Oeuvres complètes de Gustave Flaubert*, ed. Louis Conard (Paris, 1910), XIII, 201.

51. *Axel's Castle*, p. 11.

52. *Gustave Flaubert* (Paris, 1935), p. 119. Harry Levin employs Thibaudet's term in commenting on aspects of Flaubert's habit of "lyric impulse" and "satiric reservation" from a much broader perspective on his works—*The Gates of Horn* (New York, 1963), pp. 232, 286, *et passim*.

53. For the passages from Flaubert's letters to Colet quoted in this paragraph, see C, II, 365; III, 25; III, 143 (italics mine).

54. "Isabel, Gwendolen, and Dorothea," pp. 244–257.

55. U. C. Knoepflmacher, *George Eliot's Early Novels: The Limits of Realism* (Berkeley, Cal., 1968), p. 138. Knoepflmacher's account of "The Lifted Veil" occurs at pp. 128–161. Quotations in the remainder of the paragraph are taken from pp. 149, 151.

56. See especially Victor Brombert, *The Novels of Flaubert: A Study of Themes and Techniques* (Princeton University Press, 1966), pp. 9, 24–25, *et passim*. "If Flaubert the realist exists, so does Flaubert the escapist, and even Flaubert the mystic. Ecstatic reveries are for him a permanent temptation" (p. 9).

57. "*Daniel Deronda*: A Conversation," in *A Century of George Eliot Criticism*, p. 110.

58. *George Eliot's Life as Related in Her Letters and Journals*, ed. J. W. Cross (New York, 1884), I, 80–81. Referred to hereafter as Cross.

59. For a much fuller account of George Eliot's successive attitudes toward religion, see Bernard J. Paris, *Experiments in Life: George Eliot's Quest for Values* (Detroit, 1965), especially his first chapter.

60. Lewes had condoned his wife's adultery at a period somewhat earlier and was therefore unable to obtain a divorce.

61. The distinction between the "science of religion," its insistence on theological dogma and the "poetry of religion," its appeal to the imagination and the human spirit, was to be a crucial one in Arnold's writings on Higher Criticism. See, for example, his "Preface" to *God and the Bible* (1875).

62. Cross, I, 127. The second quotation from Eliot's letters occurs in Cross at I, 137.

63. *The George Eliot Letters*, ed. Gordon S. Haight (New Haven, 1954–55), IV, 13.

64. *The George Eliot Letters*, III, 366 (the italics are Eliot's).

65. "George Eliot in the 1860's," *Victorian Studies*, 5 (1961), 93–108. The same process seems to be at work in Eliot as early as the late eighteen-fifties.

66. Gordon S. Haight, *George Eliot: A Biography* (New York, 1968), p. 446. Barbara Bodichon had at the time read only Book I but felt already with a "sort of horror" the "terrible foreshadowing" of Dorothea's descent from bright faith into dark bafflement.

67. U. C. Knoepflmacher, *Religious Humanism and the Victorian Novel* (Princeton, N.J., 1965), p. 22.

68. Haight, *George Eliot*, p. 451.

69. Quoted in Knoepflmacher, p. 74.

70. For an excellent discussion of Flaubert's use of detail for ironic commentary, see Brombert, pp. 44–55, *et passim*.

71. *Middlemarch*, ed. Gordon S. Haight (Boston, 1956), chapter xxvii, pages 194–195. Subsequent quotations from *Middlemarch* are followed by chapter and page numbers of this edition in parentheses.

72. Ian Milner discusses at some length the special meaning of the myth of Prometheus for George Eliot, particularly as she develops it in her notes for her poem *The Spanish Gypsy* and in the poem itself. The ideal is to accept the iron bonds necessity assigns the individual within an indifferent universe but to work within the limits fate assigns, struggling heroically for the good of humanity: "Here, in short, is the rationale of the hero in George Eliot. Neither the wise submitter nor the spectacular rebel but one who, while recognizing necessity within and without, achieves moral freedom by conscious and active commitment to the struggle for human welfare."—*The Structure of Values in George Eliot* (Prague, 1968), p. 4. Dorothea, Casaubon, Lydgate share at the start a Promethean vision so far as desiring to promote human welfare is concerned, but they have yet to learn more about the nature of necessity.

73. *The Romantic Agony*, trans. Angus Davidson (London, 1962), pp. 170–181.

74. *Adam Bede*, ed. Gordon S. Haight (New York, 1964), pp. 179–180. Subsequent quotations from *Adam Bede* are followed by chapter and page numbers of this edition in parentheses.

75. See, for example, her long review-essay "Die bürgerliche Gesellschaft," in the *Westminster Review* for July–October, 1856: "The greatest benefit we owe to the artist, whether painter, poet, or novelist is the extension of our sympathies. . . . Art is the nearest thing to life; it is a mode of amplifying experience and extending our contact with our fellow-men beyond the bounds of our personal lot" (p. 54).

76. Leavis, p. 48. Professor Leavis finds such weakness to a degree even in moments of Eliot's presentation of Dorothea, though it is hard to agree with him there. In Casaubon, Leavis decides, Eliot has grown "wholly strong" (p. 85), and he feels that the force of Rosamond's destructive power has its pronounced impact upon the reader precisely because Eliot is by the time of *Middlemarch* able to achieve an effective distance: ". . . the destructive and demoralizing power of Rosamond wouldn't have seemed so appalling to us if there had been any animus in the presentment" (p. 87). E. M. Forster (*Aspects of the Novel* [1927; New York, 1954], pp. 127–133) apparently assumes that Eliot remains a "preacher" throughout her career, unable to rise to the levels of Dostoevsky. It is the scene from *Adam Bede* in which Dinah Morris (a *bona fide* Methodist preacher) confers with Hetty in prison that Forster chooses to illustrate his point, which seems to be loading the dice when a fair game would have answered.

77. "George Eliot," pp. 82–94. "*Middlemarch* resumes [summarizes] the observation and experience of a lifetime. Until this book George Eliot often strains after things beyond her capacity, as Dorothea Casaubon strained after a spiritual power beyond her nature. But now in *Middlemarch* the novelist is reconciled to her experience" (p. 91).

78. Quoted in J. Isaacs, *An Assessment of Twentieth-Century Literature* (London, 1951), pp. 111–112.

79. *The Novel and the Modern World* (1938: Chicago, rev. ed., 1965), pp. 4–5.

80. *The Novels of Flaubert*. See especially pp. 24, 32, 43–44, 71; but this is a frequent theme in Brombert's invaluable study.

81. J. Isaacs, p. 81.

82. *The Structure of Values in George Eliot*, p. 87.

83. *Religious Humanism and the Victorian Novel*, p. 22.

84. "*Middlemarch*: Touching Down," in Bedient's *Architects of the Self* (Berkeley, Cal., 1972), p. 87. The quotation that follows later in the paragraph occurs at p. 90.

85. Introduction to *Middlemarch*, p. xii.

86. "Henry James and the Trapped Spectator," *Explorations* (New York, 1964), p. 189.

87. Appendix to *The Portrait of a Lady*, ed. Leon Edel (Boston, 1956), p. 485.

88. "Preface," *The Portrait of a Lady*, pp. 14–15.

II

MADAME BOVARY: ILLUSION, COUNTER-POINT, AND THE DARKENED UNIVERSE

S EEN FROM ANOTHER CENTURY, FLAUBERT'S METHOD FOR DEALING WITH
the interior life of his heroine does not appear so boldly experi-
mental as it did to his contemporaries. By the early nineteen-hundreds
James Joyce had enlarged space and exploded time in the imaginative
worlds of his protagonists in ways Flaubert would scarcely have com-
prehended; and Proust, in the special manner of his idiom, had given
dimensions to the psychological novel that make the world of Emma
Bovary seem confined indeed. Combray and Yonville l'Abbaye are
geographically at no great distance, but in the realm of the imagination they are regions apart. By the 1930's Virginia Woolf and Doro-
thy Richardson had gone so far beyond Flaubert's tentative adventures with the ebb and flow of human consciousness (or beyond
Henry James's, for that matter) that the path by which they have
come is often faint or problematic. It is still possible to maintain,
however, that in the century and more since the appearance of Emma
Bovary no single character in fiction has had his pattern of imaginative
life so graphically imprinted on the minds of readers. Joyce's focus
is not upon the peculiarities of any single inner world; Stephen-
Telemachus and Leopold-Ulysses are in ways important and calculated larger-than-life in a particular segment of space and time. In
Proust, also, the art is of a sort that expands the individual conscious-

ness into something cosmic in implication. Where Joyce and Proust are expansive, Flaubert is intensive. His powers for concentrated vision and for lyrical expression are all channeled into rendering by relatively traditional resources the experience of a single obscure village doctor's wife and the tract of outer world that she inhabits. But it is not the discipleship of naturalists like Zola that makes J. Isaacs speak of Flaubert as more modern than Conrad and impels Henry James to distinguish *Madame Bovary* as a novel from which there is "endlessly much to be learned." If Flaubert's history of Emma Bovary is a long remove still from the novels of Joyce and Proust, it is nevertheless a revolutionary work—in important ways the first modern novel. It is already a narrative that reverses the traditional movement and does not end with a marriage but begins with one. Falling out of rather than into love is the subject of prominence, and loneliness rather than the defeat of loneliness is what love accentuates in Emma Bovary's experience no less than in Lady Chatterley's. With *Madame Bovary* the "drama of incommunicability" is already a dominant fact of the novel. The mind has turned inward; the private world has already become a brightly colored but insubstantial world of illusion, and the activity that matters most takes place not on the world's great stage but in that internalized theater. The immediacies of private thought and feeling have taken precedence over the immediacies of the shared life. Already outside the brightly lighted inner chamber, moreover, lies a dark reality in which the individual human experience inescapably ends in nothingness. Like the Lady of Shalott, the human consciousness must leave her web and loom and perform her journey into extinction. Except that in the novelist's realm as opposed to the poet's there take place a number of less extreme exposures of inner world to outer that prefigure the ultimate finality. Flaubert's correlatives endow Emma's experiences of disillusion with something like heroic form only in her death scene. Earlier she is an unheroic heroine presented according to a theory of "impersonality" that explores in rich and richly ironic "modern" terms her attempts to find fulfillments of her imagined world in a provincial Norman reality. It is above all literature that fosters her private vision and channels its fascinating twists and turns—literature that in one way or another flatters human expectations with romantic versions of what purports to be a shared and verifiable human reality. "Literature" in her girlhood experience means such reading as sentimental novels and saints' legends. Later the term must broaden to encompass a wide variety of sources for flattering pictures that gloss over the darker facts of the human condition.

The betrayals of literature constitute a major theme in *Madame Bovary*, and a theme of significance in *Middlemarch* as well. It is a theme that graphically reflects the position of the author between two worlds but facing toward the twentieth-century world. The theme is still prominent in James's *The Portrait of a Lady*, and it plays a not inconsiderable part in Conrad's *Lord Jim*. George Eliot's Lydgate is to be betrayed by his sentimental reading in ways not dissimilar from Emma's; but it is in *Madame Bovary* that the betrayals of romantic literature figure centrally in an intensely centralized narrative of human alienation and human illusion in a darkly factual world. Another great novelist had written about the betrayals of literature a half-century earlier; but to think of *Northanger Abbey* is to see the better how far Flaubert's heroine had by 1857 traveled in the direction of Marcel or Mrs. Dalloway.

Though Flaubert could speculate to Louise Colet that even as he was writing, there were Emma Bovarys doubtless weeping in at least twenty French villages, it is inconceivable that any one of the twenty could actually be mistaken for Flaubert's particular Emma. The tenacity with which Emma Bovary holds her individual life in the imagination of the reader is the more remarkable when emphasis is given (as it will have to be here) to the fact that throughout the novel Flaubert characteristically employs his second vision to undercut his heroine's assumptions of superiority to her environment. Readers and critics are likely to go on (and with excellent reasons of a kind, provided the author's purpose is not the major question) seeing her as to a considerable degree an artist *manqué*, a sensitive spirit deserving of the happiness she vainly pursued. Shortly after *Madame Bovary* was published, Sainte-Beuve in a distinguished critique accused Flaubert of wielding a pen in the way his father before him, as a surgeon, had employed a scalpel, dissecting without compunction the dreams of his heroine: "Shall I confess it? One feels more indulgent toward her than does Flaubert himself."[1] A few months later Baudelaire carried a good deal farther this paradox of the heroine whom the reader wants to rescue from her creator. Baudelaire imagined Flaubert resolving to confront the vulgar reading public (a public that had become jaded while remaining trivial) with a vulgar subject to match, "since the choice of too lofty a subject is an impertinence for the nineteenth-century reader."[2] At the same time Flaubert (so runs Baudelaire's critique) resolved to play a game of setting subject and style in opposition to each other: "We shall apply a style that is sinewy, picturesque, subtle, and exact upon a banal canvas. We shall put the most passionate feelings into the most trivial adventure. The solemnest words will escape from the stupidest mouths." But Baudelaire, like so many critics to follow, though he sees so much of what his friend Flaubert has put on the canvas, cannot resist taking up the brush himself to end with a very different picture. He insists on endowing Flaubert's obscure housewife with all the gifts and graces that the novelist has so pointedly denied her. "In short, this woman is truly great. She is, above all, deserving of our pity, and in spite of the systematic hard-heartedness of the author, who has made strenuous efforts to be absent from his work and to play the role of a showman of marionettes, all *intellectual* women will be grateful to him for having raised the female to so high a power, so far from the pure animal, and so near to the ideal man . . . ." Baudelaire makes his own prose-poem of Emma's girlhood in Flaubert's despite—the maiden "deliciously intoxicated" by the gemmed hues of church windows, by the light cast upon her prayer book, by the music of vespers, confusing her budding sexual fantasies with her religious visions.

No writer since Baudelaire has gone quite that far in celebrating Emma Bovary at the expense of Flaubert, but critics have with some consistency been inclined to regard her as to a greater or lesser degree a victim of bourgeois society through her very superiority to the persons who surround her.[3] This is a tribute to the vitality with which Flaubert managed to endow her, a vitality nearly sufficient to render her independent of the context in which she draws her breath. Emma's imagination is, to be sure, far more agile than the imaginations of her neighbors, and the strength of her desires is presumably far greater than theirs. The pursuit of ecstasy is a failing readers will always view with much more sympathy than they are likely to bring to the pursuit of money or of property. But Emma is the victim of her lovers as well as of the townsmen, and her excess of desire, if it is often presented poetically, is also presented pathologically. When the focus of concentration is the nature of her inner life and her special pattern of illusion, as it is to be here, it becomes plain that she is designed by her creator—as opposed to the creative reader—to be something less admirable though not less meaningful than a heroine betrayed by the superiority of her mind and tastes. Emma is the victim of a disease, of a virulent strain of romantic egoism. In Emma's case the disease is studied with an intensity worthy of Flaubert's surgeon father from its first stages to the moment of her death. And indeed well beyond her death, for the contagion displays a curious virulence thereafter in her husband. The lyrical sensitivity to life remembered as that of the heroine is (as Baudelaire more or less implies) the sensitivity of the narrator. Flaubert's achievement is greater than has often been allowed. Balzac had made absorbing art of the exterior world of commonplace social life. Flaubert's achievement was to make absorbing art of the interior world of commonplace illusion.

i. Emma and the Pursuit of Art

There are clues to Emma's particular distortion of reality even in the early pages of the novel. It is not simply that she finds life on the family farm uncongenial, a fact that would not need to conflict with Flaubert's making her an artist *manqué*; but it is significant that she finds summer on the farm even more boring than winter: "She would have dearly liked, even if only for the winter, to live in town, although the length of the fine days made the country perhaps more boring still in the summer. And, in accordance with what she was saying, her voice was clear, or sharp, or would suddenly become filled with languor, trailing off in slow modulations that ended almost in murmurs as if she spoke to herself—one moment joyous, opening big naïve eyes; the next with her eyelids half closed, her look drowned in boredom, her thoughts wandering."[4] To Charles such conversation and conduct seem merely characteristics of a charming girl's behavior; but these sudden shifts in mood, even while in process of talking to Charles, and Emma's inclination for living half in a dislocated dream world and half in the pleasure of self-drama in the present moment, with Charles as her audience are significant indications of what will come later on.

It is not until chapter six, after Emma's first sense of disappointment in marriage, however, that we are provided an ambitious account of what her private world has been like. It has been occupied by an amazing jumble of romantic visions formed from her reading and scarcely modified as time has gone on from its first naïveté and passionate self-absorption. The subject is of the greatest importance for the character of his heroine, and Flaubert had prepared himself with personal discomfort for writing this part of his book. "I have just reread several children's books for my novel," he wrote Louise Colet in March, 1852. "I am half crazy tonight, after all that has gone on in front of my eyes today—from old keepsakes to accounts of shipwrecks and buccaneers." And farther along in the same letter: "For two days now I have been trying to live the dreams of young girls, and for this I have been sailing in milky oceans reading of castles and troubadours in caps of velvet with white plumes" (C, II, 370–371). In his extended catalogues of Emma's girlhood dreams—lists that occupy several pages in his final fiercely rationed text—Flaubert presents a touchingly ludicrous series of pictures, pointing up their absurdities by fantastic juxtapositions and mocking turns of phrasing: "They were all about love, lovers, mistresses, persecuted ladies swooning in lonely pavilions, postilions killed at every relay, horses ridden to death on every page, gloomy forests, broken hearts, vows, sobs, tears, and kisses, boats rowed by moonlight, nightingales in shady groves, gentlemen brave as lions, gentle as lambs, virtuous as no one ever is, always well dressed, who wept like fountains." At fifteen, for a half-year, Emma "dirtied her hands with the dust of old lending libraries," and after a time discovered the world of historical romances:

> With Walter Scott, later on, she became infatuated with historical events, dreamed of oak chests, guardrooms, and minstrels. She would have liked to live in some old manor-house, like those long-waisted chatelaines who, in the shade of pointed arches, would spend their days, elbow on parapet, chin in hand, watching a white-plumed knight come galloping out of the distant countryside on his black horse. At that time she worshiped Mary Stuart and deeply venerated illustrious or unhappy women. Joan of Arc, Héloïse, Agnes Sorèl, the beautiful

Ferronière, and Clémence Isaure stood out to her like comets in the dark immensity of history, where also there stood out, here and there, though less clearly, and all unrelated, St. Louis and his oak tree, the dying Bayard, some atrocities of Louis XI, a little about St. Bartholomew's Day, the crest of the Béarnais, and always the memory of the painted plates glorifying Louis XIV. (I.vi.50–51)

The ballads she had learned in the Convent's music classes were "all about little angels with golden wings, madonnas, lagoons, gondoliers." Inane in style and subject, they were potent to fill Emma's quick imagination with exciting images—"seductive phantasmagoria of sentimental realities." The painted plates glorifying Louis XIV had persisted in Emma's memory from the time of her entering the convent school, and her remembering them so well suggests that her predisposition to romantic phantasmagoria was with her even then. She had dined with her father the night before at an inn where the dishes illustrated the story of Mademoiselle de la Vallière (I.vi.49). Flaubert's brilliant counterpointing of the world of illusion and the impingements of the world of shared reality is seldom achieved with more economy than in his single sentence in which scenes that speak of tenderness of the heart and the glamor of life at court are overlaid and partly obliterated by the scratching of tableware at a public hostelry: "The explanatory legends [on the inn's plates], obliterated here and there by the scratching of knives, all glorified religion, the tenderness of the heart, and the pomps of the Court."

Beyond seeing herself as the heroine in historical romances, learning ballads about angels and madonnas and gondoliers, and acquiring a gallery of unassorted pictures from saint's legend and historical anecdote, Emma Bovary while in the convent school began exploring the world of "keepsakes," the sentimental volumes of poetry and short prose pieces profusely illustrated, bound in satin or gilded paper, and sold like flowers or candy as fashionable gifts, especially for young ladies.[5] "She trembled as she blew back the tissue paper over the engraving and saw it rise in a half fold and fall gently against the opposite page. Here behind the balustrade of a balcony was a young man in a short cloak, who locked in his embrace a young girl in a white dress with an alms-purse at her waist" (I.vi.52). The scenes of the keepsakes offered her what passed for glimpses of aristocratic leisure, scenes depicting a life as far removed from the chores of the barn or dairy at the family farm as it was from the daily regimen of the convent school. English ladies lolled in carriages, or glided through parks in handsome equipages driven by two postilions, or were discovered in moments of elevated sentiment, lounging abstractedly on sofas, gazing at the moon, cooing at a dove in a Gothic cage, or smiling while they plucked leaves from a daisy. Dreams of a shadowy but alluring *haute monde* are mixed with Emma's fantasies of inhabiting the pages of historical romances. They prefigure the pivotal chapter in which Emma and Charles are to visit overnight the aristocratic estate of Vaubyessard, a setting in which Emma's ideal world seems suddenly and with a transforming impact to enter her waking experience. The keepsakes also furnish Emma pictures more exotic—mainly oriental but (like her chaotic version of history) made up of masses of absurdly jarring data that interact among themselves in such a way as to provide their own eloquent commentary. Descriptions of this sort, in which the apparent pointlessness of juxtapositions becomes Flaubert's resort for an "impersonal" means of making his point (often, as here, with a phrasing that is far from objective) are a major hallmark of his style in *Madame Bovary*: "And you, too, were there, sultans with long pipes swooning in arbors in the arms of dancing girls: Giaours, Turkish swords, fezzes; and above all, you, pallid landscapes of dithyrambic foreign lands, that often show us at one and the same time palm trees and firs, tigers on the right, a lion to the left, then some kneeling camels—the whole framed by a well-tended virgin forest, and with a great perpendicular sunbeam quivering in the water, where, standing out as white scratches here and there on the steel-gray background, swans are swimming." Emma reads of such phantasmagoria at night by the illumination of an oil lamp which "lighted up all these pictures of the world" while the sound of the real world is hushed except for the distant noise of carriages passing along the boulevards outside the convent.

In his pages devoted to Emma's girlhood reading, Flaubert has given his most elaborate account of Emma's private world as it existed at the time of her marriage. Her reading had not tempered her well for life as the spouse of a provincial doctor, a point that Flaubert dramatizes by placing his ambitious detailed itemization of it immediately after Emma's first dismayed survey of Charles's house with its many vestiges remaining of his deceased first wife and the humble debris of Charles's day-to-day occupation. Her first sight on opening the door was of "a cloak with a small collar, a bridle, a black leather cap, and on the floor, in a corner . . . a pair of leggings, with the dried mud still on them" (I.v.43). From the kitchen she was soon to hear the grotesque noises of Charles's patients in his consulting room. The contrast between the world around her and the world of her reading was nearly total: "Before her marriage she had thought herself in love; but the happiness that should have followed had failed to come. She must, she supposed, have been mistaken. And Emma wondered what one meant exactly in life by the words *bliss*, *passion*, and *rapture* that had seemed to her so beautiful in books."

Her life at the convent had offered no such painful discontinuities. Her grief at the death of her mother had found appropriate channels without much difficulty. The passage, it is worth remarking, follows directly the extended account of Emma's absorbed reading of the keepsakes as "pictures of the world." There is no break in tone, for Emma's mind passes easily from the patterns of her reading to what she imagines to be the patterns of "life." She "had a memorial picture made with the hair of the deceased, and, in a letter sent to Les Bertaux [the family farm] filled with sad reflections on life, she asked to be buried later in the same grave" (I.vi.53). There is a special irony to Flaubert's comment following this passage. "Emma was secretly gratified to feel that *she had reached at a first trial the rare ideal of sensitive beings, never attained by mediocre hearts.* She let herself meander along with Lamartine, listened to harps on lakes, to all the songs of dying swans, to the falling of the leaves, the pure virgins ascending to heaven, and the voice of the Eternal discoursing down the valleys" (italics mine). It is worth reminding oneself that Flaubert himself was a devotee of art as the most exacting of disciplines—that he was, even in his moments of portraying his heroine who found herself rising to the level of poetic expression at a first try, undergoing the agonies of the artist creating art, the *affres de l'art* of which he complains so often and so feelingly in his letters to Louise Colet. The passage continues: "She gradually grew tired of all this but wouldn't admit her boredom, continued from habit first, then out of vanity, and at last was surprised to feel her grief appeased, and with no more sadness in her heart than wrinkles on her brow." "My cursed Bovary is torturing me and tiring me to death," Flaubert wrote Louise Colet in January, 1852. "Ah but I am terribly worn out and discouraged!" (C, II, 339). And in March, while he was laboring hard at the first draft of his description of Emma's girlhood dreams, he complained to Colet: "I have been working like a mule for fifteen long years. . . . Oh, if ever I produce a good book I'll have worked for it" (C, II, 372–373). Such patient self-subordination to art was as alien to Emma's nature as it was cruelly present in the experience of her creator. She could not easily lose herself, Flaubert makes explicit, even in her reading. Quiet scenes bored her. "She had to extract some personal profit from things and she rejected as useless whatever did not yield immediate gratification—*being of a temperament more sentimental than artistic*, looking for emotions, not landscapes" (I.vi.50, italics mine). When, at Yonville, Emma undertakes projects calculated to keep her at a level superior to the village life, they all come to untidy conclusions. She had an ambition to learn Italian and bought dictionaries, a grammar, and a packet of white paper. She attempted serious reading and the study of history and philosophy. All such pursuits required a tenacity that was not in her temperament, and "her books fared like her pieces of embroidery, all of which, only just begun, were stuffed into her cupboard; she took them up, left them, passed on to something else" (II.vii.174).

When at Tostes, in the early days of her marriage, she had tried to relieve her boredom by practice at the piano, practice itself soon became tedious: "What was the good of playing? Who would hear her? Since she could never dress in a velvet gown with short sleeves, her fingers touching lightly the ivory keys of an Erard piano, and feel the murmurs of ecstasy circulate round her like a breeze, it was not worth the effort of boring herself with practicing" (I.ix.88).

"I am leading an austere life, deprived of all exterior pleasure," Flaubert wrote Colet in April, 1852, "one where I have nothing to sustain me but a kind of permanent rage, in which I sometimes weep at my impotence, but find no escape. I love my work with a love that is frenzied and perverted, as an ascetic loves the hair shirt that scratches his belly. Sometimes when I find myself empty, when I cannot manage expression, when, after scribbling long pagefuls, I discover that I haven't created a single [good] sentence, I collapse on my divan and lie there dazed, in a mental swamp of despair and dullness" (C, II, 394). Such exclamations—and there are many of them in Flaubert's letters of the time—lend added point to passages of *Madame Bovary* in which Emma finds herself reaching at once the rarefied strata inhabited by artists, or dreams of becoming (if only practice were less boring) a concert pianist. So does Flaubert's well-considered statement that his heroine is of a temperament "more sentimental than artistic." Emma Bovary is meant to be in significant ways the antithesis of the author as he writes about her. Her sentimental reading is to a large extent the sort of pseudo-art for which Flaubert had a vehement and acutely personal contempt.

The fantastic tiered cake that brings cries of admiration from the guests at Emma's and Charles's wedding is almost without question intended—in Flaubert's intensely unified novel with its ideal of total relevance enforced by throwing out by far the greater part of what he created—to challenge the reader to discover meanings beyond the incident in which it appears. It is a masterpiece of hedonistic clutter that anticipates and resonates with other images memorably embodying the tastelessness, absurdity, and hedonism of petit-bourgeois society in general and the world of Emma's imagination in particular. The details of Emma's reading are to appear a few pages later. The cake is the product of a sugar-baker's inspiration run rampant. A confectioner who had just started his shop in the district had created it as a sample of the magnificences he was capable of. It had a base of blue cardboard made to represent "a temple with porticoes, colonnades, and stucco statuettes all round" with an additional effect produced by pasting on gilt paper stars. On the tier above this came a castle-keep comprised of Savoy cake and ornamented with small fortifications done in candied angelica stems, almonds, raisins, and quarters of oranges. On the third level appeared a green meadow with lakes of jam on which rode boats made of nutshell, and surmounting all there was a Cupid in a swing made of chocolate, its supporting poles, however, terminating in natural rosebuds (I.iv.39). Taken all together, Flaubert's prose poem of the wedding cake anticipates the method of the Symbolist Poets. Vehicle is divorced from any satisfactory tenor, and the perceptive reader must supply for himself the relation (rich in its ramifying implications) between the wildly heterogeneous facts of the tiered cake and the absurd non sequiturs that are to be presented shortly afterward, layer by sugared layer, of Emma's reading, in which "immediate gratification" was the one thing she demanded.

61

ii. Vaubyessard

With her visit to the estate of the Marquis d'Andervilliers, Emma's inward experience enters upon a new life. There is more than a faint suggestion of blasphemy in Flaubert's way of presenting her initial moment of epiphany at Vaubyessard. What she undergoes is in essence an experience of conversion such as saints had undergone in the legends that formed a portion of her reading. The scales fall from her eyes, and she beholds, while waking, the truths of a new way of life made manifest—except that for Emma it is not a waking to the way of the Cross: ". . . in the splendor of the present hour her past life, so clear until now, vanished entirely, and she almost doubted having lived it. She was here, at the ball. Beyond, overspreading all else, was only shadow. She was eating a maraschino ice that she held with her left hand in a silver-gilt cup, her eyes half-closed, and the spoon between her teeth" (I.viii.72). Emma's conversion, like many conversions to sainthood, follows lines of thought and emotion long building in her imaginative life. It is, of course, a detail of importance that she is eating a maraschino ice from a silver-gilt cup with the spoon between her teeth at the precise moment when her past life suddenly becomes unreal. What Emma sees as the overpowering splendor of Vaubyessard has nothing much more suggestive of distinction (of a sort Flaubert himself would accept as distinction) than the pictures of fashionable life Emma had studied in the keepsakes, where ladies and gentlemen enjoyed uninterrupted lives of wealth and luxury. The details Flaubert selects as points of Emma's special observation leading up to her moment of revelation—delicate pomades . . . the shimmer of satin . . . diamond brooches . . . exquisite foods . . . handkerchiefs that exude a subtle perfume—evoke an atmosphere of lavish sensuosity which Flaubert further underlines in two pointed passages. In one he generalizes upon the aristocratic gentlemen that have dazzled Emma: "Their indifferent glances had the appeased expression of passions daily gratified, and through all their gentleness of manner pierced that peculiar brutality that bespeaks a dominance over half-tame things . . . the handling of thoroughbred horses and the pursuit of loose women." In the second passage (which occurs earlier) the ancient Duke de Laverdière is presented as a species of death's head at the feast—a man with a notorious past, who has now so worn out his faculties that a servant must shout in his ear "in reply to his mumblings" the names of the dishes that he points to. Emma sees no lack of glamour in this decayed aristocrat. Flaubert, however, allows the reader two perspectives. The Duke de Laverdière is seen both as a deaf old man whose lips dribble gravy while he eats, and, through Emma's dazzled perception, as a nobleman of the Court who has "lain in the bed of queens."

In earlier manuscript sheets of *Madame Bovary*, among passages that Flaubert omitted from the final version, there appears a conversation among other members of the bourgeoisie who along with Emma and Charles have been invited to the dinner and ball. Their conversation concentrates on the food about to be placed on the table and upon the price of the dinner service. One of them estimates that the silver alone would be worth a full thirty thousand francs, and though a second citizen voices his awe and astonishment at such a figure, a third is certain that, if the coffee spoons are counted in, the whole would run to a good forty thousand.[6] If the silversmith had endowed his work with any special grace, it is lost on the beholders. Luxury and wealth are what impress these gentlemen in this relatively lame scene that Flaubert had once thought of including in his detail of bourgeois wonderment.

At three o'clock in the morning the cotillion begins. Though Emma does not know how to dance a waltz, one of the gentlemen of Vaubyessard, a Viscount (never to be identified further, though Emma keeps him always in her memory and even thinks she sees him momentarily at Rouen in the final decline of her fortunes [III.vii.412–413]) comes to urge her a second time to join him in the waltz, assuring her that she would get on very well with him to guide her. He is significantly left faceless—a representative of all the aristocratic young gentlemen, faultlessly clothed and exotically perfumed, who live at ease in the atmosphere of Vaubyessard. Georges Poulet has devoted an essay to Flaubert's preoccupation in *Madame Bovary* with circular forms.[7] Certainly a series of richly nondiscursive images circular in pattern occupy positions of importance in the novel, and among them is the waltz at Vaubyessard, which seems to perform symbolically Emma's removal from the realities of her domestic life to a passionate engagement with experience of a sort that can be hers only in her newly active life of illusion. "They began slowly, then moved faster. They whirled: all things around them whirled—lamps, furniture, the walls, the floor—as with a disk turning on a pivot. As they passed near the doors, the train of Emma's gown clung to his trousers; their legs intertwined. He looked down at her; she raised her eyes to his. A torpor came over her, and she stopped dancing. Then they began again, and with a swifter movement the Viscount swept her off to the very end of the gallery, where, out of breath, she nearly fell for an instant, and leaned her head against his chest." But it is not Flaubert's intention to allow the overtones of the scene to go farther toward any actual involvement between Emma and the Viscount, who is to remain symbolic in effect and never individualized: "Then, still whirling but more slowly, he guided her once more to her seat. She sank back against the wall and covered her eyes with her hands." The music of the orchestra goes on echoing in Emma's mind after the ball has ended, and "she struggled to keep herself awake so she could prolong the illusion of this luxurious life that she would so soon have to give up." As she and Charles drive home next day, she imagines she sees the Viscount in a group of horsemen. Charles picks up from the road where they have passed a "cigar case trimmed in green silk, with a crest in the center like the door of a carriage." For Emma the cigar case is to serve as a medallion or saint's medal commemorating her visit to Vaubyessard, her place of revelation. Her imaginative world—peopled by keepsakes with their English ladies lolling in carriages or inhabiting sumptuous interiors, Lamartine's poetry, Scott's heroines in gothic castles, the painted plates with scenes of Madame de la Vallière, the ballads with all their "seductive phantasmagoria of sentimental realities"—now circled about the Viscount as a central figure. She took to drawing the cigar case from the cupboard where she concealed it among the linen to inhale (like a ceremonial incense) its odor of verbena and tobacco. She preferred to think it had been a present from the Viscount's mistress. "Of what had they spoken as he stood resting his elbow on one of those elaborate mantelpieces adorned with flower vases and Pompadour clocks?" (I.ix.79). Since she assumed the Viscount had by now left Vaubyessard for Paris, the very name of Paris began to enchant her and "rang in her ears like the great bell of a cathedral." Paris "glittered before her eyes," even (Flaubert adds with his characteristic counterpointing note of irony) "on the labels of her jars of pomade." Emma is sent into a search through magazines and novels to discover vicarious pleasures in the world of fashion and luxury. The figure of the Viscount is present to her in all the accounts she reads of race meetings, soirées, and first nights at the theaters. Gradually memories of his figure become less vivid to her, though even more pervasive in lending reality to her illusionary world: ". . . the circle of which he was the center gradually widened around him; and the halo she had endowed him with spread beyond his image and gilded her other dreams."

Both the overtones of religious worship and the considerable play of circular images surrounding the Viscount are calculated to make Emma's fantasies at the one time religious and sexual. Emma's visions of Parisian life widen to take on Olympian overtones. Writers and actresses luxuriate at an immense remove from the life of Tostes: "They lived far above all others, among the storms that rage between heaven and earth, partaking of the sublime." She had been confined by fate to an island of "petit-bourgeois stupidity" inhabited by mediocrities while "beyond stretched as far as eye could see the immense land of raptures and passions." In her longing, Flaubert tells us in a lapse from his principle of "impersonality," she confounded "the sensuous pleasures of luxury with the joys of the heart, and elegancy of social manners with delicacy of sentiment." The distanced moonlight raptures of the keepsakes now became absurdly mixed in her fantasies with concrete details of material wealth drawn from Vaubyessard and magazines of fashion. "Sighs in the moonlight, long embraces, tears flowing over yielded hands, all the fevers of the flesh and the languors of tenderness seemed to her inseparable from the balconies of great mansions, where leisure abounds, from boudoirs with silk curtains and thick carpets, well-filled flower stands, and a bed on a raised daïs, from the flashing of jewels and the glitter of golden braids on servants' liveries."

An important aspect of Flaubert's rich and subtle irony in *Madame Bovary* is Emma's conception of her private world as something altogether distinct from the petit-bourgeois society she inhabits at Tostes and at Yonville l'Abbaye. Her vision at Vaubyessard is exactly a petit-bourgeois vision, as the deleted scene involving the three guests' wonderment at the value of the dinner service would have implied overflatly. When the merchant Lheureux later exploits Emma's fancy for buying scarves, rings, seals, silks, and other luxuries, he is on ground he well understands even while he flatters Emma's assumptions of aesthetic superiority. She scarcely reveals in such scenes the "refinement of taste" that critics have sometimes observed as characteristic of her.

It is unlikely that Flaubert thought there was a possibility of finding at Vaubyessard anything markedly more elevating to the spirit than the luxuries that had dazzled Emma and the other bourgeois guests. He took a pessimistic view of the society of his time whether lower, middle or upper class. Writers who enjoyed the greatest success with the public, he wrote Louise Colet, were those that pandered to "the passions of the day, the concerns of the moment." People still gave lip service to the classics as they did to religion, but no longer understood them and found them boring. The bourgeoisie, he declared, now included all of mankind (C, III, 52). "Seventeen eighty-nine demolished royalty and nobility," he wrote at another time, "1848 the bourgeoisie, and 1851 'the people.' Nothing remains except the vulgar and stupid mob. We are all mired to the same depth in mediocrity. Social equality has invaded the mind. Our books, our Art, our science, are aimed at serving everybody, as one constructs railroads and public shelters. Mankind has a rage for moral abasement, and I resent being a part of it" (C, III, 349–350).

It was not only Emma Bovary who, in the months following her visit to Vaubyessard, felt a captive isolated from the life of fashion in the monotony and dinginess of Tostes. The village hairdresser experienced a melancholy that Flaubert plays in pointedly ironic parallel to Emma's own. His shop, its windows decorated with an old fashion-plate stuck against a pane and displaying the wax bust of a woman with yellow hair, lay close to the house of the Bovarys. Like Emma he sighed for other worlds: "He, too, the hairdresser, lamented his wasted talents, his hopeless future, and dreaming of a shop in a big town—Rouen, for instance, overlooking the harbor, near the theater—he paced back and forth all day from the mayor's office to the church, sombre and waiting for customers." When Emma looked up, "she always saw him there, like a sentinel on duty" (I.ix.89–90).

Immediately following his paragraph devoted to the vignette of the hairdresser Flaubert places his vignette of the organ grinder, also a paragraph in length: "Sometimes in the afternoon the head of a man appeared outside the living-room window, a swarthy head with black whiskers, that smiled slowly, with a broad, gentle smile that showed his white teeth. A waltz began, and atop the barrel-organ, in a little drawing room, dancers the height of a finger, women in pink turbans, Tyrolians in jackets, monkeys in black frock coats, gentlemen in knee breeches, whirled, whirled among the armchairs, the sofas, the tables, reflected in small bits of looking-glass held together at the corners by strips of gold paper."

"They whirled: everything around them whirled—lamps, furniture, the walls, the floor—*as with a disk turning on a pivot.*" These details from the waltz at Vaubyessard are pointedly paralleled in the fantastic burlesque of fashionable waltzing that is enacted atop a disk connected, one assumes, by a pivot to the instrument of the organ grinder, where bits of mirror and gold paper form ironic equivalents for material wealth, and monkeys in frock coats substitute for gentlemen of rank.

The organ grinder is a creator of illusion. Emma's dreams are set in motion like the little figures atop the organ: "the music issued from the box, droning through a curtain of pink taffeta . . . . They were tunes played in other places—at the theaters, sung in drawing-rooms, danced to at night under lighted chandeliers—echoes of the world that reached Emma in this way. Sarabands ran continuously through her head, and like an Oriental dancing-girl on a flowered carpet, her thought leaped with the notes, swung from dream to dream, from sadness to sadness." The organ grinder himself, the swarthy man with black whiskers, occasionally "spat out a long squirt of brown saliva against the milestone" as he turned the handle. Finally he collected some pennies in his cap and drew a cloth over the little world of music and dancers and left. The organ grinder thus moves disturbingly across Emma's vision and the reader's mind as a mysteriously nondiscursive image, a sinister manipulator of a world of dancers and dreamers who pivot round and round atop his organ, or who listen with sighs at the windows of houses. Flaubert is nothing if not careful to the point of obsession in his concern for freighting with meaning each scene he chooses to elaborate in his much-deleted and much-revised final manuscript. It is fairly safe, taking into account the author's idiom, to associate Flaubert's vignette of the organ grinder with the producers of sentimental literature and art whom Flaubert saw with indignation playing upon the emotions of the public. Art, Flaubert complained to Colet in September, 1853, was now aimed at serving everybody, and everybody had become a vulgar and stupid mob. Such sentiments were much in his mind, it is evident, during the writing of *Madame Bovary*.

The final version of *Madame Bovary* was indeed the result of agonizing compression of a great mass of materials. For four years and eight months—from September, 1851, into April, 1856—Flaubert worked at his novel. He prepared numerous plans and outlines; he wrote a total of 1,788 pages of rough draft; and these sheets are crossed and recrossed, so that parts of the manuscript even in its advanced stages witness the agony with which Flaubert arrived at his final decisions. Great amounts of material that he had worked into more or less final form were omitted from the novel as it eventually appeared —so many of them that a running account of the action of *Madame Bovary* has been edited and prepared from them, a volume that is of value to anyone trying to see the purposes underlying the novel.[8]

One deleted section dealing with Emma's experiences at Vaubyessard is particularly helpful in its implications. In the omitted scene, Flaubert had caused Emma to wander from the chateau after the ball to walk at dawn in the grounds. Eventually she came to a little summer house in a small wood. Entering, she found the place picturesquely furnished, with bamboo chairs and a green marble table and cages with parakeets. Most enchanting of all to her were the small square panes of one window of the little house. These were of various colors. Emma found a special fascination in viewing the landscape through these colored lenses. "Through the blue all seemed sad. An azure haze suffusing the air lengthened the meadow and made the hills seem far away." Shifting to the yellow, she beheld a world of feathery golden clouds and brilliantly illuminated sky, a world "joyous and warm." The green made earth, lawn, water, flowers all seem to fuse into one element, while the shadows became black and forbidding. It was the red pane, however, that she preferred above the others. It "devoured all else with its color." The stream became rose-hued, the grassy banks looked "like seas of curdled blood" and the sky turned to one immense conflagration.

Though she at last became frightened and turned away to see the countryside through another window that had panes of clear glass, thus returning to "ordinary daylight," Flaubert's purpose in designing the incident seems evident. It may be that Flaubert ultimately rejected the scene as too patently and artificially embodying Emma's habit of viewing the world through the vari-colored panes of her reading. In any event, it seems significant that she stayed longest in front of the red pane. One remembers that even at an early age Emma had found nothing of much interest in nature unless nature was in tumult, "being of a temperament more sentimental than artistic, looking for emotions, not landscapes" (I.vi.50).

iii. RODOLPHE: THE LANGUAGE OF SENTIMENT; THE LANGUAGE OF SATANISM

In the earlier stages of Emma's married life, before the appearance of Rodolphe, her illusions though often implicitly sexual in overtone are still centered in the fashionable life of Paris or the glamour of more distant places, their remoteness from her daily life constituting an important element in the fascination they have for her. The Viscount is scarcely an exception, for he is, for Emma, a perfumed symbol rather than a man of flesh and blood. It is only in the later stages of her course following the advent of Rodolphe that Emma's visions become deeply colored with sexual experience in itself. Even in her most bizarre scenes with Rodolphe and later with Léon at Rouen, *illusion* remains at the very heart of her demands, despite the increasing tones of Satanism that then color her experience. There are still times when she reverts to dreams of a lost paradise that never existed. When she has abandoned the respectable married life of Yonville so far as to dance through the night with Léon to "the wild sounds of the trombones," attired in masculine costume, with velvet breeches, carmine stockings, and a wig and a three-cornered hat—a costume that might come from the pages of the Marquis de Sade or, later, of Huysmans—Emma finds herself capable of being shocked when the voices of other women betray them as females of the "lowest class" (III.vi.403). She imagines herself escaping the present through a return to youth and innocence: "Everything, herself included, was now unbearable. She would have liked to fly away like a bird, to go away to become young again somewhere far off in the regions of immaculate space."

In the early weeks of her marriage, she had tried to picture for herself an ideal setting for the first experience of married love. The scene is touchingly sentimental, distanced, and pastel: "To taste the full sweetness, one would no doubt have to travel to those lands with resounding names where the days following marriage are spent in delicious idleness. In post-chaises behind curtains of blue silk one slowly ascends the mountain roads, listening to the song of the postilion as it is re-echoed by the mountains amid the sounds of the little bells of goats and the far-off roar of waterfalls" (I.vii.56). As if she were turning pages in one of the keepsakes that supplied her with pictures of the world, Emma's fantasy leaves this lithograph of Switzerland for a more exotic setting to the south: "At sunset on the shore of a bay they would breathe the perfume of lemon trees; then in the evening on the villa terraces above they would gaze hand in hand at the stars and make plans for the future." Flaubert has already told us how, during the period of courtship, Emma in her conversations with Charles would abruptly shift from one mood to another, "her voice . . . clear, or sharp, or . . . filled with languor, trailing off" as if she spoke to herself (I.iii.31). In a similar way her fantasy takes sudden turns of scene and mood. She shifts from her vision of "regions that produce happiness" to those that induce melancholy: "Why could she not now be leaning over the balcony of some Swiss chalet, or enshrining her melancholy in a Scotch cottage, with a husband clad in a black velvet coat with long tails, and soft boots, a pointed hat and ruffles?"

Emma's wistful vision of the slow-paced carriage shared with a loved one behind silk curtains sets up ironical echoes in her later vision of galloping away in the arms of Rodolphe drawn by four horses. It resonates with greater irony, as has often been observed, to the famous scene with Léon, in which their love is consummated for the first time in a public cab with drawn blinds circulating monotonously through the streets of Rouen.

To adjust the world of her illusion to the world of Tostes, in which her husband cupped blood and prescribed pills, was, of course, an impossibility. But Flaubert (himself in his one aspect equally addicted to romantic visions) views Emma's desires for living a romance with a special delicacy at this stage of her experience, if one judges from the tone of his presentation: "Perhaps she would have wished to confide all these thoughts to some one. But how speak about an uneasiness so elusive, changing shape like the clouds, unstable as the winds? Words failed her, and also the occasion, the courage. But if Charles had only wished it, if he had guessed, if his eyes had only once read her thoughts, it seemed to her that her heart would have opened its wealth to him, suddenly, as ripened fruit falls from a tree at the touch of a hand. But even as their outward familiarity became greater, so did her aloofness from him in her inward life" (I.vii.57).

It is easy to understand how some critics have inclined to the view that Emma represents to an important degree an island of refined aesthetic and spiritual yearnings surrounded by elements not only alien but distinctly inferior to her own in the bourgeois village life in general and the dullness of her husband in particular, and that that is the way Flaubert has arranged for us to see her. The lyricism of such passages as the one last quoted seems to imply a nature attuned to delicate perceptions, a nature that, planted in finer soil, would have flowered without danger of blighting. It is necessary, however, to make a distinction: The diction and the lyrical movement of such passages are not Emma's. They are Flaubert's working as ventriloquist. It may be worth noting in the passage just quoted that when Emma thinks of confiding her fleeting visions, not only the occasion and the courage fail her, but the words as well. Flaubert's use of the indirect free style (*le style indirect libre*), his employment of various devices of phrase and structure to evoke Emma's felt presence—not merely her attitudes but an impression that we are hearing her voice in the moment of her silent speaking to herself[9]—is somewhat more complicated than it is often considered. The accents Flaubert assigns his heroine in such passages as that quoted in the preceding paragraph represent her unspoken yearnings. They conjure up for the reader an impression of overhearing a musical voice in lyrical accents quite in keeping with what we have learned of her charms of face and figure. But Flaubert is playing Cyrano for Christian de Neuvillette; we are endowing Emma (as Roxane endowed Christian) with poetical graces that belong elsewhere. And it is better so. Much later Emma is to pour out her love for Rodolphe Boulanger in words designed to represent her own idiom (at a time, it is true, when her imagination is colored by more vivid experience) and not Flaubert's translation into the language of her inward yearnings. Emma's idiom when it reaches the reader from her own lips is passionate, but it is not poetical: " 'Oh, I love you, I love you,' " she exclaims to Rodolphe (who is embarrassed by her asking him, a jaded roué, to declare he has never loved any one else). " 'I love you so much I couldn't live without you, understand? . . . I'm your slave, your concubine! You're my king, my idol! You're good! You're beautiful! You're wise! You're strong!' " (II.xii.264–265). If I have not managed here to be entirely fair to Emma's accents in my translation (the original will be found in the notes[10]), it is in any event clear that Rodolphe does not find her exclamatory language distinctive from that he is used to hearing in such situations and that Flaubert intended the passage to be full of feeling but lame in its diction and rhythms. Rodolphe for his part had "heard these things uttered so often that they had no freshness for him. Emma was like all his other mistresses; and the charm of novelty, falling away little by little like a garment, laid bare the eternal monotony of passion, that always assumes the same forms and the same language." But Flaubert, as narrator, even in his published version of his novel, in which on theory he so carefully represses remarks that might be labeled an obvious deviation from his mask of "impersonality," comments in what amounts to an open authorial intrusion on the part of the narrator: "He did not perceive, this man so versed in experience, the differences in emotions underlying the same expressions. Since libertine or venal lips had murmured to him phrases like Emma's, he believed only slightly in the sincerity of her words. One ought, [Rodolphe] thought, to discount exaggerated phrases used to cloak an ordinary love affair . . . ." And Flaubert's observation completing the passage suggests rather clearly that despite his famous avowal of purpose to Louise Colet—"no lyricism, no author's reflections, the personality of the author not present" (C, II, 361)—he must at times have been conscious that he was intervening in his work as authorial commentator: ". . . as though the fullness of one's soul did not sometimes overflow in empty metaphors, since no one ever is able to give the exact measure of his needs, his concepts, or his sorrows. Human speech is like a cracked kettle whereon we beat out tunes to set a bear dancing when we would aspire to move the stars to tenderness." If Emma's speech, outside the special language of love, is of a quality above that suggested by thumping on a cracked kettle to produce rhythms for a dancing bear, it is nevertheless the narrator who supplies her oftentimes with translations in a prose that might, if a poet's hyperboles were facts, move the stars to tenderness. Flaubert, working at the one time as both realist and lyricist, had, indeed, no choice. Emma—ostensibly the mind doing the perceiving—must assume the spotlight while the author himself sings behind the scenes; for, as Donald Fanger points out, realism has to appear objective by nature and the "lyrical material has to be attributed or attributable to a character—a procedure that keeps it under narrative control, keeps it judged."[11]

A passage that occurs on the first night of the Bovarys' removal from Tostes to Yonville also suggests that Emma's familiarity with sentimental reading has not given her speech distinction—at least beyond the clichés of such literature. She and Charles converse with Léon and Homais at the chief inn of the town, and Emma and Léon find they speak a common language. Léon, it is worth observing, though like Emma he cultivates sentimental reading, is an attorney's clerk, a petit-bourgeois. He is, much later in the novel, to be her second lover. In the early months at Yonville, however, before the appearance of Rodolphe, Léon shares sentimental scenes with Emma on a Platonic level. Like Emma, he assumes his superiority to the general citizenry of Yonville because of his sensitivity to literature and to music. He dresses neatly; he cleans his fingernails. A passage near the end of the novel, after his months as Emma's lover at Rouen, synthesizes Flaubert's conception of his nature. The liaison has by that time run its course; Léon has been reprimanded by his employer for neglect of work and scandalous conduct. He promises to reform and thinks of all the trouble Emma may still stir up for him. He thinks, too, of all the jokes his fellow clerks will make: "Besides, he was going to be promoted to head clerk; it was time to be serious. So he gave up his flute, his exalted sentiments, his romantic imagination; *for every bourgeois in the warmth of his youth, were it for only a day, a moment, has believed himself capable of immense passions, of high enterprises*. The pettiest libertine has dreamed of sultanas; *every notary bears within him the debris of a poet*" (III.vi.400–401, italics mine).

There is not much reason to suppose, therefore, that when Emma enjoys a sense of communication and kinship with Léon at Yonville, she is conversing with a spirit possessed of unusual refinement, or that her own responses to Léon's words are to be thought of as those of an especially sensitive nature. Indeed the dialogue that Flaubert gives to Léon and Emma contrasts significantly with the lyrical quality that invests his language when he is translating Emma's thoughts and emotions into his own lyrical idiom for her. Charles Bovary in the scene at the inn remarks that his wife is not fond of exercise, for she " 'prefers always sitting in her room reading.' " Léon replies that he also prefers such occupation. " 'And indeed, what could be better than to sit by one's fireside of an evening with a book, with the wind beating against the window and the lamp burning?' " The words strike a ready response in Emma: " 'What, indeed?' she said, gazing at him with her large black eyes wide open."

Encouraged by such response from a woman of obvious refinement who is also very pretty, Léon expands his thought in clichés fostered by the popular book trade, clichés that Flaubert himself could only consider absurdly bourgeois: " 'You forget everything else,' he continued; 'the hours slip by. Without moving from your chair, you travel through the countries of your imagination, and your thought, blending with the fiction, relishes the details, or rushes forward with the adventures. It mingles with the characters, and it is you who are living their lives, your own heart beats in their breasts.' " Emma exclaims, "How true! how true!" It is splendid to discover one's own sentiments expressed in books, but she prefers novels to poetry, which is in the long run boring. Her delight is "stories that rush breathlessly along, that frighten one." She has no use for novels that have commonplace heroes and deal with the concerns of everyday life. (Flaubert, of course, is writing a book in that general vein as she speaks.) Léon agrees: " 'Indeed,' observed the clerk, 'since these works fail to touch the heart, they miss, it seems to me, the true aim of art. It is so sweet, amid all the disappointments of life, to be able to dwell in the imagination upon noble characters, pure affections, and pictures of happiness. For myself, living here far from the

world, this is my sole distraction. Yonville has so little to offer' "
(II.ii.114–115). By degrees, Flaubert tells us, while Charles and Homais talked of medical and civic matters, Léon and Emma "entered
into one of those vague conversations where random turns of phrasing
keep bringing you back to a core of shared sympathies." But lest the
reader should think that this implies a distinguished power of intellect
in Léon and Emma, Flaubert specifies the things that they discoursed
about—the theaters of Paris, "titles of novels, new dance tunes, *and
the world they did not know*" (italics mine).

The pains that it took Flaubert to enter into the world of Emma's
reading and Emma's imagination are evident in his letters to Louise
Colet while he was suffering his agonies of art in creating the earlier
chapters of *Madame Bovary*. The contempt he felt for sentimentality,
as opposed to sincere sentiment, was during this period very intense
in him. His work on this part of the novel progressed with excruciating slowness. "Tonight I finished scribbling the first draft of my
young girl's dreams. I have another fortnight to put in sailing on
these blue lakes, after which I'll attend a ball and then endure the
rainy winter, following which I'll close with a pregnancy" (C, II,
381). The "young girl's dreams" are clearly Emma's early readings
and her imaginative life as they are described in retrospect between
her marriage to Charles and the winter following the ball at Vaubyessard. The pregnancy of Emma spans the last months at Tostes and
the first at Yonville. Such material continued to exact agonizing
effort. Though Flaubert had intended to complete his novel as far
as the visit to Vaubyessard in a fortnight, he had just managed to
carry his manuscript that far at the end of four weeks: "I have now
come to my ball, which I will commence on Monday," he wrote
Louise Colet on April 24, 1852. "I hope it will go better." He had
managed only twenty-five pages in the last six weeks, averaging a
little more than half a page a day (C, II, 394). His natural inclination,
he wrote in July, was not at all toward the sort of material that he
was dealing with (C, II, 461–462); and it was only, one infers, by an
enormous effort of empathy that he could manage to see through the
eyes of Emma in the earlier stages of her career. Some months later
but still when only a little over the first year of the four years and
eight months he was to spend on *Madame Bovary* had gone by,
Flaubert was still feeling the great difficulty of creating the imagina-

tive world of his novel: "I am working fairly well, I mean with some confidence; but it is hard to express well something one has never felt" (C, III, 53, November 22, 1852).

Such complaining was to come to a halt. A change in tone takes place with Flaubert's letter to Louise Colet at the end of December, 1853. He has at last reached the scene of Emma's seduction by Rodolphe. She is now "my little woman" rather than the embodiment of a problem; Flaubert is able to throw himself into the scene of his narrative. He exults over his task that has overwhelmed him for nearly all of the last twelve hours, from two in the afternoon until two the next morning. "I am in the midst of lovemaking," he writes Louise Colet. "I am sweating and my throat is choked. This has been one of the rare days of my life which I have passed entirely in illusion from end to end." Flaubert is no longer occupied with the "dreams of young girls" or troubadours in caps of velvet: "At six o'clock, just as I wrote the words 'fit of hysterics,' I was so carried away, was bellowing so loudly and felt so deeply what my little woman was going through, that I was afraid of having hysterics myself." For the time the agonies of art were displaced by joy in his power to write—"to be no longer yourself but to move in an entire world of your own creating. Today, for instance, man and woman together, lover and beloved, I rode in a forest on an autumn afternoon under the yellow leaves, and I was the horses, the leaves, the wind, the words that were spoken, and the red sun that made them half-close their love-drowned eyes" (C, III, 404-405).

What had happened was that Flaubert had at last arrived at a point in his story where he could sometimes enter into the imaginative life of his heroine without cramping his own imagination. As Mario Praz illustrates at length in *The Romantic Agony*, Flaubert by nature had much in common with such writers as de Sade, Baudelaire, and Huysmans.[12] Even through her affair with Léon before he leaves Yonville for Paris—an affair made up of sighs and glances—there is much restraint in Emma's imaginings as well as in her conduct. Her thoughts at this point are indeed complicated; they reveal a good deal about Flaubert's agonies in trying to chart precisely his heroine's intricate moods. Emma was quite conscious, he tells us, of being enamored of Léon and entertained fancies of a physical consummation. "But the more she became aware of her love, the more she repressed

76

it, hoping to conceal it, and make it lessen" (II.v.150). Part of her reluctance, Flaubert says, came from modesty, part from fear of consequences, and part from sheer indolence! There was also the pleasure she obtained during this affair from playing the drama of virtue under duress: "Then pride and the pleasure of saying to herself, 'I am virtuous,' and of studying herself in the mirror assuming poses of resignation consoled her a little for the sacrifice *she thought she was making*" (italics mine). Flaubert's difficulties were to last through the departure of Léon for Paris and even (with qualification) through the early part of Emma's experience with Rodolphe.

Once Emma has surrendered to Rodolphe, there is, as has been intimated, a change in the color of her inner world, though the change is not the abrupt *volte-face* and total abandonment of bourgeois attitudes and values that she fancies it to be. She begins to identify herself with the more lurid of the heroines of history and literature—the "lyric legion of adulterous women." The life of permanent bliss she had so often read about is, she feels, soon to become her reality. "She was about to enter a world of wonders where all would be passion, ecstasy, delirium. An azure immensity surrounded her and ordinary life appeared distant and far beneath her wrapped in shade, visible only at moments from these heights" (II.ix.225). Such visions do not, however, inspire her tongue with language to suit them. She achieves expression only in traditional clichés of respectable bourgeois life that Rodolphe finds flattering but absurd. "Besides, she was getting dreadfully sentimental. She had made him exchange miniatures, handfuls of hair had been cut off, and now she was asking for a ring—a veritable wedding-ring, in token of eternal union. Often she spoke to him of the 'chimes of evening,' of the 'voices of nature.' Then she would go on and on about her mother, and his. Rodolphe's had been dead for twenty years; nevertheless Emma consoled him with affected phrases of the sort one would use with a bereaved child. Sometimes she would even say, gazing at the moon: 'I am sure that somewhere up there they both give their blessing to our love' " (II.x. 235–236). Their love, far from supporting a state of permanent ecstasy as Emma had assumed, tames down in the course of six months to a routine resembling marriage. Temporarily Emma leaves off seeing Rodolphe and explores novel sensations in playing the role of virtuous wife and mother, to abandon it only after the humiliations attending

Charles's disastrous operation on Hippolyte's clubbed foot. It is only during this second pursuit of ecstasy with Rodolphe that Emma's inner world assumes at last positive colorings of Satanism. When Emma dreams of eloping with Rodolphe, abandoning Charles and her respectable life once and for all, her fantasy, as Flaubert elaborates it, significantly parallels the pattern of her earlier fantasy (during her first weeks of marriage) of what the honeymoon would have been like if it had touched perfection. The details, however, are much altered. In the earlier fantasy she and her husband would have ridden in a post-chaise at a leisurely pace through the mountains of Switzerland while the mountains echoed to the postilion's song, the sound of goat's bells, and the far-off roar of waterfalls. Or they would have gazed hand in hand at the stars, breathing the perfume of lemon trees, or would have savored a haunting melancholy in a Swiss chalet or (it might be) a Scotch cottage. Now, she fancied, she was soon to hurtle away with Rodolphe in a carriage drawn by four horses. They would gallop for a week toward some novel land, never to return. They would travel "on and on, their arms entwined, without speaking a word." Splendid cities would suddenly appear, with domes, bridges, ships, "whole forests of lemon trees, and cathedrals of white marble, their pointed spires bearing storks' nests." They would ride down a wide pavement where their path would be strewn with bouquets of flowers offered by women dressed in red. Chiming bells, neighing mules, strumming of guitars, and the hiss of fountains would greet them. Heaps of fruit would be piled in pyramids at the foot of pale statues that smiled beneath sprays of water. "They would row in gondolas, swing in hammocks, and their life would be as easy and free as their loose silken gowns, warm and star-studded as the nights they would contemplate." Days, all of them magnificent, would go on and on like waves. The vision "hovered on the horizon, infinite, harmonious, azure, and washed in sunshine" (II.xii.271–272).

This is all a long distance from Emma's early fancies. Her fantasy of life with Rodolphe is much closer to the tone of many passages in Flaubert's *The Temptation of Saint Anthony*, which he had laid aside unpublished when he started *Madame Bovary*, and still closer to the voluptuous romanticism and overt Satanism of *Salammbô*, the work that was to follow *Madame Bovary*. Emma now luxuriates in the atmosphere of illicit love, Flaubert tells us, and she increases in voluptuous beauty like a flower nourished on rain, wind, sunshine, and—the counterpointing detail claiming its place—manure. "Her cravings, her sorrows, her sensual ecstasies and her ever-youthful illusions had gradually developed her, and she blossomed out in the fullness of her nature, like a flower nourished on manure, on rain, wind, and sunshine." Her outward appearance assumes a sensual allure to match the preoccupations of her inner world. "Her half-closed eyelids seemed expressly shaped for the long amorous glances that issued from beneath them, while her sighs dilated the fine nostrils and raised the fleshy corners of her lips . . . . Some artist skilled in corruption seemed to have designed the shape of her hair as it fell on her neck, coiled in a heavy mass, casually rearranged after being loosened every day in adultery" (II.xii.269–270). In contrast to the eloquence of her flesh, her language has become coarsened; its plethora of lame clichés—no longer clichés of bourgeois life but now clichés of frankly erotic love—disgusts Rodolphe, who at last allows his contempt to enter even into his love-making. "He threw aside all modesty as inconvenient. He treated her as he pleased, and made her into something pliant and corrupt. It was an idiotic species of infatuation, full of admiration on his part and voluptuousness on hers, a beatitude that left her drugged; and her soul sank deep into this drunken state, drowned and shrivelled in it, like the duke of Clarence in his butt of malmsey" (II.xii.265–266). Later, in Emma's liaison with Léon at Rouen, religious symbols and connotations are fused with sexual in a manner especially reminiscent of Flaubert's *The Temptation of Saint Anthony*. Their place of assignation before the first consummation of their love is the cathedral, where Léon sees the church surrounding Emma "like a huge boudoir." Stained glass, a silver lamp, a painting of Salome dancing, sounds that resemble sighs of love, the aroma of incense set up voluptuously ambiguous overtones. "The arches bent down to shelter in their darkness the avowal of her love; the windows shone resplendent to illumine her face, and the censers would burn that she might appear like an angel amid perfumed clouds" (III.i.331).

Love gifts for Rodolphe and later for Léon account for many of Emma's debts to Lheureux, a bourgeois Mephistopheles who offers her all manner of luxuries on easy credit. She borrows recklessly until, "all absorbed in her passions, she had no more worry over money matters than an archduchess" (III.vi.393). She progresses by degrees from dunning Charles's patients and thus collecting money without his knowledge, to falsifying records. In her last desperation, she tries to force Léon to steal from his employer. As her imaginative world deepens in its colors and increasingly absorbs her, she is less and less able to face her reality; and when her resources for evading reality are gone she eventually escapes by suicide.

v. Rodolphe, Homais, Bournisien, and Other Dealers in Illusion

The language of illusion figures so large in *Madame Bovary* as to occupy a major part of the novel. In counterpoint to Emma, who is the willing dupe of sentimental language, Flaubert presents us with a number of personages who consciously exploit such language, weaving illusions for others by means of it. Usually, though not always, they are immune to being deceived to any extent by their own language. Indeed, critics have generally treated Emma as the only person in the novel who becomes the victim of sentimental language.[13] There is a good deal of evidence, however (as I shall show later), for placing Charles Bovary significantly in this category. In *Middlemarch*, to a far greater extent, characters will be seen to be victims of the illusions they weave, and of their own language. Flaubert's scene at the agricultural fair in Yonville has justly been made much of. It has often been pointed out that the sentimental language of Rodolphe, pursuing in the council-room on the second floor of the town hall the initial stages of his plan for seducing Emma, is played by Flaubert in counterpoint to the earthy language of the Chairman awarding agricultural prizes on the platform outside just beneath the window:

"A hundred times I wanted to leave, and yet I followed you, I stayed . . . ."
"For manures!"
"—As I would stay tonight, tomorrow, all the days to come, all my life!"
"To Monsieur Caron of Argueil, a gold medal!"
"—For I've never found in any one such perfect charm."
"To Monsieur Bain of Givry-Saint-Martin!"
"But then I'll always have my memories of you."

"For a merino ram . . . ."

"—But you will forget *me*, I shall pass out of your life like a shadow."

"To Monsieur Belot of Notre-Dame."

"No! Isn't there some place for me in your thoughts, in your life?"

"For a hog! First prize divided equally between Messieurs Lehérissé and Cullembourg, sixty francs!"

Equally worthy of notice, however, is the fact that in the earlier part of this scene the even more elaborate love-making of Rodolphe is played in counterpoint to another sort of sentimental language weaving false illusions—the speech of the Councilor, wooing his constituency with empty flattery about the power and dignity of peasants tilling the land:

Then she looked at him in the way one looks at a traveler who has journeyed in exotic lands and she continued:

"—We haven't even this distraction, we poor women."

"—A miserable distraction, for there's no happiness to be found in it."

"—But does one ever find happiness?" she asked.

"—Yes. One day it comes," he answered.

"And this is what you understand," said the Councilor. "You, farmers, tillers of the fields! You, peaceful pioneers in the march of civilization! You, men of progress and morality. You understand, I say, that the storms of political strife are even more dreadful than those of nature . . . ."

"—Yes. One day it comes," repeated Rodolphe. "One day, suddenly when one has given up hope. Then new horizons open. It is as if a voice cried: 'Here it is!' You feel the need of confiding the whole of your life to that person, of giving all, of sacrificing all! There is no need for explanations. Each understands the other by intuition. They have met before, in their dreams."

There is much more of both Rodolphe's practiced play-acting of sentiment on the upper level and the politician's facile rhetoric below before the section ensues where prizes are awarded and Rodolphe continues with his love-making.

Still another kind of empty rhetoric, however, is to be associated with the agricultural fair; for Homais, a frequent contributor, is to write an account of the Fair for the *Fanal de Rouen*:

"Why these festoons, these flowers, these garlands? Where was the crowd running, like the waves of a sea in storm, under the rays of a tropical sun that poured its heat upon our fertile meadows?"

Then he spoke of the condition of the peasants. . . . Then, touching on the entry of the Councilor, he did not forget "the martial air of our militia," nor "our sparkling village maidens," nor "the bald elders, the patriarchs" who were there . . . . (II.viii.212–213)

Homais pictures the awarding of medals as a time of deep emotion: " 'Father embraced son, brother embraced brother, the husband his wife.' " Many another on his return to his " 'good housewife . . . wept tears of joy as he hung up his medal on the modest walls of his cottage.' " At the banquet the " 'utmost merriment reigned throughout.' " And nighttime brought on a fitting climax: " 'After nightfall a brilliant display of fireworks all at once lighted up the heavens. It was a veritable kaleidoscope, a scene from an opera. For a moment our humble locality might have thought itself transported into the midst of a dream from the "Thousand and One Nights." ' "

The fact (as opposed to Homais' gilded version of it) is that the fireworks had been stored for safety in the mouldy cellar of Monsieur Tuvache, as Flaubert had told us two pages earlier. The powder of many pieces had become too damp to ignite, and the crowning work of the evening, supposed to exhibit a dragon biting its tail, turned out a complete failure, though the public, Flaubert intimates, did not greatly mind. "Now and then a meagre Roman-candle went off; then the gaping crowd gave a roar that mingled with the little shrieks of women who were being tickled in the darkness" (II.viii.211).

Homais' clichés can on occasion not merely gild the truth but demolish it. A prime example is his report for the *Fanal de Rouen* (it is presumably no accident that *Fanal* rhymes with and is only a single letter away from *banal*) on the success of Charles's operation before Hippolyte's foot has yet had time to develop gangrene: Charles is " 'one of our most distinguished practitioners,' " his operation upon Hippolyte is " 'an act of loftiest philanthropy,' " and the operation has been performed without pain and with merely the appearance of a few drops of blood. Hippolyte's condition " 'up to the present time leaves nothing to be desired. Everything tends to show that his convalescence will be brief . . . .' " Homais conjectures it may well be that " 'at our next village festal occasion we shall . . . see our good Hippolyte figure in the midst of a bacchic dance, surrounded by a group of gay companions, and thus bear witness to all eyes, by his spirit in his dancing, of his complete recovery.' " Only a few lines below this psalm to modern surgery we learn that a livid tumescence has covered the limb and "a black liquid oozed at one place and another from several blisters" (II.xi.246–247). Even in Flaubert, the language of illusion and the irony of fact are seldom played in more devastating counterpoint.

Monsieur Homais cannot, however, be dismissed as a completely cynical manipulator of language. To an extent he believes the ideas he presents with so much sciolistic zest. He talks a jargon of scientific progress on occasions when there is no profit to be gained from it. Especially notable is his extended debate with the Abbé Bournisien carried on as they sit up with the corpse of Emma Bovary. Flaubert expends considerable space in his carefully rationed final manuscript on this fantastic dialogue between religion and science on the part of representatives who know little of deeper implications or deeper experience in the two gospels they preach. Meanwhile the corpse itself is deteriorating, and neither the apostle of religion nor the apostle of science can do anything to reverse the horrible process of dissolution (III.ix.453–461). When Charles at last lifts the veil from the face of the corpse and shrieks at the horror of what he sees beneath, they are of no help to him in his moment of black epiphany.

Though Homais believes in his religion of science and though his professions of faith border on zealotry, he is not, on the other hand, at all willing to undergo martyrdom. The fact is obvious at many points. When the Surgeon Canivet, brought at last from Neufchâtel to remove Hippolyte's gangrened leg, condemns outright the stupidity of trying to straighten club feet and denounces Charles for having thought he could do so, Homais is discreetly silent. Though the idea of the operation had been his, Homais "did not take up the defense of Bovary, nor did he demur in the slightest." Canivet sometimes sent prescriptions to be filled by Homais; and the pharmacist, "abandoning his principles, sacrificed his dignity to the more serious interests of his trade" (II.xi.252). Rhetorical flourishes are one thing, business is another. At the end of the novel, after the decline and death of Charles Bovary, Homais continues to prosper. Pharmacist in legal status, he is actually the village's chosen healer and physician. Flau-

bert elects to devote the closing lines of his novel to this sciolistic but
magniloquent disciple of progress and science in a final irony:

> Since the death of Bovary three doctors have followed one another
> at Yonville without being able to succeed there, so fiercely has M. Ho-
> mais routed them. He has had the devil's own success with his clientele
> [*Il fait une clientèle d'enfer*]; the authorities treat him with respect, and
> public opinion protects him.
> He has just been awarded the cross of the Legion of Honor.[14]

Rodolphe, Emma's lover, is a far more cynical manipulator of sentimental language than Homais in that he calculates his stratagems. At
the same time—and this is a paradox that Flaubert makes more of
than has often been observed—he is in good part the victim of his
own pretenses. At thirty-four he "combined brutality of temperament
with shrewdness of intellect, being something of a connoisseur in
women, having had much to do with them" (II.vii.181). He is caught
up in the pursuit, as if it were a way of life, a profession which he
must follow to live whether he wishes to or not. He is satiated with
his current mistress, an actress in Rouen, at the time of meeting
Emma; but his words to himself suggest that enthusiasm and novelty
in entering upon a new adventure have long been lost for him: "She's
panting for love, like a carp gasping for water on a kitchen table.
Three words of gallantry and she'd adore you, I'm sure. It would be
tender! charming! Yes, but how to get rid of her afterward?" (II.vii.
181). Like a carp on a kitchen table! The thought of such fare does
not induce Rodolphe to enter headlong into the new adventure. He
waits six weeks before again calling on Emma, in the meantime—
with appropriate symbolism—occupying himself with hunting game.

At the termination of the affair as in its early stages (especially—
as we have seen—at the agricultural fair) Flaubert employs with
brilliant results his characteristic counterpoint of the language of
sentimental cliché and the language of realism. In this instance, however, both voices are Rodolphe's. He composes his calculatedly sentimental letter of farewell bit by bit, interspersing between portions of
his writing his voiced reflections to himself:

> "You were coming away in blind trust, fearless, believing in happi-
> ness . . . . Ah, wretched, irrational creatures that we are!"

Rodolphe paused here to try to find some good excuse.

—If I tell her I've lost all my money? . . . No. That wouldn't settle anything for good. It would all start over again later. How can one make such women listen to reason!

He thought a moment and then added:

"I shall not forget you, believe me; and I shall always be deeply devoted to you . . . . Forget me! Why did we have to meet? Why were you so beautiful? Is it my fault? Oh, *mon Dieu*, no, no! Blame only Fate!"

—"There's a word that's always effective," he said to himself.

A drop from a tumbler of water completes the letter, blurring the ink at one spot to simulate the tear Emma will have expected him to have shed over his page.

Before sitting down to write, Rodolphe had searched through a box for some of Emma's own letters—a box in which he kept, along with such letters, other mementos of his former loves. There were "bouquets, a garter, a black mask, pins, and locks of hair—masses of hair! Some dark, some fair, some, catching in the hinges of the box, broke even as he opened it" (II.xiii.279). About some of the former mistresses who had bestowed these relics he could remember nothing whatsoever. "All these women, crowding his consciousness at the same time, seemed diminished in size, leveled to a uniformity in his feeling." He shuffled various old love letters from hand to hand for a moment; but they made him feel "bored and drowsy" and he put them back exclaiming, " 'What a lot of nonsense!' "

Flaubert's Abbé Bournisien appears, though a priest, to have himself felt little or nothing of the illusions that by profession he dispenses like pharmacopoeias to those among his congregation who are receptive to them. In his way he is not unlike the organ grinder who, by a turn of the crank, had set the sighs and yearnings of Emma in motion at Tostes. Emma's experiences with religion have, as we have seen, been a subject for irony with Flaubert from the early chapters of the novel. The plaster priest in the garden of the house in Tostes anticipates the ineffectiveness of religion for her later on, as does the cracked bell of the church at Tostes and its "monotonous ringing" that dies away across the field while a dog howls. Symbolically, over the winter following the visit to Vaubyessard, the little plaster image of the priest had lost his right foot "and the very plaster, scaling off with the frost, made white scabs on his face" (I.ix.89). On the journey from Tostes to Yonville, the plaster priest falls out of the carriage and breaks "in a thousand pieces" on the pavement of a town they pass through (II.ii.121–122).

When Emma, after Léon has left Yonville for Paris, stirred by her memories, tries to recapture the religious visions of her days at the convent, the Abbé Bournisien cannot even comprehend what she is looking for. While he speaks to Emma, he must also shout threats from time to time at the unruly children who insist on running up and down the aisles instead of learning to repeat by rote the words of the catechism. The Abbé appears grotesquely unaware that the words of the holy rites can have special meaning for anyone who is not in physical distress. His first thought when Emma tells him she is "suffering" is that she is complaining of the heat (which bothers him also), and his second is that she has indigestion. When she assures him fervently that he, as priest, has the power to "solace all sorrow," he replies, apparently without the remotest intention of being evasive, with an anecdote of going to a neighboring village to talk to some peasants who believed their cow was under a spell. They had expected him to relieve its misery with his white magic. The scene between the Abbé Bournisien and Emma is made up of such non sequiturs of dialogue. By degrees Emma's faith in his ability to provide the illusion she seeks is dissipated, and she sees him as he is—an unkempt old man with grease and tobacco stains spotting his cassock: "And she had the air of one awakening from a dream" (II.vi.158).

Later, however, following Rodolphe's rejection of her, she becomes desperately ill, and a time ensues in which she and the Abbé speak less at cross purposes. He exhorts her to religion "in a playful, gossipy tone that was not without charm," and she was comforted through old religious associations set in motion at the sight of his cassock, stained though it might be (II.xiv.295). The Abbé had talked to poor Hippolyte during his period of excruciating suffering in much the same way, suggesting a Hail Mary and an Our Father as Homais might prescribe palliative medicines, coming back from day to day to joke and tell anecdotes and dispense a little more of his formulas to the sufferer (II.xi.250). Baudelaire pours contempt upon the Abbé Bournisien in his critique of *Madame Bovary*[15]; but the Abbé seems on the whole a well-intentioned man albeit an insensitive one oblivious to the poetry in the rites he performs. He is perhaps Flaubert's most honest practitioner among the dispensers of illusion that play a part in *Madame Bovary*.

Emma's own religious visions have by the time of her second experience with the Abbé become inextricably confused with her memories of erotic love. At the height of her illness she asks the Abbé to administer communion. The ceremony, even as performed by this prosaic practitioner (once he has cleared from the chest of drawers its array of medicine bottles and converted it into a makeshift altar) creates a magnificent illusion in her: "Emma felt some powerful force passing over her that freed her from all pain, all perception [of the world around her], all feeling. She no longer thought of her body. Another life began. It seemed to her that her being, mounting toward God, would lose itself in His Love, as incense disperses itself in vapor. The sheets of her bed were sprinkled with holy water; the priest took the white Host from the sacred pyx, and almost swooning with celestial joy she parted her lips to receive the body of the Savior as it was presented to her" (II.xiv.295). A blasphemous irony takes place in Emma's world of illusion. Her spiritual and her earthly lover become confused in her own mind in a manner more than a little reminiscent of the voluptuous hallucinations of Flaubert's Saint Anthony. "The curtains of the alcove floated softly about her, like clouds, and the rays of the two candles burning on the chest of drawers appeared to her as dazzling glories. Then she let her head fall back believing she heard through space the harps of seraphs and beheld in an azure heaven, on a throne of gold, in the midst of saints bearing branches of green palm, God the Father resplendent in majesty, who ordered angels with wings of flame to descend to earth to carry her aloft in their arms." Emma now turns wholeheartedly to her religion. Sure that she is seeking Christian humility (though the vision is, of course, as intensely ego-centered as Flaubert could well have made it), she "saw within her the destruction of her will, which opened wide the gates for heavenly grace to conquer her." She buys rosaries, wears holy medals, and purchases (one would judge at a reckless expense) a "reliquary set in emeralds that she might kiss it every evening."

The Abbé Bournisien is delighted with her piety but somewhat troubled by her fervor. Emma demands literature that will clarify her mind on matters religious, and the Abbé, quite without insight into such matters, writes Monsieur Boulard, the bishop's bookseller, to send "something of note for a lady with a very distinguished intellect." The bookseller throws together a random package of "whatever happened to be popular in the current religious book business." The incident suggests that the bookseller, like the Abbé Bournisien himself, dispenses the materials of religious illusion without much understanding of the nature of the articles he sells. There is in the packet an absurd variety: "They included little manuals of questions and answers, supercilious pamphlets in the manner of M. de Maistre, and novels of a sort, in rose-colored bindings and a sugary style, turned out by sentimental seminarists or repentant blue-stockings." Flaubert has not been altogether impersonal in assigning names to them. "There were titles like *Think on This Carefully; The Man of the World at the Feet of the Virgin Mary, by M. de ***, Decorated with many Orders; Some Errors of Voltaire, for the Use of the Young*, etc." (II.xiv.297). Such reading, even under less ambiguous titles, could hardly absorb the attention of a woman who was able to visualize God the Father ordering down angels with wings of fire to carry her aloft to him.

By degrees Emma begins to lose the vividness of her religious illusion, though, Flaubert tells us, she "addressed to the Lord the same suave words that she had once murmured to her lover in the transports of adultery." Emma is temporarily to abandon religion for (first) the brief but memorable illusion, at the opera, of love for the star tenor Edgar Lagardy when the world of canvas scenery and footlights momentarily overwhelms her and (second, and much more important) her feverish and prolonged liaison with Léon. But Flaubert has already prepared us for Emma's final religious vision in which the Abbé Bournisien will administer the last rites of the Church and Emma will bestow upon the Host, "the body of the Man-God," the "most passionate kiss of love that she had ever given" (III.viii.446).

vi. CHARLES, BERTHE, AND THE THEME OF ISOLATION

Middlemarch has more to do with the theme of isolation of individual from individual in the modern world than does *Madame*

Bovary. Yet with forms of illusion in *Madame Bovary* as the chosen focus, it becomes abundantly evident that the theme figures as a strong undercurrent throughout most of the novel. It is, indeed, so fully realized as an integral part of the narrative that it is not easy to isolate. The theme is prominent in the treatment of the various purveyors of the language of illusion. Rodolphe does not himself believe in the language that he employs, though the main part of his stock of sentimental clichés deals with human isolation. The scene between Emma and Rodolphe at the agricultural fair stresses, as we have already seen, three kinds of rhetoric that do not convey truth from mind to mind but merely make the telling of truth impossible. Rodolphe is, indeed, the most sinister of the three manipulators of language, the most cynical and the most predatory. The beginning of this dialogue—before Rodolphe and Emma have arrived at the town hall—suggests how much Rodolphe depends upon the theme of isolation in his practiced language of seduction:

"Anyway," he said, "when one lives in the country . . ."

"Any trouble you take [on dress] is wasted," said Emma.

"True!" replied Rodolphe. "To think that not a person here is capable of appreciating even the cut of a coat!"

Then they talked about the mediocrity of provincial life, of the lives that it stifles, of the noble dreams that perished there.

"That is why," said Rodolphe, "I am sinking into such a state of gloom."

"You!" she exclaimed astonished. "I thought you were lighthearted."

"Ah, yes, on the surface. Because I know how to wear a mask of mockery in public. But how often, viewing a cemetery in the moonlight, I've asked myself whether it wouldn't be better for me to join those who sleep there . . ."

"Oh! and your friends?" she said. "Don't you think of them?"

"My friends? What friends? Do I have any? Who cares about me?"

And he accompanied the last words with a kind of indrawn sigh. (II.viii.192–193)

Rodolphe soon takes up the theme again: "Yes, I have missed so many things. Always alone! Ah! if I had some aim in life, if I had met with affection, if I had found some one!" Rodolphe is, of course, first implying and later all but stating that he and Emma have been destined to discover in each other a unique means of defeating isolation. It is a sentiment that sets up strong vibrations in her, even as he has calculated.

Emma has been dreaming of an ideal companion, who will intuitively know her fancies, ever since the disenchantments of her early days with Charles, when it had seemed to her that "if his eyes had only once read her thoughts . . . her heart would have opened its wealth to him, suddenly, as ripened fruit falls from a tree at the touch of a hand" (I.vii.57). It is one of the persistent ironies of *Madame Bovary* that while Emma vainly searches for someone who will defeat her sense of isolation—in Rodolphe, in the Abbé as representative of religion, in her vision of Edgar Lagardy the operatic hero, in Léon, no one of them really concerned with her individual point of sight—she habitually rejects as if by reflex the love and sympathy that are always waiting attendance on her. Charles tries humbly if ineptly to understand her. He happily subordinates his own concerns to hers. With a delicacy that gives the novel special depths of mood and meaning, Flaubert plays with the stock situations of the cuckold husband of fabliau or farce. Charles urges Emma unknowingly into the arms of her lovers. It is Charles who encourages Emma to stay overnight at Rouen to find needed diversion in another evening of opera and thus effects a second and crucial meeting with Léon in that city.

With the birth of Berthe, her daughter, Emma is offered a second opportunity for normal human resource in defeating her sense of isolation. But though Emma is willing on an impulse to play for a time the role of mother, she habitually rejects her child. On Emma's first taking Berthe in her arms at the cottage of the wet-nurse Mère Rollet, the infant soils the collar of her silk dress, and the drama of motherhood is abruptly broken for her by this impact of reality. Emma hurries to get away from the child and from the cottage (II.iii.128–129). When Emma returns home after finding her escape into religious illusion frustrated by Abbé Bournisien's inability to comprehend her language or her needs, she meets little Berthe tottering toward her, trying to tug at her mother's apron strings. She rejects this little appeal for communication violently, pushing the child from her with such force that Berthe cuts her cheek. Emma is momentarily alarmed at the sight of blood, but it is Charles who puts plaster on the wound— effecting a temporary disfigurement that makes Emma soon reflect on how ugly her child is, and how little the daughter has inherited of her mother's beauty (II.vi.160). It is of Berthe that Charles is thinking in a later scene rich in implications. He has crept to bed lest he awaken Emma, who is actually feigning sleep while she entertains fantasies of a future with Rodolphe.

> When he returned home in the middle of the night, he never dared to wake her. The porcelain globe of the night lamp cast a flickering round of light upon the ceiling, and the drawn curtains of Berthe's little cot made it look like a tiny white hut standing out in the shade by the bedside. Charles looked at his wife and daughter. He thought he could hear the light breathing of his child. She would soon grow big now; every season would bring progress. Already he saw her in his mind's eye returning home from school at the end of the day, laughing, her blouse spotted with ink, her satchel on her arm. Then they would have to send her to a boarding-school. That would cost a lot—how would they manage? He pondered the problem. He thought of hiring a little farm in the neighborhood that he himself could supervise every morning when he rode out to see his patients. He wouldn't spend what it brought in; he would put the money in the bank. Then he'd invest in some stock of one sort or another. Besides, his practice would grow. He was counting on that, for he wanted Berthe to be well-educated, to be accomplished, to take piano lessons. Ah, how pretty she would be later, at fifteen, when, resembling her mother, she would wear one of those same broad-brimmed straw hats in the summer time! At a distance they'd be taken for sisters. He pictured her sewing by their side of an evening under the light of a lamp. She would embroider slippers for him; she would look after the house; she would fill all the home with her charm and her gaiety. They would find her some good young fellow with a solid business, who would make her happy. And her happiness would last always. (II.270)

This is by far the most extended and most intimate view that we are to have of Charles's inner experience—his touching illusion of domestic security and a solid future—from the early chapters until the concluding chapters of the novel. Flaubert, in one of the most eloquent of his many statements by implication, places Charles's vignette upon Berthe's future immediately before and in contrapuntal arrangement with his parallel passage portraying what is going forward in Emma's imagination as she merely feigns sleep, lying by his side. While Charles envisions the stages of Berthe's growing up and plans a happy bourgeois domestic future, Emma is living in imagination her fantasy of galloping away in the arms of Rodolphe to exotic lands never to return. Robed in silken gowns spangled with stars, they will pursue a life of undomestic bliss.[16]

Seen against the plan of the novel as a whole, Charles's selfless vision assumes still greater pathos; for Berthe, even more than Charles, is to be the victim of her mother's destructive illusions. Instead of the secure life Charles has pictured for her, Berthe, as her mother's debts mount, is to be deprived of any schooling (though Charles pathetically tries to teach her to read, employing as her primer the pages of his medical journal [III.vi.398]); and after Charles's early death she is to be last heard of as a common laborer in a cotton mill.

The extent to which Flaubert himself sympathized, or intended the reader to sympathize, with Charles Bovary is a point that must continue to be a vital and debated question. There is scarcely a doubt that at times Charles's conduct is meant to be tasteless, even ridiculous; and there are many indications that his level of intelligence is not high. In the early days of their marriage, Emma is depressed by his conversation, which she finds "flat as a street pavement." Everyone's ideas "passed through it in their ordinary clothes, without exciting emotion, laughter, or reverie" (I.vii.57). She is probably giving a fair estimate—the precision of the phrasing suggests Flaubert's analytical voice as narrator rather than the lyrical idiom he typically provides for Emma's unspoken thoughts—and there is nothing later to intimate that Charles thinks originally or possesses intelligence greatly above that of the peasants or townsmen that he lets blood from or doses with drugs. He is persuaded by Homais and Emma to attempt the blundering operation on Hippolyte; and he is almost unbelievably blind in his trust in Emma during the course of her infidelities. These become so open as she grows more frantic in her pursuit of ecstasy that his refusal to see what is going on comes perilously close to broad comedy. Nevertheless, Victor Brombert seems eminently right in arguing that Charles's love for Emma is presented as not ludicrous, but essentially "deep and tragic."[17] Brombert, however, seems to be confusing narrator and character, attributing to Charles the author's own lyricism in the opening chapters, in Flaubert's eloquent portrayal of the early scenes through which Charles passes, just as critics often tend to ascribe to Emma later in the novel the lyricism into which Flaubert translates her impressions.

Flaubert's letter to Louise Colet, in January, 1853, more accurately reflects his view of Charles while he was writing the novel:

> I maintain, however, that ideas are action. Thus I now have fifty consecutive pages in which there is not a single event. It is an uninterrupted picture of a bourgeois life and of a love that remains passive—a love all the harder to portray because it is at the same time both timid and profound but, alas! without inner disturbance, because my gentleman is of a tranquil disposition [*nature tempérée*]. I have already had something like this to deal with in the first part: my husband loves his wife in a manner not unlike her lover. They are both mediocrities in much the same milieu, but I must differentiate between them . . . . (C, III, 85–86)

Charles is not, it would appear, intended to be cleverer or more original than another young mediocrity would be. It is the greater success for Flaubert that he is able to portray a commonplace mind experiencing a blind love that is revealed as something deep and tragic.

The depth and tragedy of Charles's love for Emma is seen fully only when we have in mind the episodes following Emma's death. The fate of Emma's and Charles's daughter Berthe is crucial to an interpretation of the final chapters of the novel. The motif developed with so many variations and such effective use of detail in these closing chapters is announced in an early sentence of the chapter following Emma's funeral: Emma "corrupted him from beyond the grave" (III.xi.472).

There is little in Charles as we see him during a large part of the novel to prepare us for his final deterioration. His delight in Emma during the early days of their marriage reflects his sense of security in an ordered bourgeois existence. He takes pride in his wife's outstanding beauty, but a part of his pleasure is seeing her as a clever manager as well, cooking for her husband delicate dishes, keeping a tidy house furnished with exceptional attractiveness (Charles does not see the unusual expenses involved, though his mother does when she comes visiting), even making out the patients' accounts in "well-phrased letters that had no suggestion of a commercial flavor about them" (I.vii.58). As the novel progresses and Emma more and more pursues her own way in isolation from Charles, we are given practically nothing of Charles's inner experience. When she is ill, he assumes that it is a question of "nerves" and has nothing to do with problems not confined to his household. He himself urges her to go riding with Rodolphe, thus hurrying on the seduction scene, because he is sure that more exercise is what she needs to recuperate her health. Even the disaster of his operation on Hippolyte only momentarily interrupts his illusion of an ordered and pleasant life. The one extended view of his private world that we are permitted in the middle of the novel, his projection of Berthe's future (significantly played against Emma's lurid fantasy of elopement with Rodolphe) imagines Berthe, as we have seen, going through the stages of a secure bourgeois life, her education in a proper boarding school (for which he must provide in advance by making more money and investing it in some sort of stocks), her young maidenhood, and her eventual marriage to "a good young fellow with a steady business." Charles, in sum, is pursuing his constructive life as the town's doctor, happily taking pride in his distinguished wife (whom other men pay the compliment of admiring) and assuming a tranquil future even while his actual welfare and that of his daughter and wife are progressively sliding toward an abyss that will include financial ruin and suicide.

It is not until Emma's ghastly death by arsenic that we again enter Charles's private experience. The first really startling evidence of how much Charles's imaginative life has changed is given us in the note he writes specifying exactly how Emma's corpse is to be prepared for interment: "I wish her to be buried in her wedding dress, with white shoes and a wreath. Her hair must be spread out over her shoulders. Three coffins, one oak, one mahogany, one lead. Let no one oppose me. I shall have the strength to see this through. Cover her with a large piece of green velvet. This is my wish. See that it is done" (III.ix.452). Homais and the Abbé Bournisien are "taken aback by Bovary's romantic ideas"; but they find with a shock that Charles, who has always been complaisant in his relations with other townsmen, has undergone a remarkable change. Homais, knowing the disastrous condition of the household's finances, protests the expense; but Charles is passionately bent on carrying through his design. And when the priest tries to calm Charles, offering him the consolation of religion, Charles blasphemously cries out, "I hate your God!"

Charles's bourgeois illusion has yielded place to romantic rebellion. His image of Emma has remained, however, essentially as she appeared to him in the first days of their marriage. While Homais and Bournisien go through the form of sitting up with the corpse (in reality, after their preliminary debate on science and religion, they spend much of their time nodding in sleep), Charles comes into the room to bid a last farewell. He is engulfed by a tide of recollections evoking with poignant detail earlier happy scenes of their life. "For a long time he stood, recalling his lost joys, her poses, her gestures, the tone of her voice" (III.ix.459). It is then that Charles lifts the veil from the horribly decomposing face. Flaubert has already given the reader details of the degeneration that is going on beneath the veil—the mouth "like a black hole at the lower part of her face"; the eyes that are beginning to "disappear in a viscous pallor"; the black liquid that has issued from what used to be her lips. There has been time for further decay in the intervening hours; so it is understandable that Charles, once he has looked beneath the veil, utters a cry of horror. It is interesting that George Eliot, also portraying a character undergoing an extreme experience of isolation and loss, should entitle her tale "The Lifted Veil."[18] But Eliot's extended tale contains no such moment of sudden fusion of theme and emotion. Flaubert's scene is a masterpiece in miniature of the sort of poetic "madness" that he is capable of in counterpointing illusion and reality.

Charles's cry marks the final collapse of his accustomed world. The spasm of energy that had enabled him to defy Homais and the Abbé Bournisien in his first grief abandons him. He takes to enacting in a recurrent nightmare the experience of lifting the veil and seeing the dead mass beneath: ". . . every night he dreamed of her; it was always the same dream. He approached her; but when he was about to embrace her she fell into decay in his arms" (III.xi.476). In his demoralized sense of isolation from the life and personality he had loved, he makes pathetic attempts to preserve the illusion of her presence. "To please her, as though she were still living, he adopted her tastes, her notions; he bought himself patent leather shoes and took to wearing white cravats. He began waxing his moustache and, just as she had done, signed more promissory notes." Emma has indeed "corrupted him from beyond the grave," working her contagion into nearly every corner of his life. Meanwhile Berthe becomes the living embodiment of the contagion's destructive power. Charles beholds his daughter's neglected state but remains powerless to effect any real remedy. "He suffered, poor man, at seeing her so badly dressed, with her shoes unlaced, the armholes of her smock torn clear to the hips, for the cleaning woman took no care of her. But she was so sweet, so gentle, and she bent her little head so gracefully, letting her fair hair fall over her rosy cheeks, that he was flooded with infinite pleasure, a happiness mixed with bitterness, like those ill-made wines tasting of resin." His efforts, pathetic in size and direction, to alleviate matters often trail away into fits of reverie. "He mended her toys, made puppets for her out of cardboard, sewed up the torn stomachs of her dolls. But if his eyes fell upon the sewing-box or a piece of loose ribbon or even a pin caught in a crack of the table, he would begin to dream and he would look so sad that she, too, grew as sad as he" (III.xi.473). In her neglected and disordered life with Charles, Berthe is given to frequent coughing, and her cheeks bear the unnaturally red patches associated with tuberculosis (III.xi.477).

Charles eventually discovers all of Léon's love letters and not long thereafter Rodolphe's as well. They do not apparently lessen his obsession with the memory of Emma or start him on a course more likely to improve his own state or that of his daughter. He refuses to visit patients and shuts himself in his house. People who, out of curiosity, climbed the garden hedge beheld him in amazement "wild-eyed, long-bearded, shabbily clothed" as he walked about the garden weeping aloud to himself (III.xi.479). His seclusion is broken in the summer by his visits to Emma's grave, taking Berthe with him, returning only after nightfall. Charles's main occupation in life has become "to savor his grief to the full," a process that is frustrated since no one is any longer willing to listen. At Argueil, where Charles in his poverty has gone to sell his horse, "his last resource," he meets Rodolphe. Charles is shocked to find that, despite a momentary sense of fury, his dominant feeling is one of envy: "He would have liked to have been this man." At last in mournful weariness, Charles says, as they sit sharing a bottle of beer: "I can't blame you for it . . . . No, I can't blame you any longer" (III.xi.480). It is a point of significance for Flaubert's conception that even in such a moment Charles must frame his final words in a sentimental cliché—one that Rodolphe had employed with effect in his dialogues with Emma and in his letter of farewell[19] but one that sums up the depths of Charles's own confused and diseased inner experience:

> He added a great phrase, the only one he had ever uttered.
> —"It is the fault of Fate."
> Rodolphe, who had fashioned that Fate, thought him very meek for a man in his situation, comic even, and slightly contemptible.

The next day little Berthe finds Charles dead, a long black tress of Emma's hair grasped in his hand.

It is Berthe who lives on, though probably, it seems implied, destined for an early death from tuberculosis. The sale of what household effects remained brought only a few francs, barely enough to ship the little girl off to her grandmother. After the death of the grandmother, within the same year, Berthe is put in the charge of an impoverished aunt who sends her to work in a cotton mill.

vii. Visions of Chaos

Both Flaubert and George Eliot, as was observed at some length in the first chapter, were very much aware of the world that science was documenting with more and more compelling data—a world Carlyle had feelingly portrayed as early as 1833 in his "Everlasting No" as a dead universe that revealed no vestige of personality outside of man and gave no scrap of evidence of man's surviving his present life. Nothing more sharply differentiates the qualities of *Madame Bovary* from those of *Middlemarch* (or from the Gwendolen Harleth half of *Daniel Deronda*) than the divergent ways in which the French author and the English embody in their fiction this profound awareness they share that rationality can no longer place man at the center of his universe as a part of an immortal whole. For both Flaubert and Eliot the hopes and consolations of Christianity are gone. The Platonic or Neo-Platonic visions that so engaged the English romantics are gone as well. For Flaubert, there is left on the one hand his rebellious anti-rational romanticism—his courting, more or less in the manner of his confrere Baudelaire, of anti-rational visions, often visions that celebrate the horror of life itself. On the other hand, and often in vital tension with his bent toward romantic rebellion, there is for Flaubert (and especially during the years in which he was composing *Madame Bovary*) his cultivation of a life of artistic discipline—his creation of an ordered universe of his own, a microcosm that he is able to endow with harmony through his "agonies of art." But neither avenue of escape—the rebellion against fact on the one hand or the attempt to lose himself as artist in his own ordered microcosm—is able to free Flaubert from a nagging sense of loss, a tendency (shared with George Eliot and with many other intellectuals of the second half of the nineteenth century) to feel the fact of outer darkness as a recent and personal experience, something that required embodying in images that could help define it and make it bearable. This troubled sense of loss—sometimes expressed in images of disgust rather than of grief—runs throughout *Madame Bovary* and pervades both the art and the substance of the novel.

Flaubert's curiously elaborate description of Charles's cap, so prominent in the opening paragraphs of *Madame Bovary* and yet so lacking in obvious meaning to justify itself in pride of place or length, has been a challenge for critics. Whatever other interpretations may be entertained, the passage serves on an important level as an eloquent nondiscursive symbol, an initial prose poem of Flaubert's upon the confusion, tastelessness, and ultimate meaninglessness of the world he saw around him. It is an initial prose lyric upon the chaos of modern life.

> It was one of those headgears of composite order in which one can discover traces of the bearskin hat, the lancer's hat, the ordinary bowler, the sealskin cap, and the cotton nightcap; one of those poor things, in sum, *whose mute ugliness contains profundities of expression, like the countenance of an imbecile.* Ovoid and stiffened with whalebone, it started out with three circular strips; then came in succession, divided by a red band, lozenges of velvet and of rabbit's fur. After that came a kind of bag that terminated in a cardboard-lined polygon covered with intricate braiding, from which there hung, at the end of a long, extremely thin cord, a little tassel of gold threads. The cap was new; its peak shone (I.i.2–3, italics mine)

It is probable that Flaubert in preparing the final manuscript of his much-revised novel fully intended the considerable affinities between the grotesque multi-layered cap of Charles and the remarkable wedding cake he introduces three chapters later—also a multi-layered cylindrical object presented in far more detail than the narrative level would justify. This cake, I have suggested earlier, serves as an effective correlative for Emma's sugared and sentimental reading; but it is not, of course, uncommon for an effective image to resonate to more than a single theme in an intensely conceived work of literature. The cake, like Charles's cap, is a masterpiece of bizarre non sequiturs containing a pasteboard temple with porticoes, colonnades, statuettes, and constellations of gilt paper stars, a castle keep in Savoy cake, with fortifications of candy, almonds, raisins, and quarters of oranges, a meadow with rocks, lakes of jam, nutshell boats. Surmounting all there is a small cupid in a chocolate swing "whose two uprights terminated in real rosebuds for ornamental knobs at the top" (I.iv.39). Perhaps it is possible to see both images as functioning not merely as visions of chaos but as images of Emma's reading as well; for the modern maker of caps, like the modern maker of cakes, has assembled his materials in accordance with the quality of his imaginative life to form a tasteless clutter of absurd non sequiturs. And so has Emma.

"I have a hatred of life," Flaubert wrote Maxime du Camp in October, 1851, at the time when he was in the first stages of his composition of *Madame Bovary*. "I've written it, and I won't cross it out. Yes—of life, and of everything that reminds me that it must be borne. It's boring to eat, to dress, even to stand on my feet. I have carried this hatred with me everywhere—at school, in Rouen, in Paris, on the Nile . . . ." (C, II, 321). This is with Flaubert not a mere pose assumed for the moment, but an attitude that is reflected often in his letters and elsewhere. In *Madame Bovary* the juxtaposition of Emma's sentimental yearnings and the sense of an underlying dark world that in one way or another destroys human aspiration and makes man cousin to the dust beneath his feet is a subject for many kinds of irony. It is intimately a part of Flaubert's double vision. The sense of the futility of religious hopes, as we have seen, runs from the beginning to the end of the novel. It underlies Flaubert's portrayal of Emma's early egocentric confusion of religious symbols and images of personal love; it is embodied in the decomposition of the plaster curé of the garden at Tostes and the stupidity of the Abbé Bournisien. It figures strongly in Emma's confusion of her god with her lover as she pours out the sensual phrases she had addressed to Rodolphe in her idolatrous worship of God the Father. Flaubert's most disturbing correlatives for man's relation to the dark universe he inhabits are embodied in his powerful scenes dealing with Emma's death and the decomposition of her body. There is no more suggestive image of Flaubert's view than the scene in which Charles lifts the veil from the decomposing face of Emma's corpse. He has anticipated this scene in the incidents involving the operation on Hippolyte's club foot. The aspirations of both Charles and Emma are for the time centered in the success of this operation. There ensue the grotesque descriptions of the progressive spread of gangrene and decay from the foot through the whole limb. And then, when Charles and Emma sit in their living room awaiting the shrieks of Hippolyte as the Surgeon Canivet removes the putrefied limb, there is a preliminary moment of insight that anticipates the last scenes of the novel. Charles experiences a brief but vivid premonitory vision of the defeat of all his hopes: "He saw himself dishonored, ruined, lost. And his imagination, assailed by multitudes of hypotheses, tossed amid them like an empty cask dragged out to sea and rolling helpless on the waves" (II.xi.255). For Emma, the moment is one of a succession of life's refusals to live up to expectation; and characteristically the fault as she sees it is not of her own making: "How could she (she who was so intelligent!) have let herself be deceived again? Moreover, what deplorable mania had driven her to ruin her life with continual sacrifices? She recalled all her instincts of luxury, all the privations of her soul, all the sordid details of her marriage, of the household, her dreams falling into the mire like wounded swallows; everything she had longed for, everything she had denied herself, all that she might have had! And for what—for what?" The tapping of Hippolyte's wooden leg on the pavements of Yonville becomes for Charles almost unbearable. The sound heard even from a distance is enough to send him hurrying off in another direction (II.xii.262). When Emma returns to Yonville from Rouen after her first infidelity with Léon, Charles has just learned of the death of his father. Both he and Emma hear from their living room "the sharp tap of a wooden leg on the boards of the entrance hall. It was Hippolyte bringing back Madame's luggage" (III.ii.347). Like Poe's raven, Hippolyte's artificial limb seems to announce the irrevocability of time past and the blankness of time future. During the funeral service for Emma, Charles hears once more the sound of Hippolyte's leg, this time upon the very stones of the church's pavement (III.x.464–465).

Among the figures in *Madame Bovary* that in their various ways embody Flaubert's nagging sense of outer darkness one may well count the sexton Lestiboudois. His funereal associations as gravedigger as well as sexton to the church are given added force by the macabre fact of his growing potatoes in the enriched soils of the cemetery lots. " 'Lestiboudois,' " the Curé remarks to him, " 'you feed upon the dead' " (II.i.100). But a character who serves more directly as a memento mori and plays a more important part in the novel is the blind beggar. This grotesque figure is not introduced until Emma is already engrossed in her affair with Léon and entering the final despairing stages of her entanglement with debt. He makes a sort of living by stationing himself at the steepest hillside on the road out of Rouen, where passengers customarily alight and walk to spare the horses (though Emma remains inside the carriage):

> There was on this hillside a wretched beggar who would place himself with his stick in the midst of the carriages. A mass of rags covered his shoulders and an ancient battered beaver hat, turned down like a round basin, hid his face. But when he took it off he revealed two bloody sockets in place of eyelids. The flesh was continually shredding off in red bits, and from the flesh there oozed liquid which congealed into green scales that extended down to his nose, whose black nostrils snuffed convulsively. Whenever he spoke he threw back his head with the laugh of an idiot. Then his bluish eyeballs, rolling perpetually, round and round, would rub against the edges of the live wounds.
> As he followed the carriages he sang a little song:
>> *Often the warmth of a fine day*
>> *Makes a young girl dream of love.*
> And the rest of it was all about birds and sunshine and green leaves. (III.v.369–370)

It is typical of Flaubert's "binocular vision" that the beggar's song should be of sunshine and green leaves. The disharmony of Nature with the mood of men and women is a recurrent motif in the pages of *Madame Bovary*. Emma's funeral will take place in a world that provides a setting more appropriate for a wedding. "A fresh breeze was blowing; the rye and colza were turning green and tiny dewdrops hung from the hawthorn hedges at the edge of the road. All sorts of joyous sounds filled the air . . . . The clear sky was flecked with rosy clouds" (III.x.466).

The beggar appears frequently like a species of death's-head during Emma's trips back to Yonville after her liaisons with Léon:

> Often the coach was already in motion when his hat would suddenly come in at the window while he clung with his other arm to the footboard . . . . His voice, at first feeble and quavering, would grow shrill. It trailed off into the night like an indistinct lamentation over some vague despair . . . with something remote in it that filled Emma with dread. It went to the depths of her soul, like a whirlwind in an abyss; it carried her away into the vast spaces of a melancholy without limits. But Hivert [the coachman], noticing a weight on one side, would strike out savagely with his whip. The lash would cut his sores and he would fall back with a howl into the mud. (III.v.370)

The portent of the beggar's apparition would stay with Emma through the rest of the trip. While the other passengers nodded or slept, "Emma, drunk with sadness, shivered under her clothes and felt her feet grow colder and colder, with death in her soul."

Homais, who on one return to Yonville is in the coach with Emma, sees nothing of ill omen in the beggar but rather an affront to science. He pronounces on the nature of the beggar's disease (scrofula), throws him a sou, and demands that he "put on [his] act." "The blind man squatted on his haunches with his head thrown back, and rolling his green-scaled eyes and sticking out his tongue, he rubbed his stomach with both hands meanwhile uttering a sort of low howl like a famished dog" (III.vii.415). The introduction of the gruesome spectacle at this point serves to announce a critical stage in the decline of Emma's fortunes. The Bovary household effects are already subject to seizure for her debts. With a dramatic gesture, she throws the apparition her last five-franc piece. Homais has boastfully offered to cure his blindness if the creature will look him up in Yonville. Motivation is thus provided for the blind beggar's appearance in Emma's death scene, which is rapidly approaching.

The long scene in which Emma goes to her death is a masterpiece of devastating ambiguities. In part it is made up of conventional phrases for describing the ending of a life in Christian piety—phrases that may well have figured in some of the books and pamphlets the Abbé Bournisien had procured for Emma from the bishop's bookseller. "She turned her face slowly, and when her eyes beheld the violet stole she seemed filled with joy. She was doubtless recapturing, in this moment of singular peace, the lost ecstasy of her first mystical flights, mingled with the visions of eternal blessedness that were now beginning" (III.viii.446). When Flaubert was brought into court for publishing *Madame Bovary*, as atheistic and immoral, one of the scenes dwelt upon was the death scene of Emma Bovary. This description of Extreme Unction, Flaubert wrote Madame Schlesinger in January, 1857, was "only a page from the *Rituel de Paris*, put into decent French" (C, IV, 146); but this characterization hardly takes care of the obvious ironies of the rites as Flaubert describes them, administered by the Abbé Bournisien, in phrases eloquently underlining the sensuality that has played so prominent a part in Madame Bovary's life:

> The priest rose to take the crucifix; then she stretched out her neck like one suffering thirst, and gluing her lips to the body of the Man-God, she pressed upon it with all her failing strength the fullest kiss of love that she had ever given. Then [the priest] recited the *Misereatur* and the *Indulgentiam*, dipped his right thumb in the oil, and began the unctions. First, upon the eyes, that had coveted all sumptuous things of the world; then upon the nostrils, that had been so fond of warm breezes and amorous perfumes; then upon the mouth, that had spoken lies, moaned in pride and cried out in lust; then upon the hands, that had reveled in voluptuous contacts; and finally upon the soles of the feet, once so swift when she had hastened to slake her desires, and that would now walk no more. (III.viii.446–447)

Bournisien makes his accustomed exhortations; but in the midst of them Emma asks for a mirror. Tears fall from her eyes as she sees her altered face; she has not yet, apparently, taken to heart the whole of the renunciations of this world that are contained in the ritual just performed over her. A moment later her decline begins to set in more rapidly. The "whole of her tongue protruded from her mouth; her rolling eyes grew pale, like the globes of two lamps that are going out, so that one might have believed her already dead except for the fearful laboring of her ribs . . . as if the soul were struggling to get free" (448). The persons gathered around her assume attitudes of prayer. "As the death-rattle grew stronger the priest prayed faster," and Bournisien's Latin syllables resemble the tolling of a bell amid the sobs of the attendants and the bizarre sounds of the body's dissolution.

It is at this point that a third element comes into the scene—the song of the blind beggar:

> Suddenly from the pavement outside came the sound of heavy wooden shoes and the scraping of a stick; and a voice rose—a raucous voice—singing:
>
> *Often the warmth of a fine day*
> *Makes a young girl dream of love.*
>
> Emma raised herself like a corpse galvanized, her hair disheveled, her eyes fixed and staring.
>
> *To gather up with busy care*
> *The stalks of wheat reaped by the scythe.*
> *Nanette bends over as she walks*
> *Along the furrows where they lie.*
>
> "The blind man!" she cried.
>
> And Emma began to laugh, an atrocious, frantic, desperate laugh, thinking she saw the hideous face of the beggar looming up in the eternal darkness like a menace.
>
> *The wind blew very hard that day*
> *And snatched away her petticoat.*
>
> A spasm threw her back upon the mattress. They all drew near. She had ceased to exist.

It is hardly surprising that the scene was attacked as "atheistic" despite its inclusion of details from the *Rituel de Paris*. The beggar (in himself an awesome commentary), his song that appears to blend earthly love, springtime, and the sickle of death, the raucous travesty of the human voice in which the song is sung, and Emma's own "atrocious, frantic, desperate laugh" at the face that, standing out against the eternal darkness, replaces her "visions of eternal blessedness" as her last sight on earth, combine to end the chapter with a devastating enactment of Flaubert's own sense of a dark universe where all things—springtime and love and beauty included—disintegrate into nothingness. Following the details just noted, the concluding sentence—"She had ceased to exist"—which might by itself continue Flaubert's play of ambiguities earlier in the chapter, is reduced to a single meaning: there is nothing left of Emma—as Emma—in the whole of the universe. When Charles later lifts the veil from Emma's corpse, he enacts another symbolic equivalent of Emma's death scene. And neither the Abbé Bournisien's sprinkling of the room with holy water as a representative of the Church and its promises of immortality, nor Homais' administering of chlorine to the floor as a representative of science and the improvements of health and sanitation it is progressively offering to man do anything to console Charles or to alter Emma's destiny. The dialectic of human illusion with its warmth, light, and vanity, and the unresponsive exterior reality in which it must find what life it can for its brief moment has, for Emma, ceased to exist.

NOTES

1. Charles Sainte-Beuve, "Madame Bovary," *Causeries du Lundi* (Paris, 1853–62), XIII, 352, 363. The critique appeared originally in 1857.

2. "Madame Bovary," *Oeuvres complètes de Charles Baudelaire*, ed. Y. G. Le Dantec (Paris, 1964), pp. 647–657.

3. There have, of course, always been notable exceptions. James and Maupassant, for example, early observed that Flaubert's style far exceeded his trivial subject in *Madame Bovary*. Percy Lubbock's notable analysis of the novel in his *The Craft of Fiction* (1921; New York, 1957, pp. 59–92) finds Emma's "intelligence . . . much too feeble and fitful to give a sufficient account of her world" (p. 86). Edmund Wilson in *The Triple Thinkers* (1948; New York, 1963, p. 103) assumes that Flaubert "*intends* all his characters to be 'middling' and that the greatness of his work arises from the fact that it constitutes a criticism of something bigger than they are." Harry Levin (*The Gates of Horn* [New York, 1963], p. 251) notes that "empathy is seasoned with antipathy" whenever Flaubert speaks of Emma in his letters to Colet; and Victor Brombert, in his *The Novels of Flaubert* (Princeton, N. J., 1966), especially in his pages 74–91, comments valuably upon the way Flaubert's "impersonal" method of narrative suffuses *Madame Bovary* with the author's own personality and point of view.

4. Gustave Flaubert, *Madame Bovary, Oeuvres complètes*, ed. Louis Conard (1910; Paris, 1930), VIII, part I, chapter iii, pages 30–31. All quotations are keyed to the pages of this edition, in which *Madame Bovary* constitutes volume VIII. References will be made hereafter by part, chapter, and page numbers in parentheses. For a general statement regarding the principles and aims of my translation from Flaubert's works, see Foreword.

5. "Keepsakes" as a type of annual publication flourished in France as in England.

Le keepsake français was published from early in the 1820's, and similar volumes under a variety of titles—*Paris-Londres Keepsake Français, Keepsake de Génie et Bienfaisance, Keepsake Breton, Annales Romantiques, Les Belles Femmes de Paris,* and the like—were widely circulated up to mid-century. Many of them depended heavily on plates first used in the English keepsakes. See Frédéric Lachèvre, *Bibliographie sommaire des keepsakes et autres recueils collectifs de la période romantique, 1823–1848* (Paris, 1929), 2 vols., *passim.*

6. Gabrielle Leleu and Jean Pommier, eds., *Madame Bovary, Nouvelle Version précédée des scenarios inédits* (Paris, 1949), pp. 209–210.

7. Georges Poulet, *Les métamorphoses du cercle* (Paris, 1961), p. 375.

8. Leleu and Pommier (see note 6) provide a full account of Flaubert's process.

9. For definitions or descriptions of Flaubert's *style indirect libre*, see especially R. J. Sherrington, *Three Novels by Flaubert: A Study of Techniques* (Oxford, 1970), pp. 89–94; and Harry Levin, pp. 252 ff. For a more elaborate treatment, see Stephen Ullmann, *Style in the French Novel* (Oxford, 1964), pp. 112 ff. For a most interesting analysis of George Eliot's employment of a variety of indirect free style in her presentation of Dorothea Brooke, see Derek Oldfield, "The Language of the Novel: The Character of Dorothea," in *Middlemarch: Critical Approaches to the Novel,* ed. Barbara Hardy (New York, 1967), pp. 63–86.

10. "—Oh! c'est que je t'aime! reprenait-elle, je t'aime à ne pouvoir me passer de toi, sais-tu bien? J'ai quelquefois des envies de te revoir où toutes les colères de l'amour me déchirent. Je me demande: 'Où est-il? Peut-être il parle à d'autres femmes? Elles lui sourient, il s'approche . . . [sic]' Oh! non, n'est-ce pas, aucune ne te plaît? Il y en a de plus belles; mais moi, je sais mieux aimer! Je suis ta servante et ta concubine! Tu es mon roi, mon idole! tu es bon! tu es beau! tu es intelligent! tu es fort!" (II.xii.264–265).

11. *Dostoevsky and Romantic Realism* (Chicago, 1967), p. 7.

12. Mario Praz, *The Romantic Agony,* trans. Angus Davidson (1933; London, 1962), p. 170. "Baudelaire and Flaubert are like the two faces of a Herm planted firmly in the middle of the century, marking the division between Romanticism and Decadence, between the period of the Fatal Man and that of the Fatal Woman, between the period of Delacroix and that of Moreau." Elsewhere Praz treats the sadistic elements in *Madame Bovary:* "Madame Bovary, in order to excite her imagination felt the necessity of reading 'des livres extravagants où il y avait des tableaux orgiaques avec des situations sanglantes' (an obvious allusion to de Sade)" (p. 171).

13. See, for a notable example, Anthony Thorlby, *Gustave Flaubert and the Art of Realism* (New Haven, 1957), pp. 39–46.

14. Flaubert had earlier planned a much more elaborate treatment of Homais' struggles to receive the decoration of the Legion of Honor. See Leleu and Pommier, pp. 639–642.

15. Baudelaire, p. 656.

16. Emma's vision is detailed at some length as an example of Flaubert's voluptuous lyricism earlier in this chapter (p. 78). It is a curious fact that Emma proposes carrying Berthe along on the elopement; but there is nothing to suggest that Emma is thinking of Berthe's welfare. Rather, in the context of the passage, she is merely casting recklessly aside an objection Rodolphe has raised to their eloping at all.

17. Brombert, pp. 42–43.

18. See my chapter I, pp. 23–24.

19. See above, page 85. Flaubert is undoubtedly mindful, and probably expects the reader to be mindful, of Rodolphe's comment after he has written "Blame only Fate" in his letter of farewell to Emma: " 'There's a word that's always effective,' he said to himself." Charles had presumably encountered the word (though as a doctor he must

have heard it often elsewhere) in Rodolphe's letter of farewell when he had found Rodolphe's letters after Emma's death. The great irony is that Charles discovers in this word, so often thrown out by others as a hollow bit of rhetoric, a means of summing up for the first time his agonized reflections over an extended period. Emma is the dupe of sentimental phrasing, but it is Charles alone who is capable at the last of giving to a single cliché all the depth of his experience in the months since Emma's death.

III

FROM *SALAMMBÔ* TO *THE SIMPLE HEART*

FOLLOWING THE TURMOIL SET OFF BY THE PUBLICATION OF *Madame Bovary*—the trial of Flaubert for immorality and atheism based on the impieties, real and surmised, of that work, and a period of celebrity and social living in Paris upon his being acquitted, Flaubert began work on *Salammbô*. Here he threw off the restrictions that had held him to his ideal of "impersonality" for *Madame Bovary* and let his gorgeous romantic phantasmagoria derived from the more lurid pages of Carthaginian history lead him where they might. The intensity of double vision that had played so important a part in *Madame Bovary*, with his lyrical impulses chained to a contrapuntal ironic view of French provincial life in Yonville l'Abbaye, went to the winds; and with it went the distinctive qualities that had made the publication of Flaubert's first novel so remarkable an advance in the field of psychological narrative. "*Madame Bovary*," Henry James declared in 1876, in the year of his own first novel (*Roderick Hudson*), "is fortunately an inimitable work." Flaubert's earliest novel had remained "altogether his best." Though anything Flaubert wrote repaid attention, *Salammbô* was a work of genius in an altogether different vein, and *Sentimental Education*, the later work that was most nearly to follow the path of *Madame Bovary* in style and theme, was in comparison "mechanical and inanimate."[1] Returning to the subject a quarter of a century later, James had not altered his judgment. There was, he said, nothing of the "near, of the directly observed," in Flaubert's *Salammbô* or his *The Temptation of Saint Anthony* and little of the sort of "extravagance of illusion" worth remarking on in *Sentimental Education*—"that indefinable last word of restrained and cold execution." Nothing in Flaubert's later work touched his first great work, which James considered "absolutely the most literary of novels," the exemplar of style and form that continued to distinguish Flaubert as "the novelist of the novelist."[2]

In view of his own preference for building his novels around fine central intelligences, James's judgments on Flaubert seem fully understandable. Francis Steegmuller, to be sure, sees in the priestess-heroine of *Salammbô* "another victim, like Emma Bovary, of the insoluble, always fascinating conflict between dream and reality, one of Flaubert's fundamental themes," and considers *Sentimental Education* Flaubert's "most masterly treatment" of this same theme.[3] Read in his own context, Steegmuller's observations may be considered reasonable; but the differences between Flaubert's treatment of the theme of illusion in conflict with reality in *Madame Bovary* and his handling of the same theme in *Salammbô* and *Sentimental Education* are so great as to constitute a distinction in kind. If *Sentimental Education*, as a number of critics maintain today, is comparable to *Madame Bovary* as a fictional masterpiece, it is a masterpiece of a distinctly different variety. The Flaubert we see at work in the pages of *Salammbô* or in *The Temptation of Saint Anthony* (written in its first form before *Madame Bovary* but left for revisions and publication until a much later date) is reveling in licenses quite alien to his mood and purposes in 1852 when he confided to Louise Colet regarding *Madame Bovary*: "Never in my life have I written anything more difficult than what I am doing now—trivial dialogue. . . . My characters are completely commonplace, but they have to speak in a literary style. . . ."[4] Flaubert looked back with envy (as in his letter to Colet in April, 1853) to the ease with which he had written of the visions of Saint Anthony: "*Saint Anthony* didn't demand a quarter of the mental tension that *Bovary* is causing me. It was an outlet for my feelings; I had only pleasure in writing it . . . ." In contrast: "Think of me now, having constantly to be in the skins of people for whom I feel aversion" (C, III, 156). The tension between lyrical vision and ironic vision which is at the very heart of the superb effectiveness of *Madame*

Bovary is not to be found in *The Temptation of Saint Anthony*. All is viewed from Saint Anthony's point of sight as he remains in one place, almost as impassive as a mirror reflecting endless clouds of illusion and hallucination. Margaret Tillett finds a close kinship between Flaubert's *Saint Anthony* and Baudelaire's *Flowers of Evil*, in both of which she discovers a "horrid fascination of the grotesque, the obscene, and hideous in life . . . ."[5] Certainly horror and brutality abound in the scenes of *Saint Anthony* even as they do in *Salammbô*, and the contrast with *Madame Bovary* is obvious and great.

The differences between *Madame Bovary* and *Sentimental Education* (1869) are less obvious and perhaps worth exploring at greater length. Despite its merits as a realistic social history of its period, *Sentimental Education* is in marked contrast to *Madame Bovary* judged as a novel about the inner experience of a central protagonist. Frédéric Moreau figures at the center of *Sentimental Education*, but he resembles the quiet center of an active hurricane. Stirring events surround him but rarely impinge upon his private world. Baudelaire insisted that though Flaubert had succeeded in making vivid the imaginative life of Emma Bovary, he had actually given his heroine much of the vitality of a masculine mentality. "A marvelous thing resulted from this: in spite of all his zeal for dramatic creation, he could not help infusing virile blood into the veins of his creature, and because of her energy and ambition and capacity for reverie, Madame Bovary remained a man."[6] It would be scarcely too much to say that compared to Emma Bovary, Frédéric Moreau possesses more of the passivity in his nature, the yielding to events rather than forming them, that is (or has been!) generally thought to be characteristic of the feminine temperament than does Emma Bovary. When Emma takes to running at early morning across the fields to surprise Rodolphe in the seclusion of his own chateau, there is really a reversal of roles. It is impossible to recall any single scene in which Frédéric Moreau pursues any one goal as aggressively as this. As Raymond Giraud observes, Frédéric "is neither a subjectively drawn Rousseauistic hero nor an impassively observed laboratory specimen," but

110

the implication seems to be that he tends toward the second state. Flaubert, recalling his own student days, has made Frédéric in considerable extent autobiographical; the central subject is not, however, Frédéric's inner experience. It is instead a whole generation seen against the events of the time. *Sentimental Education* is Flaubert's assessment of his era and generation—"his condemnation of the entire bourgeois civilization of the late July Monarchy and early Empire, an important document for the study of the evolution of the artist's alienation from society."[7] Flaubert himself wrote: "I want to do a moral history of the men of my generation—'sentimental' history might be more exact. It is a book about love, about passion, but only the kind of passion that is possible nowadays, *that is, inactive passion*" (C, V, 158, italics mine).

Frédéric Moreau seems, indeed, to have "inactive passion," or passion that is never strong enough to drive him into intensive action, at the very heart of his nature. For a while as a young student, he regularly attends lectures in the pursuit of a law career, but two weeks are enough to discourage him. He attempts, during the course of *Sentimental Education*, to find a career as a lawyer, a writer, a painter, a politician. All attempts are short-lived, and he continues to wander aimlessly through a period in which stirring events are happening all around him. This seems to be an important part of Flaubert's conscious plan in the novel. While the February, 1848, Revolution is going on, Frédéric is preparing for a liaison with Madame Arnoux which does not take place; while bloody battles are raging in Paris and history is being made, Frédéric is strolling the paths and avenues of Versailles with his mistress Rosanette. Even while Louis Napoleon's *coup d'état* is taking place, Frédéric is absorbed in pursuing other interests. "Political events," Flaubert observes in passing, "left Frédéric indifferent, so preoccupied was he with his own affairs."[8] To the degree that his character is developed, Frédéric, like Emma Bovary, is a romantic egoist as he pursues his illusory ideal of romantic love symbolized by Madame Arnoux, on the one hand, and engages in a frankly sensual relationship with Rosanette on the other. The large number of characters, the various strata of society which are presented, the detailed portrayals in the riot scenes all compete for the center of interest, and Frédéric's character is by no means awarded the intensive treatment afforded Emma Bovary.

111

Central to the sentimental aspects of Frédéric's education and to the design of the work is Frédéric's unusual relation to Madame Arnoux in an affair that extends throughout the length of the novel and that ultimately—in line with Flaubert's irony upon the tendencies of the age—ends in nothingness. It is surely an extreme of "inactive passion" even among the variants Flaubert may have considered in planning his book.

When Frédéric first sees Madame Arnoux on shipboard during a journey from Paris to Nogent, he is immediately infatuated with her. It is strongly representative of the differences between *Madame Bovary* and *Sentimental Education*, however, that whereas in the former novel the revelation Emma experiences at Vaubyessard, perhaps her strongest experience of infatuation, is to send her imaginative life into fierce activity, occupying pages filled with details of her search for knowledge of fashion and with symbolic correlatives for her state of mind (the organ grinder, the silk cigar case, the scaling of the plaster priest, the cracked bell of the church at Tostes, and so many more), Frédéric's vision of Madame Arnoux passes with little comment calculated to render memorable this epoch-making first appearance of her in his life. We hear no more of Mme. Arnoux and her impact upon Frédéric's imagination for many pages—and even then there is in the treatment only the faintest resemblance to the sort of vital particularity that Flaubert had invested in *Madame Bovary*. This is, of course, simply to say that Flaubert had chosen to write a very different novel from that which reveals with such intensity, lyricism, realistic counterpointing, and effective symbolism the inner life of Emma Bovary.

Sentimental Education is in certain respects a novel in the manner of Balzac. Frédéric's courtship of Madame Dambreuse, a wealthy woman who can help him to realize a political career, is reminiscent of Rastignac in his courtship of Delphine in *Père Goriot*. Like Rastignac, Frédéric is introduced to many strata of society and many types of people. Among his immediate reference group there are an unsuccessful painter, a writer who has written nothing of significance, a teacher of mathematics who devotes most of his time to preaching socialistic theory, an obscure actor, a lawyer without clients, and the husband of Madame Arnoux, an art dealer at the outset of the novel, but a man who frequently changes occupations without great improvement of his fortunes. Frédéric is exposed to provincial life in his native village of Nogent as well as to Parisian upper-middle-class society in the Dambreuse family. He carries on a sustained relationship with his mistress Rosanette, but while Rosanette is giving birth to his child, he is already in half-hearted pursuit of the widowed Madame Dambreuse, though eventually he cannot bring himself to take the hand she offers him: To do so would be to commit himself to an active life as a politician. By degrees, as life continues year by year, Frédéric attains middle age without ever having carried out a significant purpose. He is an early prototype of the non-hero, the central figure uncertain of aim or motive that is to reach extremes of statement in such twentieth-century novels as Camus' *The Stranger* or Sillitoe's *Saturday Night and Sunday Morning*. Flaubert sums up much of Frédéric's later years in a famous passage:

> He traveled.
> He knew the melancholy of steamboats; of cold awakenings in tents; the tedium of landscapes and ruins; the bitterness of interrupted friendships.
> He returned.
> He went into society. He had other loves. But the ever-present memory of the first made them insipid; and then vehemence of desire, the flower of the sensation itself, had withered. His intellectual ambitions were equally toned down. Years passed; and he endured the idleness of his mind and the stagnation of his heart. (III.v.600)

Immediately following this swift vignette of seasons passed without fruition, Madame Arnoux appears to him for the first time in several years. She wears a black lace veil, and as they walk together she is obscured by shadow, so that Frédéric obtains only vague glimpses of her—they promenade "like people walking together in the country over a bed of dead leaves." On their return to his rooms, Madame Arnoux for the first time takes off her hat and veil. In the lamplight Frédéric sees that her hair has turned white, and the sight strikes him "like a blow full in the chest." Frédéric attempts to conceal his distress with gallantry; Madame Arnoux for her part accepts eagerly "this adoration of the woman she had ceased to be." For the moment, they revive much of the old sense of mutual attraction; but the moment cannot last. The pattern of illusion that has been at the heart of this

113

affair without fruition has always been pastel in its coloring; and the ending of the illusion is in keeping with what it has been. "They had nothing more to say to each other." The scene concludes with her cutting and giving Frédéric a lock of her white hair. The closing sentence is simply "And that was all." This particular scene is not altogether remote from one James—and especially the later James—might have conceived. His judgment that *Sentimental Education* represents an "indefinable last word of restrained and cold execution" suggests his own failure to recognize the novel's best qualities, but it serves at least to emphasize the remoteness of *Sentimental Education* from the intensity of inner experience that Flaubert had achieved in *Madame Bovary*.

Flaubert's last ambitious work, *Bouvard et Pécuchet*, left uncompleted at his death and not published until 1881, is a curiously chaotic piece combining burlesque and satire with a few passages of intense lyrical beauty. Though the two chief characters in this strange work, the Bouvard and the Pécuchet of the title, are indeed the victims of gross illusions, it is hard to see in the chaotic treatment of them anything that can be reduced to a significant pattern. Flaubert, an intense admirer of Rabelais, has given a Rabelaisan exuberance to parts of the work, especially those following the retirement of the two characters to the country to make an ambitious study of such varied subjects as horticulture, agriculture, landscape gardening, preserving and distilling, chemistry, anatomy, physiology and medicine, hygiene and dietetics, zoology, geology, archaeology, history, literature, declamation, aesthetics; politics and social theory; lust and its dangers, gymnastics, table-turning and magnetism, hypnotism, magic, philosophy (including the systems of Spinoza, Descartes, Locke, etc.), metaphysics, theology and martyrology; educational method, phrenology, and town-planning. It is a work of extreme and massive disparities. Passages of power and beauty vie with expanses of appalling dullness; islands of real wit are interspersed in sections of heavily labored attempts at comedy. The flatnesses unfortunately cover far more territory than the areas of wit and beauty. Flaubert's good friend Turgenev advised him to deal with his subject briefly and with concision, in the manner of Swift or Voltaire; but Flaubert, though he protested his great respect for Turgenev's judgment, believed that bulk was essential to his conception and asserted, moreover, that for him brevity was an impossibility. There would be time thereafter for selecting and abridging. (C, V, 178)

Flaubert was wrong on two counts: He was never to be granted enough time to complete the elaborate plan of his book—the compression and cutting he projected were never to take place. And he was wrong also in his saying that he could "never write anything short." In 1875–76 while he was still struggling with *Bouvard et Pécuchet* and suffering from acute depression, he turned for relief to the writing of his *Three Tales* (*Trois Contes*), in which all three stories are distinguished work, and one of them is among the world's supreme achievements in the field of the short story. The resemblances between *A Simple Heart* (*Un Coeur simple*) and *Madame Bovary* in subject and style are remarkable considering the twenty years that separate them and the great divergences of the subjects and ways of treating them that had absorbed Flaubert in the years between. Especially so since Flaubert apparently felt—or was soon to feel—that he had renounced *Madame Bovary* from his affections. "*Bovary* bores me," he wrote George Charpentier in 1879. "People insist on talking about it. For them nothing I have written since matters. I assure you that if I didn't need money I would take steps to see that it was never reprinted" (C, VIII, 207).

A Simple Heart is a short story of approximately eleven thousand words or something under thirty pages; but into this space Flaubert has compressed with almost miraculous concision the essentials of a profoundly symbolic pattern of illusion. The mind of the protagonist is, as the title would suggest, curiously uncomplicated and, to superficial view, an unprofitable subject for an author to choose for the center of his story. It is the triumph of the piece that Flaubert succeeds in making the imaginative activity of this very simple serving maid, who cannot even read, an exciting and deeply moving subject. In the first part, indeed, the passage of external events is quite rapid as we cover the earlier years of Félicité's life, including a love affair in which she suffers a betrayal. Flaubert's theory of impersonality, so consciously exercised in *Madame Bovary*, is again manifest in the detachment of the narrator. When Félicité discovers that her lover has rejected her for an old woman he has married for her money, she "threw herself on the ground, cried out again and again, called aloud to God, and moaned alone in the fields till daylight came."[9] Flaubert makes graphic use of concrete particulars to evoke state of mind throughout the first third of the story detailing Félicité's devoted service to the family of the Widow Aubain; but it is with the first account of the effect of a sermon (or a synthesis of sermons) upon Félicité that we are provided an extended view of her internal life:

> The priest started with an outline of sacred history. It was as if she beheld with her own eyes the Garden, the Flood, the Tower of Babel, cities in flames, dying nations, and overturned idols. The vision left her filled with awe for the Most High and fear of His wrath. Then she wept, hearing the story of the Passion. Why had they crucified Him— Him who so loved the children, fed the multitudes, healed the blind, and had wished, in His meekness, to be born among the poor, on the dungheap of a stable? The sowings, the harvests, the wine-presses, all these familiar things the Gospel speaks of, were familiar to her life. God's passing had sanctified them; and she loved the lambs more tenderly for love of the Lamb, and the doves because of the Holy Ghost. (iii.23–24)

The problem of visualizing God himself among the many familiar evidences of His handiwork baffled Félicité.

> She found it hard to imagine Him in person, because He was not simply a bird, but at times a flame, and a breath at other times. It might be His light, she thought, which flickers at night about the edge of the marshes, His breathing which drives the clouds, His voice which gives harmony to the bells; and she would stay rapt in adoration, enjoying the coolness of the walls and the quiet of the church.

Such moments of insight into Félicité's private life are played against the ironical detail of her servitude to the Aubain family, who take her devotion as a matter of course. On the occasion of the daughter Virginie's confirmation, Félicité so identifies with the girl that she feels she herself is participating in the rite:

When it was Virginie's turn, Félicité leaned forward to see; and with an imaginativeness born of deep and tender feeling it seemed to her that she herself was this child—Virginie's face became hers, she was dressed in her clothes, it was her own heart beating so loudly in her breast. At the moment of opening her mouth for the wafer, she closed her eyes and nearly fainted. (iii.25–26)

It is the pattern of the story that all things Félicité loves are one by one to be taken from her. Virginie is placed in a convent as a boarder for her further education. Her leave-taking from her mother involves much show of emotion; but there is apparently no time for a farewell to Félicité, though it is the servant who "put six pots of preserves, a dozen pears, and a bunch of violets" under the seat of the van that took Virginie away and who, one surmises, felt most deeply Virginie's absence. When, some years later, Virginie (who has always been frail) dies at the convent, it is Félicité who sits up for two nights with the body. When Félicité and Mme. Aubain go to Virginie's room to take away the belongings of the dead girl, Flaubert provides one of his prose lyrics such as had given part of the special tone to *Madame Bovary*, where the details juxtapose different periods of time and where concrete objects become poignant symbols of times dead and past (as with Rodolphe rummaging through his souvenirs of past loves, Emma viewing the desiccated bridal bouquet from Charles's first marriage, or Charles searching the dead effects of Emma Bovary in the last pages of the novel) : the mood of nature, as often in *Madame Bovary*, is presented as a jarring counterpoint to the mood of the two women:

Virginie's dresses were in a row beneath a shelf on which there were three dolls, some hoops, a set of toy pots and pans, and the basin that she had used. They took out her petticoats as well, and her stockings and handkerchiefs, and stretched them out on the two beds before folding them up again. The sunshine lit up these poor objects, bringing out their stains and the creases once made by the body's movement. The air was warm and blue, a blackbird warbled, all life seemed to breathe a deep sweetness. They found a little plush hat with thick, chestnut-coloured pile; but it was eaten all over by moths. Félicité begged to keep it for her own. (41)

Félicité had already lost her nephew Victor, on whom she had showered her affection after the departure of Virginie for the convent, an affection he and his impoverished parents found it profitable to encourage. On each visit from Honfleur he brought things for her to mend and, at his parents' instruction "to get something out of her," took home "a packet of moist sugar, or perhaps a cake of soap, spirits, or even at times money." When Victor goes to sea as a cabin boy, Félicité suffers vicariously all the perils she imagines him subjected to. When at the end of six months she mentions her worries to Madame Aubain, her mistress shrugs off concern for this mere "scamp of a cabinboy." But it is not long until Victor is dead.

After the deaths of Victor and Virginie, Félicité transfers all her great fund of affection to a parrot. Her delusions about Loulou sustain her in her illness, poverty, and old age. For Loulou becomes inextricably confused in Félicité's mind with the Holy Ghost, and it is before Loulou that she comes in time to say her prayers. It is one of Flaubert's triumphs that he is able to keep his bizarre subject in the realm of deep pathos despite the fact that his "binocular vision," as in *Madame Bovary*, provides the reader with vivid, grotesque particulars of the reality surrounding Félicité's internal experience. Félicité's concentration upon Loulou as the focus of her affection occurs a short time after she and her mistress have put away the clothes of the dead Virginie. The parrot is a gift to Madame Aubain from a family that is leaving the city and finds this a convenient way of getting rid of him. "His body was green and the tips of his wings a deep pink; his forehead was blue and his throat golden. But he had the tiresome habit of biting his perch, tearing out his feathers, sprinkling his ordures about, and splashing out the water of his tub. He annoyed Madame Aubain, and she gave him to Félicité" (iv.45). Flaubert supplies a pungent counterpointing of Loulou's habits that would, for anyone except Félicité, utterly disqualify him for apotheosis.

Félicité pours her affection upon this unresponsive object. When he disappears she wears her slippers to shreds searching for him. Her severe exhaustion from the search brings on an attack of quinsy, followed by earache; and in three years' time she is deaf. With her deafness, Félicité's "little circle of ideas contracted farther still; the peal of church-bells, the lowing of cattle for her no longer existed. All living beings moved with the silence of ghosts" (iv.48–49). Only one sound now reaches her, and that is the piercing voice of the parrot. "As though to amuse her, Loulou reproduced the tick-tock of the turn-spit, the shrill cry of the fish vender, and the whine of the saw in the joiner's house opposite; and when the bell rang he imitated Madame Aubain's 'Félicité! the door! the door!' They carried on dialogues, he monotonously reciting the three phrases in his repertoire, and she replying with words just as disconnected but pouring out what was in her heart." Flaubert, who had earlier interpreted Emma's halting phrases into poetic periods commensurate with their depth of feeling, now presents Félicité's love for Loulou in language that if simpler is often eloquent. "In her isolation Loulou was almost a son and a lover. He climbed her fingers, nibbled at her lips, and clung to her kerchief; and when she bent her forehead and moved her head gently back and forth, as nurses do, the great wings of her bonnet and the bird's wings flapped in rhythm together."

Only once does Félicité suffer an experience of bleak epiphany. The death of Loulou brings on a grief so intense that Madame Aubain suggests Félicité have the little body stuffed. Walking to Le Havre to carry out the purpose, Félicité is nearly run down by a mail coach whose approach, in her deafness, she has not been aware of. The angry driver lashes her in passing with his whip. The experience under a dark winter sky, with ice whitening the ditches and the trees that line the road leafless in their winter barrenness, anticipates Félicité's isolation and descent to death in the closing pages of her story; but it is only in the present episode that Félicité herself reviews for a moment her life as it might appear from the outside:

> Her first act, when she regained consciousness, was to open her basket. Loulou happily was not injured. She felt a burn in her right cheek, and her hands when she touched it were red; the blood ran.
>
> She sat down on a pile of stones and bound up her face with her handkerchief. Then she ate a crust of bread which she had put in her basket as a precaution, and found a consolation for her wound in gazing at the bird.
>
> When she reached the crest of Ecquemauville she saw the lights of Honfleur sparkling in the night like a host of stars; beyond, the sea stretched vaguely. Then a feebleness overtook her; and her wretched

childhood, the disillusion of her first love, her nephew's going away, Virginie's death—all came back to her together like the waves at flood-tide, and rose to her throat and choked her. (iv.51)

Margaret Tillett considers the scene overlooking Honfleur "absolutely out of tune" with Félicité's character.[10] But it is a part of Flaubert's theory in this story as in *Madame Bovary* that the author often serves legitimately as the translator of emotions for which the character has no adequate words. Moreover, the experiences which Félicité is evoking in this rare or unique synthesis—the accumulated griefs of her life—are so much a part of her consciousness that even with her limited powers of generalization it seems plausible that she should undergo this moment of modest epiphany. With the wound of the lash still burning her cheek, with the impression of being cut off in a frozen world from the human world lying below her, with the little corpse of Loulou at her side, there is reason for her to find her universe grown suddenly alien and indifferent. The scene represents a needed enactment in miniature, with Félicité for once in witness, of the theme of alienation that plays so prominent a part in this short story, as it does in *Madame Bovary*.

Loulou's body newly stuffed is returned looking even more beautiful than Loulou had appeared in life, his head tilted to one side, his beak now biting a gilded nut, his one foot in the air and his other enclosing a branch screwed into a pedestal. Félicité finds him a place of honor in her room. Flaubert, whose fascination with meanings to be found in clusters of absurd non sequiturs figures so eloquently in *Madame Bovary*, makes of Félicité's chamber a temple for a religion of love. Deep selfless devotion, cut off from transcendental response, has been obliged to bestow itself on inanimate clutter. A perceptive court might have found stronger evidences of impiety in Flaubert's short story than in his first novel. "On the walls there were rosaries, medals, several Virgins, and a vessel for holy water made from a coconut; on the chest of drawers, draped with a cloth like an altar, was the box ornamented with seashells that Victor had given her, together with a watering-can, a toy-balloon, exercise-books, the illustrated geography, a pair of young lady's boots; and, fastened by its ribbons to the nail of the looking-glass, the little plush hat [of Virginie]" (iv.52–53). It is not long before Félicité is beginning to observe resemblances between Loulou and the Holy Ghost as represented in one window of the church; and she sees still stronger similarities to Loulou in a crude color print portraying the baptism of Our Lord. "With his purple wings and emerald body he was the very image of Loulou." The Holy Ghost, Félicité reasoned, must have appeared not, as was generally thought, as a dove—"for such creatures cannot speak." Rather, it had surely been one of Loulou's ancestors.

It must have been a challenge, even for Flaubert, to manage such subject matter without reducing it to the level of burlesque. Part of the dignity that Flaubert achieves is archetypal in character. After the suicide of Madame Aubain's lawyer, who has stolen her funds, and then the death of Madame Aubain herself, the rooms are stripped of furniture, and only Félicité remains in the otherwise empty dwelling. The house, with strong overtones of Chapter Twelve of Ecclesiastes, is in its abandonment and decline made to render universal in import the isolation and decay of Félicité herself. The building continues falling farther and farther into ruin without either buyer or tenant. Félicité lives on in it by means of her small pension.

> She scarcely ever went out, for she did not like to pass the shop where some of the old furniture was displayed for sale. Since her fit of giddiness she dragged one leg; and as her strength diminished Mère Simon, whose grocery shop had collapsed, came every morning to split wood and pump water for her.
>
> Her eyes grew feeble. The shutters no longer were opened. Years passed, and the house was neither rented nor sold.
>
> Félicité never asked for repairs for fear of being turned out. The boards of the roof rotted; her bolster was wet for a whole winter. After Easter she spat blood. (iv.57)

Though Félicité is too deaf to hear more, she does make out the one word "pneumonia" shouted by the doctor Mère Simon has brought to her bedside.

The final scene centers in the custom of placing festal shrines at places along a route taken by a religious procession bearing the Holy Sacrament. A rivalry among the women of the parish ends in their choosing as a compromise the placing of the third shrine in the courtyard of Madame Aubain's empty house. In her fevered condition, Félicité asks to place her parrot among the articles of beauty that will decorate the shrine. Though the neighbors object, the priest consents. Félicité's condition worsens so much that she requests and receives extreme unction. Later Mère Simon brings Loulou to her so that she may bid him good-bye. "Although Loulou was not a corpse, the worms devoured him as if he were. One of his wings was broken, and the stuffing was coming out of his stomach. But she was blind now; she kissed him on the forehead and held him close against her cheek. Mère Simon took him back from her to put him on the altar" (iv.59). The procession reaches the shrine in the courtyard just at the moment when Félicité's death agony begins.

> A death-rattle that grew more and more acute made her sides heave. Bubbles of froth emerged from the corners of her mouth and her whole body trembled. . . .
>
> The clergy appeared in the courtyard. Mère Simon clambered onto a chair to reach the attic window, and so looked down directly on the shrine. Green garlands hung about the altar, which was adorned with a flounce of English lace. In the middle was a small frame enclosing relics; two orange-trees stood at the corners, and there were silver candlesticks and china vases, with sunflowers, lilies, peonies, foxgloves, and tufts of hortensia. This heap of blazing colour descended in steps from the altar down to the carpet which extended along the pavement. Rare objects caught the eye. There was a silver-gilt sugar-basin with a crown of violets; pendants of Alençon stone glittered on the moss, and two Chinese screens revealed their landscapes. Loulou, buried under roses, showed nothing except his blue forehead, like a plaque of lapis lazuli. (v.62–63)

A brief paragraph follows describing the ceremony performed before the magnificent clutter of the shrine—a paragraph that seems intended to serve as a transition from the world outside to the world once more of Félicité's experience; for the ceremony is described with something approaching an imaginative participation in it: "The wardens, the singers, the children took their positions along the three sides of the court. The priest slowly mounted the steps and placed his great, resplendent golden sun upon the lace. Everyone kneeled, and there was a deep silence. The censers glided in full swing on their chains." There follows, as the final paragraph of the story, Félicité's culminating vision:

An azure vapor ascended to Félicité's room. Her nostrils met it; she inhaled it with a mystic sensuality [*une sensualité mystique*], then closed her eyes. Her lips smiled. The beatings of her heart lessened one by one, vaguer each time and softer, as a fountain sinks, as an echo disappears. And when she sighed her last breath she believed she saw, through an opening in the heavens, a gigantic parrot above her head, looking down from on high [*un perroquet gigantesque, planant au-dessus de sa tête*].

"The priest rose to take the crucifix; then she stretched out her neck like one suffering thirst, and gluing her lips to the body of the Man-God, she pressed upon it with all her failing strength the fullest kiss of love that she had ever given." Emma Bovary's moment of mystic sensuality is succeeded by the song of the blind beggar and her own final atrocious desperate laughter. In *A Simple Heart* Flaubert has no need for so sinister a death's head as the blind beggar. The parrot-god offers a gentler correlative for the author's sense of loss, less acute for the two intervening decades. The implications seem, however, much the same. Both are visions of human dissolution at the edge of an impersonal universe. *A Simple Heart*, like *Madame Bovary*, has traced a life-illusion with a consummate employment once again of ironical realistic counterpoint, in a manner no earlier continental novelist had approached. Five years earlier across the Channel George Eliot had published *Middlemarch*, a novel strongly contrasting with the compression and "impersonal" method of Flaubert's tale but with important factors in common.

NOTES

1. "Charles de Bernard and Gustave Flaubert," *French Poets and Novelists* (London, 1893), pp. 199, 203. The essay appeared originally in *Galaxy* in 1876.
2. "Gustave Flaubert," in *The Future of the Novel*, ed. Leon Edel (New York, 1956), pp. 134, 145. The essay appeared originally in 1902 as a preface to an edition of *Madame Bovary*.
3. *The Selected Letters of Gustave Flaubert*, ed. and trans. Francis Steegmuller (New York, 1957), p. 192 (in an interchapter).
4. *Correspondance, Oeuvres complètes de Gustave Flaubert*, ed. Louis Conard (Paris, 1926–1933), III, 24–25. Quotations from Flaubert's letters are keyed to this edition by volume and page number in parentheses preceded by the letter *C*.
5. *On Reading Flaubert* (New York, 1961), p. 83.

6. *Oeuvres complètes de Baudelaire*, ed. Y. G. Le Dantec (Paris, 1961), p. 652.

7. Raymond Giraud, *The Unheroic Hero* (New Brunswick, N. J., 1957), p. 140.

8. *L'Education sentimentale, Oeuvres complètes de Gustave Flaubert*, ed. Louis Conard (Paris, 1910), VII, part III, chapter v, page 596. Quotations from the novel are followed by part, chapter, and page number of this edition in parentheses.

9. "Un Coeur simple," *Trois Contes, Oeuvres complètes de Gustave Flaubert*, ed. Louis Conard (Paris, 1910), XV, part ii, page 10. Quotations from "A Simple Heart" are followed by part and page number of this edition in parentheses.

10. Tillett, p. 93.

IV

MIDDLEMARCH: FIVE PATTERNS OF
ROMANTIC EGOISM

G EORGE ELIOT'S ROSAMOND VINCY OF *Middlemarch*, HENRY JAMES
declares in his review of that novel for *The Galaxy* in 1873, represents "a rare psychological study." And a few sentences later he
adds: "The author's rare psychological penetration is lavished upon
this veritably mulish domestic flower. *There is nothing more powerfully real than these scenes in all English fiction, and nothing certainly more intelligent.*"[1] This is praise indeed from a young critic
not ordinarily inclined toward generosity (he had earlier pronounced
Dickens' *Little Dorrit* "labored" and *Our Mutual Friend* a work
"dug out as with spade and pickaxe"). James continues regarding
Eliot's scenes: "Their impressiveness and (as regards Lydgate) their
pathos, is deepened by the constantly low key in which they are
pitched. It is a tragedy based on unpaid butchers' bills, and the urgent
need for small economies. The author has desired to be strictly real
and to adhere to the facts of the common lot, and she has given us a
powerful version of that typical human drama, the struggles of an
ambitious soul with sordid disappointments and vulgar embarrass-
ments." It is Dorothea Brooke, however, that is for James, even more
than Lydgate and Rosamond, "the great achievement of the book."
Eight years after his review of *Middlemarch*, James was to publish his
The Portrait of a Lady. James's famous portrait of Isabel Archer is, as
Leon Edel has said, fully worthy of its place in "the great gallery of

the world's fiction" along with other eminent heroines, including Dorothea Brooke and Emma Bovary. Isabel's drama is profoundly similar to that of Dorothea—so much so that Edel's brief description would do as well for the earlier heroine. Both enact dramas "of suppressed passion, passion converted into high ideals and driven by a need for power that reckoned little with the world's harsh realities." And in both instances the portrait that remains most vividly in the reader's mind is one depicting the maiden in the "freshness of her youth—and the strength of her innocence and her egotism." If *The Portrait of a Lady* is in a certain sense (as Edel says) "a 'George Eliot novel' written by James in the way he believed she *should* have written," Isabel is nevertheless (as Edel also makes clear) a brilliantly original creation.[2] The question of the extent of James's specific indebtedness to Eliot has been much debated. It is much less important, at least in the context of the present study, than the question of how far George Eliot had gone by 1872 along paths in psychological narrative that James was to extend in *The Portrait of a Lady* and in ensuing novels. In any event, James in his critique found Dorothea Brooke, despite his pronounced enthusiasm for Lydgate and Rosamond, the great fact of the novel. She was "altogether too superb a heroine to be wasted . . . [and] of more consequence than the action of which she is the nominal center."

What James found weak in *Middlemarch*, what made it an "indifferent whole," was its vast scale and what he considered its looseness of construction. He was later to think of George Eliot, as he did of Tolstoy, as one of the creators of unwieldy novels—"loose baggy monsters"—that were full of life but deficient in unity or form.[3] The contrast between *Middlemarch* and *Madame Bovary* in regard to unity and form is indeed very great; and it is significant that whereas James learned so much from Eliot in psychological analysis, it was in Flaubert and in *Madame Bovary* specifically that he found the form of the novel "in *itself* as interesting, as active, as much of the essence of the subject as the idea." In *Madame Bovary* he found "a perfection that not only stamps it, but that makes it stand almost alone."[4] *The Portrait of a Lady* shows that James had learned much from Flaubert as well as from Eliot. And both novels could help him to understand the possibilities of concentrating for interest not upon incident but upon the inner life of the protagonists. Dorothea Brooke and Edward

Casaubon, Lydgate and Rosamond challenge us primarily, as does Emma Bovary, not through their relatively meager course of action in the outer world, but through our interest in what takes place in their private lives of thought and emotion, even as, to quote James, we follow Emma Bovary because of our fascination with "the nature of her consciousness and the play of her mind."[5] George Eliot, like Flaubert, was defensive about the emphasis she had placed upon the play of inward life as opposed to event. Both were aware of the likelihood of overtaxing the patience of their audiences in making this choice. It is interesting to see that James, while he was writing *The Portrait of a Lady* in 1881, felt that he, in turn, was risking the loss of his audience in concentrating so intently upon the inner life of his protagonist: "The weakness of the whole story is that it is too exclusively psychological—that it depends to[o] little on incident . . . . The idea of the whole thing is that the poor girl, who has dreamed of freedom and nobleness, who has done, as she believes, a generous, natural, clearsighted thing, finds herself in reality ground in the very mill of the conventional."[6]

The Portrait of a Lady is focused on the consciousness of the heroine almost as intensely as is *Madame Bovary*; but its settings are those of a sophisticated society, living the life of the upper classes in the great cities of Europe. Even by 1881 (less than a decade after the appearance of *Middlemarch*), in this first masterpiece of his career, James's style and substance are eminently his own and mark a stage in psychological fiction toward the twentieth century with its further subordination of setting and incident. The provincial town of Middlemarch is at least as important to George Eliot's novel as Yonville is to Flaubert's. The manner of presenting the world of illusion of Emma Bovary and of Eliot's protagonists depends upon playing in counterpoint to the illusion a vivid awareness of what the character and his very limited provincial world looks like from the outside. This is achieved in *Middlemarch* through the ironical voice of the narrator and through (as often in *Madame Bovary*) seeing the character through the eyes of other inhabitants of the town. When Dorothea Brooke is about to marry Edward Casaubon, we are supplied the intimate thoughts and aims of both Dorothea and her fiancé as the two rush blindly toward a disastrous union, each seeing the situation through the distorted lens of his ego, each seeing in the other qualities that do not exist there. At the same time we are given an awareness of the outer reality, the grotesque aspects of this marriage as it is seen from the outside by the narrator (whose superbly controlled irony is a vital part of the presentation) and by a variety of the inhabitants of Middlemarch. This counterpoint of inner vision with outer reality —the patterns of romantic egoism seen in double vision—is central to the psychological realism of both Flaubert and George Eliot; and it is here that they most closely resemble each other. At the same time the very significant differences between the two authors also come out strongly when we view them from this perspective. The lyricism, the "impersonality" of Flaubert are in some ways extremely different from the especially *prose* quality of Eliot's style and her emphasis on a theory of "sympathy" as opposed to "impersonality" in her presentation of her characters and their inner life. As was suggested in Chapter I, however, Eliot's particular kind of sympathetic insight is often more impersonal in its clarity and power of perception than Flaubert's "impersonality"; and Flaubert's theory of living emphatically the life of his characters (even though he professed to dislike them) comes rather close oftentimes to what Eliot meant by sympathetic insight.

i. Dorothea Brooke and Edward Casaubon

Few heroines of the novel on first thought seem less alike than Emma Bovary and Dorothea Brooke. Emma is as much a product of the Bertaux farm and the convent as Dorothea is of the English gentry and of a Swiss Protestant boarding school. Emma is involved in a hedonistic day-dream patterned by her reading in sentimental novels, and Dorothea is involved in dreaming of a life mission with her imagination channeled by her curious reading in theological works ordinarily associated not with healthy young women but with elderly ecclesiastics. Both Emma Bovary and Dorothea Brooke are, however, studies in distorted vision and frustration. Both are victims of romantic egoism. They are involved in their separate kinds of intense self-drama, their intimate life of the imagination seen in counterpoint to the absurdities of this vision as viewed from the outside.

On the surface, Dorothea Brooke appears so much a product of the author's idealism that even F. R. Leavis, writing in 1948, fails to allow for the subtleties of Eliot's irony and sees Eliot's heroine as predominantly "a product of George Eliot's own 'soul-hunger'—another day-dream ideal self."[7] It is only with Barbara Hardy in 1959, and with later critics, that the importance of irony in George Eliot's presentation of Dorothea Brooke is given greater attention.[8] When the focus becomes Dorothea's pattern of illusion, the amount of irony in Eliot's treatment becomes still more apparent.

The much-discussed "Prelude" of *Middlemarch* that Eliot sees fit to place before her first chapter has often been read as a one-dimensional proem inviting us to share the sense of pathos in Dorothea as a latter-day Saint Theresa whose "passionate, ideal nature" must demand an epic life in vain. Critics have taught us in recent years, however, to be wary of taking George Eliot's statements at face value. There is, in fact, more than a suggestion in this prelude that St. Theresa herself, despite her fame for effecting needed reforms in a religious order, may have found the epic life of an earlier century not entirely without prosaic frustrations and hard choices. The image of such opposition of the real to the ideal occurs first in the opening paragraph, where Saint Theresa and her little brother at an early age start out to seek martyrdom among the Moors. "Out they toddled from rugged Avila, *wide-eyed and helpless-looking* as two fawns, but with human hearts, already beating to a national idea; *until domestic reality met them in the shape of uncles, and turned them back from their great resolve.*"[9] It is made clear, at least, in the next paragraph that for the many Theresas born in the nineteenth century, "spiritual grandeur" must find itself "ill-matched with the meanness of opportunity," and in the third it is evident that Dorothea will be a "Saint Theresa, foundress of nothing." In juxtaposing Dorothea to Saint Theresa, George Eliot is already using a kind of irony that plays an important part in *Middlemarch*—an irony of literary or historical context of the kind Eliot will later employ in presenting Casaubon in the context of the sixteenth-century sonneteers—his own pedestrian qualities played in effective parallel against this background. Irony of context pervades *Madame Bovary*, where Emma's romantic visions based on her sentimental reading are seen so typically against the details of her life in Yonville. It figures more prominently in such scenes as Emma's witnessing the opera of *Lucia di Lammermoor* and losing herself in her fantasy of life with the star tenor, or burning incense under the influence of oriental tales, and invoking the atmosphere of the harem for her affair with Léon. To see blooming Miss Brooke of Middle-march against the august gray eminences she dreams of intimately serving—Bossuet, Pascal, the judicious Hooker, or Milton—is to feel an even stronger irony of literary context.

Dorothea is a child of Puritanism. Her uncle, Mr. Brooke, George Eliot tells us in the early pages of *Middlemarch*, felt none of this inheritance of Puritan energy, but "in his niece Dorothea it glowed alike through faults and virtues." It is almost immediately apparent that Dorothea's zest for Christian self-abnegation is actually an inverted sort of egoism. Such patterns, Eliot subtly suggests, can offer an opportunity for indulging a histrionic flair. Emma Bovary had found a channel for self-drama by proclaiming vows, fasting (or, rather, Flaubert slyly intimates, making occasional resolutions to fast—even "for a whole day") and inventing little sins in order to lengthen the drama of confession, "kneeling in the shadow, her hands joined, her face against the grating beneath the whispering of the priest."[10] Dorothea, though in a Puritan tradition, found similar outlets for bringing a sense of drama to her identity. She was a "young lady of some birth and fortune, who knelt suddenly down on a brick floor by the side of a sick labourer and prayed fervidly as if she thought herself living in the time of the Apostles—who had strange whims of fasting like a Papist, and of sitting up at night to read old theological books!" (i.7). Eliot does not allow us to take Dorothea's motives at her heroine's own evaluation. "Riding was an indulgence which she allowed herself in spite of conscientious qualms; she felt that she enjoyed it in a pagan way *and always looked forward to renouncing it*" (i.7, italics mine). Her sister's comment not long afterward is that Dorothea "likes giving up." Dorothea's reading in the classics of Protestantism is in some ways no less sinister in its effects on her youthful imagination than Emma's reading in keepsakes or romantic novels, and the author's irony in presenting such material is often equally evident. Dorothea "felt sure that she would have accepted the judicious Hooker, if she had been born in time to save him from that wretched mistake he made in matrimony; or John Milton when his blindness had come on; or any of the other great men whose odd habits it would have been glorious piety to endure . . ." (i.7). Early on, Eliot informs us that Dorothea was "enamoured of intensity and greatness, and was rash in embracing whatever seemed to her to have

130

those aspects . . ." (i.6). It is her unusual form of romantic egoism—her penchant for envisioning herself as light-bearer or handmaiden to a hero of erudition rather than as the spouse and helpmate of a more ordinary sort of companion—that leads her, a healthy girl not yet twenty, into a headlong betrothal to the Reverend Edward Casaubon, an anemic pedant of near fifty. It it worth observing that George Eliot heads the chapter in which Dorothea first meets Casaubon and pronounces him "the most interesting man she had ever seen" (ii.13) with a quotation from *Don Quixote* in which Don Quixote, despite the protestations of Sancho Panza, insists on seeing a barber with a brass basin on his head as a cavalier wearing the resplendent golden helmet of Mambrino. Dorothea's passion for remaking life to correspond to the pattern of her own illusion leads her into versions of reality that are scarcely less ludicrous.

The imperious egoism that makes Dorothea insist on seeing life as a romantic drama with herself as heroine is subtly embodied even in the first chapter of the novel when Dorothea and her sister Celia share jewels that were left them by their dead mother—a scene that might on rapid reading appear to offer nothing more challenging than the running dialogue of young girls such as filled pages in popular novels of the time. Celia is in the habit of regarding her elder sister with a measure of awe, born of Dorothea's unhesitating absoluteness in her judgments. But the reader is soon made aware of Celia's ability, like Sancho Panza's, for seeing many things undistortedly, though her vision, like his, stops near the limits of day-to-day life. When Celia proposes that they share the jewels between them, Dorothea in a tone "half-caressing, half explanatory" assures her that the two of them should be above the need for adorning themselves with jewels. When Celia pleads the point defensively, recalling that many Christians, even their former Swiss preceptress and teacher, Madame Poinçon, were not above wearing jewels, Dorothea's reply is a revealing piece of histrionic self-flattery: " 'You would like to wear them?' exclaimed Dorothea, an air of astonished discovery animating her whole person *with a dramatic action which she had caught from that very Madame Poinçon* who wore the ornaments. 'Of course, then, let us have them out. Why did you not tell me before? But the keys, the keys!' She pressed her hands against the sides of her head and seemed to despair of her memory" (i.9, italics mine). The passage is, of course, a telling example on Eliot's part of the way Dorothea makes Christian humility a means for dramas that flatter the ego and lend excitement to provincial life. Celia's efforts to persuade Dorothea to take at least a cross made of pearls enable Dorothea to keep the little morality play from coming to a close: " 'Not for the world, not for the world. A cross is the last thing I would wear as a trinket.' Dorothea shuddered slightly." And again a moment later on further urging by Celia: " 'No, I have other things of mama's—her sandal-wood box which I am so fond of—plenty of things. In fact, they are all yours, dear. . . . There—take away your property.' " Renouncing the world's baubles thus in one fine gesture may seem an impressive act of piety. But lest readers of Charlotte Yonge or other edifying novelists of the period should take this pageant of Christian "giving-up" overseriously and find its meaning in directions not intended, Eliot provides an unorthodox conclusion. Observing for the first time a splendid ring with an emerald surrounded by diamonds that the sun has just lighted up, Dorothea is suddenly reminded of how "gems are used as spiritual emblems in the Revelation of St. John." She yields easily to Celia's urging that she take the ring and the matching bracelet while meantime "her thought was trying to justify her delight in the colours by merging them in her mystic religious joy." They are the finest of the jewels, and Celia may be pardoned for feeling that Dorothea, for all her claims to superiority in things spiritual, was "not always consistent."

Emma Bovary, tempted by thoughts of Léon during their first acquaintance at Yonville but playing the role of the chaste wife, is not entirely dissimilar: "Then pride and the pleasure of saying to herself, 'I am virtuous,' and of studying herself in the mirror assuming poses of resignation consoled her a little for the sacrifice she thought she was making" (II.v.150). Closer to Dorothea in temperament and situation is James's Isabel Archer, "probably very liable to the sin of self-esteem" in her young maidenhood and often given to surveying "with complacency the field of her own nature; she was in the habit of taking for granted, on scanty evidence, that she was right; she treated herself to occasions of homage." Isabel "spent half her time in thinking of beauty and bravery and magnanimity" and sometimes "went so far as to wish that she might find herself some day in a difficult position, so that she should have the pleasure of being as heroic as the occasion demanded." James's words apply almost equally well to Eliot's heroine. For Dorothea as for Isabel—"Altogether, with her meagre knowledge, her inflated ideals, her confidence at once innocent and dogmatic, her temper at once exacting and indulgent, her mixture of curiosity and fastidiousness, of vivacity and indifference, her desire to look very well and to be if possible even better, her determination to see, to try, to know, her combination of the delicate, desultory, flamelike spirit and the eager and personal creature of conditions: she would be an easy victim of scientific criticism if she were not intended to awaken on the reader's part an impulse more tender and more purely expectant"[11] (vi.53–54).

The parallel between Don Quixote and Dorothea suggested by the motto for the second chapter of *Middlemarch* becomes more evident as the chapter progresses. Where Celia (in keeping with her part as an English provincial Sancho Panza) considers their dinner guest the Reverend Edward Casaubon merely very ugly, Dorothea has seen in him "one of the most distinguished-looking men" she has ever beheld. Celia remembers the two white moles with hair on them that mark his sallow face. Dorothea deplores this tendency in her sister to "look at human beings as if they were merely animals with a toilette, and never see the great soul in a man's face." She herself has noticed his remarkable resemblance to a portrait of Locke. "He has the same deep eye-sockets." When Celia asks with timid irony if Mr. Casaubon has a great soul, Dorothea unhesitatingly replies that such is her belief, and she adds, quite unconscious of any second meaning, "Everything I see in him corresponds to his pamphlet on Biblical Cosmology" (ii.15).

It is Celia who sees Casaubon better for what he is, and it is Dorothea who proves both literally and symbolically nearsighted. Feeling herself no interest in young Sir James Chettam, Dorothea has arbitrarily assigned all his visits and favors to an interest on his part in Celia, though it is quite plain to everyone else that Sir James is courting Dorothea herself. It is finally Celia who sets Dorothea right, gathering all her courage (and an amalgam of complacency) to reveal her sister's humiliating error—a result of her habitually "taking up notions": " 'Well, I am sorry for Sir James. I thought it right to tell you, because you went on as you always do, never looking just where you are, and treading in the wrong place. *You always see what no-body else sees; it is impossible to satisfy you; yet you never see what is quite plain.* That's your way, Dodo' " (iv.27, italics mine).

If such dialogue seems in any degree dilute young girl's talk of a sort one would expect in the lesser novels of Anne Ritchie Thackeray, it must be remembered that George Eliot is making much of *seeing* and kinds of vision and of animal images as applied to Celia (to whom Dorothea applies the nickname "Kitty") and quite probably to Doro-thea in the nickname "Dodo"; for the dodo bird, its name derived from the Portuguese for *foolish*, was already extinct (as Dorothea's special brand of piety was also an anachronism in Middlemarch in the nineteenth century). The constant intellectual companion and wife of George Henry Lewes would know about the dodo, a prominent phenomenon for biological study of the extinction of less-improved forms. Celia's reproach to Dorothea for always "treading in the wrong place" is not a phrase chosen at random. It echoes Dorothea's own words a few pages earlier in rejecting a small Maltese puppy Sir James has tried to give her in pursuing his courtship. She had always been afraid of treading on a small dog that Celia had once owned, because "I am rather short-sighted" (iii.22). Dorothea is relieved that Sir James does not offer the dog to Celia, because there was in conse-quence "no puppy to tread on." The theme is broadened a few para-graphs after Celia's speech about Dorothea's treading in the wrong place and never seeing what is plain to others. Dorothea congratulates herself upon her coming marriage to Casaubon, which will take her away from the neighborhood "and her own sad liability to tread in the wrong places on her way to the New Jerusalem" (iv.28). It is upon the sensitivities of other human beings as well as on puppies that Dorothea treads because of her short-sightedness, and the larger irony is that in leaving her home to marry Casaubon she will tread upon his own romantic ego and his jealously guarded self-image in ways that play a major part in the darkest aspects of their marriage. At a much later time when Dorothea is "innocently at work towards the further embitterment of her husband," George Eliot will com-ment: "She was blind, you see, to many things obvious to others—

likely to tread in the wrong places, as Celia had warned her . . ."
(xxxvii.272–273).

Dorothea had soon "looked deep into the ungauged reservoir of
Mr. Casaubon's mind, seeing reflected there *in vague labyrinthine
extension every quality she herself brought*; had opened much of her
own experience to him, and had understood from him the scope of
his great work, *also of attractively labyrinthine extent*" (iii.17, italics
mine). Eliot's use of *labyrinthine* twice in the short passage is calculated; for *labyrinth* along with *tomb*, *mine*, and other suggestions
of subterranean places of indefinite dimensions are to appear frequently in her descriptions of Casaubon's mental processes. Even
in the preceding chapter, as Gordon Haight observes,[12] when Mr.
Brooke asks Casaubon how he stores his voluminous notes, Casaubon replies, "In pigeon-holes partly." His reply is to prove prophetic.
Casaubon's projected great work, his Key to all Mythologies, is never
to take shape. It will remain a matter of pigeonholes and labyrinths,
for Casaubon by nature is quite incapable of ever effecting the synthesis that might give meaning to his laborious researches. Here as
so often elsewhere in *Middlemarch* the interaction among images
Eliot employs is quiet but pervasive. Unlike those characteristic of
Flaubert in *Madame Bovary*, they are, rather than self-declaring,
typically submerged in the discursive content of the sentence. Dorothea's notions about marriage, we learn, come from an exalted enthusiasm about the ends of life, "an enthusiasm which was lit chiefly
at its own fire" (iii.20). It was on Casaubon that "the radiance of her
transfigured girlhood fell" (v.32); but such fire and light can illumi-
nate in ways that are painful. Casaubon "had been the mere occasion
which had set alight the fine inflammable material of her youthful
illusions" (x.62); and the experience was not destined to be a joy for
him. It made demands upon his nature that he realized, with an
amount of disillusion and distress, struck no answering chord in his
own nature, where spontaneity and enthusiasm had long been absent.
"He has certainly been drying up faster since the engagement," Mrs.
Cadwallader observes: "the flame of passion, I suppose" (x.67). The
fire which has set alight Dorothea's youthful illusions has been of her
own making. Casaubon, "lost among small closets and winding stairs"
in "an agitated dimness," has little light to give any one. Perusing old
volumes, "with his taper stuck before him," he is satisfied with win-

dowless underground locations and "had become indifferent to the sunlight" (xx.147). The "ungauged reservoir" of his mind, into which Dorothea has the impression of peering deeply, has actually served only to provide a surface reflection, and it is her own qualities that she sees reflected, like Narcissus. Later she will find the ungauged depths of Casaubon's mind, that she has thought to be beyond her plumbing, more nearly resemble the "shallows of an enclosed basin" out of sight of the sea (xx.145).

Casaubon's explanations of his coming work to Dorothea (explanations in which Eliot makes tone and rhythm echo ominously to the reader the plodding pomposity and tangled defensive processes of thought out of which they come) captivate her by their very breadth of conception, and she is all the better convinced that in this modern scholar-hero learning and piety go hand in hand. " . . . here was a living Bossuet, whose work would reconcile complete knowledge with devoted piety; here was a modern Augustine who united the glories of doctor and saint" (iii.18). Celia reflects with reason that Dorothea is "too religious for family comfort," and even Sir James Chettam has observed an "excessive religiousness" in her. Mrs. Cadwallader is a little later to congratulate Sir James on losing Dorothea —a girl with "a great deal of nonsense in her—a flighty sort of Methodistical stuff," who would require her husband "to see the stars by daylight" (vi.42–43). Casaubon's letter of proposal is as stiffly pedantic as his conversation; but Dorothea reads it with a "glow of proud delight." "There would be nothing trivial about our lives," she has reflected earlier. "It would be like marrying Pascal" (iii.21). It is a measure of Eliot's distance from her heroine that Dorothea, possessed of a "nature altogether ardent, theoretical, and intellectually consequent" (iii.21), can utter the statement without the slightest sense of its implicit irony.

Casaubon is in his way as much a victim of illusion as is Dorothea. It is probably significant that Eliot makes frequent mention of his weak eyesight.[13] In any event, he has enough egoism in his nature, she tells us, to feel no surprise when a beautiful girl of twenty looks upon him as an eligible mate, "pouring out her joy at the thought of devoting herself to him." He was, to be sure, "touched with an unknown delight (what man would not have been?) at this childlike unrestrained ardour: he was not surprised (what lover would have been?) that he should be the object of it" (v.36). The delicate irony, combined with sympathetic insight, with which George Eliot treats this character is, as critics have observed, one of the triumphs of *Middlemarch*. Casaubon is not an heroic figure; but he is not on the other hand a simpleton or a clown. He will never gather his notes and publish his vast Key to all Mythologies, but he has worked diligently for many years and has written pamphlets that impress people. Mr. Brooke thinks Casaubon is likely to become a bishop.[14] The Reverend Mr. Cadwallader calls him "a scholarly clergyman, and creditable to the cloth" (viii.52). Sir James Chettam, to be sure, sees him as "no better than a mummy!" (vi.43) and later comments that Casaubon "has got no good red blood in his body" (viii.52). Mrs. Cadwallader, who, as we have seen, has a gift for satire, replies on the second occasion, "No. Somebody put a drop under a magnifying-glass, and it was all semicolons and parentheses." But, though Eliot gives us such views of Casaubon from the outside, she does much more to present his inner life with sympathy, though it is, to be sure, such sympathy as can accompany clarity of vision and cannot be divorced from irony. Mr. Casaubon found courtship a hindrance to progress on his Key to all Mythologies. "But he had deliberately incurred the hindrance, having made up his mind that it was now time for him to adorn his life with the graces of female companionship, to irradiate the gloom which fatigue was apt to hang over the intervals of studious labour with the play of female fancy, and to secure in this, his culminating age, the solace of female tendance for his declining years" (vii.46). Casaubon's theory of woman's part in marriage, presented here with relatively mild insistence on the complacency involved and with mere mocking echoes of Casaubon's ponderous periods and channels of thought, is to be commented on more directly a little later. Tertius Lydgate, who is at a much earlier stage of his career than Casaubon, feels he cannot think seriously of entering into marriage with the beautiful Rosamond Vincy: "He had seen Miss Vincy above his horizon almost as long as it had taken Mr. Casaubon to become engaged and married: but this learned gentleman was possessed of a fortune; he had assembled his voluminous notes, and had made that sort of reputation which precedes performance,—often the larger part of a man's fame. *He took a wife, as we have seen, to adorn the re-maining quadrant of his course, and be a little moon that would cause hardly a calculable perturbation"* (xi.70, italics mine). But Lydgate's assumptions about marriage, though more colorful, assume that the woman's place in marriage is equally that of an ornamental satellite to the male; and, like Casaubon's, they are to lead him into disastrous consequences. A single conversation with Dorothea Brooke has convinced Lydgate of her ineligibility for such a role. "She did not look at things from the proper feminine angle. The society of such women was about as relaxing as going from your work to teach the second form, instead of reclining in a paradise with sweet laughs for bird-notes, and blue eyes for a heaven." Casaubon is blind to such dangers in Dorothea but is already disturbed in another regard. He had "determined to abandon himself to the stream of feeling, and perhaps was surprised to find what an exceedingly shallow rill it was." Like other victims of theories cherished in private and untested in the outer world, Casaubon has expected to find in courtship the delights that literature seemed to promise him. "As in droughty regions baptism by immersion could only be performed symbolically, so Mr. Casaubon found that sprinkling was the utmost approach to a plunge which his stream would afford him; and he concluded that the poets had much exaggerated the force of masculine passion" (vii.46).

Three chapters later Eliot explores Casaubon's private life in greater detail. The passage is of the first importance for an understanding of Eliot's theory of sympathetic insight into her characters and her awareness that she is doing something fresh in the development of the novel in concentrating upon the internal experience of obscure and unheroic characters as a subject for fiction. The passage represents as well her first ambitious suggestion of the many she will provide as the novel progresses of the way separate egos, each with a world of its own, may collide with the worlds of other egos in the process of living, each following his own illusion on collision courses likely to lead to marital or other disasters. At the start Eliot in a sentence already quoted reminds us that Dorothea, on her part, does not really understand her fiancé at all but has assigned him a pattern that she desires him to fulfill for her—to serve as "the fine inflammable material of her youthful illusions." Eliot proposes, half ironically, to "defend" Casaubon from the disparaging remarks of Sir James, Mrs. Cadwallader, and others: "I am not sure that the greatest man of his age, if ever that solitary superlative existed, could escape these unfavourable reflections of himself in various small mirrors; and even Milton, looking for his portrait in a spoon, must submit to have the facial angle of a bumpkin" (x.62). The mirror image is Eliot's intimate and recurrent symbol for the relation of the individual ego to the exterior world. If our common reality is represented by a large pier glass or a surface of polished steel that has been rubbed until it is covered by a multitude of scratches running in all directions, and then if a lighted candle held up to its surface figures as the individual ego beholding phenomena outside itself—the relation of the individual to his outer world and the extent of his seeing all things as having a reality primarily in terms of his own particular interests is rendered in an especially effective analogy. It "is only your candle which produces the flattering illusion of a concentric arrangement" in which all the scratches rendered visible center in the one little light. This is Eliot's "parable," she tells us, for the fact that society is composed of millions of egos, each holding his special candle to the mirror and seeing all life centered in his special view of reality. This image of the mirror and the candle is employed or echoed by implication throughout the novel in a great many forms. The painter Adolf Naumann, who plays only a small part in the action, humorously but significantly (in terms of Eliot's parable) explains to Will Ladislaw his view of the place he holds in the universe: "See now! My existence pre-supposes the existence of the whole universe—does it *not*? and my function is to paint—and as a painter I have a conception which is altogether *genialisch*, of your great-aunt or second grandmother as a subject for a picture; therefore, the universe is straining towards that picture through that particular hook or claw which it puts forth in the shape of me—not true?" (xix.141).

In her presentation of Casaubon's inner life, George Eliot is working toward her pivotal statement—"Mr. Casaubon, too, was the centre of his own world . . . ."

Suppose we turn from outside estimates of a man, to wonder, with keener interest, what is the report of his own consciousness about his doings or capacity: with what hindrances he is carrying on his daily labours; what fading of hopes, or what deeper fixity of self-delusion the years are marking off within him; and with what spirit he wrestles against universal pressure, which will one day be too heavy for him, and bring his heart to its final pause. . . . Mr. Casaubon, too, was the centre of his own world; if he was liable to think that others were providentially made for him, and especially to consider them in the light of their fitness for the author of a 'Key to all Mythologies,' this trait is not quite alien to us, and, like the other mendicant hopes of mortals, claims some of our pity. (x.62)

Later in the novel, Eliot will with a similar consciousness of purpose present Tertius Lydgate as another study of obscurity and failure in a man cherishing a vision of high achievement—one of the men "who once meant to shape their own deeds and alter the world a little" but who came by slow degrees "to be shapen after the average and fit to be packed by the gross" (xv.107). Such men begin in their romantic egoism with warm illusions of their power to write a Key to all Mythologies or to discover the secrets of living tissue, but find eventually their old selves walking like ghosts to trouble their present. "Nothing in the world [is] more subtle," Eliot says, "than the process of their gradual change!" Casaubon is shown us only in the last part of his career; but she traces Lydgate's inner life as he finds himself gradually more and more ensnared in small frustrations—the tragedy of unpaid butchers' bills, as James called it. In both cases, Eliot clearly feels the novelty and significance of what she is doing in the same way that Flaubert had felt that, in his tracing minutely the gradual decline of a provincial doctor's wife, he was creating something important and unprecedented. Casaubon's plight in the time just preceding his marriage to Dorothea is one that calls forth Eliot's remarkable powers for illuminating character by means of a dry light that makes sympathy and irony work together. Casaubon, in winning the hand of a spirited girl, has found a paradoxical sort of success with disheartening parallels to his experience in scholarship. In his studies he has as years passed felt more and more the "chilling ideal which crowded his laborious uncreative hours." In love also, he has experienced a depressing awareness of duties that must be fulfilled and forms that must be carried through without joy, without spontaneity. There is nothing much in earlier English fiction that resembles Eliot's analysis, tender yet cruelly probing, of the inner life of an obscure pedant in a situation that might seem altogether laughable except that, viewed from the inside, it is rich in pathos:

> For in truth, as the day fixed for his marriage came nearer, Mr. Casaubon did not find his spirits rising; nor did the contemplation of that matrimonial garden-scene, where, as all experience showed, the path was to be bordered with flowers, prove persistently more enchanting to him than the accustomed vaults where he walked taper in hand. He did not confess to himself, still less could he have breathed to another, his surprise that though he had won a lovely and noble-hearted girl he had not won delight,—which he had also regarded as an object to be found by search. (x.62–63)

For "we all of us, grave or light," Eliot comments, "get our thoughts entangled in metaphors, and act fatally on the strength of them" (x.63). Casaubon's metaphor or analogy has to do with saving against future use, an assumption that his dedication for long years to the pursuit of scholarship "had stored up for him a compound interest of enjoyment." Now he finds only a blankness of sensibility in place of the delight he had assumed awaited him once he was ready to make withdrawals against his account.

> Here was a weary experience in which he was as utterly condemned to loneliness as in the despair which sometimes threatened him while toiling in the morass of authorship without seeming nearer the goal. And his was that worst loneliness which would shrink from sympathy. He could not but wish that Dorothea should think him not less happy than the world would expect her successful suitor to be; and in relation to his authorship he leaned on her young trust and veneration, he liked to draw forth her fresh interest in listening, as a means of encouragement to himself: in talking to her he presented all his performance and intention with the reflected confidence of the pedagogue, and rid himself for the time of that chilling ideal which crowded his laborious uncreative hours with the vaporous pressure of Tartarean shades.

Thus Casaubon is trapped in the metaphors about love even as he has been trapped in the metaphors about rewards to be won in the search for knowledge. The demoralization affects him physically. Mrs. Cadwallader decides, at a dinner given a few days preceding the wedding, that Casaubon "looks like a death's head skinned over for the occasion," and adds: "Mark my words: in a year from this time that girl will hate him. She looks up to him as an oracle now, and by-and-by she will be at the other extreme" (x.67).

Dorothea's marriage to Casaubon does not lead her into hatred, but it does, much sooner than a year, destroy her exalted image of him. When Eliot takes up the story of Dorothea and Casaubon on their honeymoon in Rome after several chapters devoted to the Lydgate-Rosamond plot of the novel, Dorothea's image of Casaubon has already given way to a bleaker reality. The "large vistas and wide fresh air which she had dreamed of finding in her husband's mind were replaced by anterooms and winding passages which seemed to lead nowhither" (xx.145). The imagery of labyrinths, blind walls, and entombment or imprisonment is to become frequent and incremental in effect. Before their marriage Casaubon's erudite talk had often seemed "like a specimen from a mine, or the inscription on the door of a museum which might open on the treasures of past ages" (iii.24), but it had become "a sort of dried preparation, a lifeless embalmment of knowledge" (xx.146). Casaubon's notes for the Key to all Mythologies are later to strike her as "shattered mummies . . . fragments of a mosaic wrought from crushed ruins" (xlviii.351). "And now you will go and be shut up in that stone prison at Lowick," Will Ladislaw, Casaubon's young cousin protests: "*you will be buried alive*" (xxii. 163, italics mine).

> She had taken all the first steps in the purest confidence, and then she had suddenly found the infinite vista of a multiplied life to be a dark, narrow alley with a dead wall at the end. Instead of leading to the high places of happiness, from which the world would seem to lie below one . . . it led rather downward and earthward, into realms of restriction and depression where the sound of other lives, easier and freer, was heard as from above, and where it served to deepen the feeling of failure.

The passage is from James's *The Portrait of a Lady*, the remarkable chapter forty-two in which Isabel meditates alone upon her life with Osmond, feeling profoundly a "sense of darkness and suffocation . . . an odour of mould and decay." Isabel is by no means a slavish imitation of Dorothea, but the parallels between them in temperament and in situation go deep. "One of the strongest feelings evoked in that long meditation of Isabel Archer's," L. C. Knights observes, "is a feeling as of being buried alive, and the strength of the book comes largely from the evoked contrast of the heroine's 'fund of life'—'her delighted spirit'—and the 'cold obstruction' that thwarts it. This is a feeling that runs through James's work from first to last."[15] To a considerable extent this is also the feeling that dominates not only Dorothea but also Gwendolen in her marriage to Grandcourt in Eliot's *Daniel Deronda*. In both Eliot and in James, I have suggested in chapter one, this sense of being buried alive has much to do with the trapped narrator as well as the trapped character—a sense of imprisonment in a dark universe that both James and Eliot, as intellectual children of the nineteenth century, share with Flaubert, and express in correlatives in the experience of their characters. Emma Bovary has, as we have seen, similar moments of bleak epiphany, though her notion of high places of happiness is not that of Dorothea or of Isabel, and though her death scene is to embody the sensation of outer blackness more directly and more graphically than would suit the manner of either Eliot or James.

During the early days of the honeymoon, Rome itself has become for Dorothea a baffling embodiment of the enigmas of her present life and the inadequacies of her girlhood theories to make any sense of it. Early in the novel Eliot had made clear that Dorothea possessed a passion for understanding experience rather than being content with merely letting it happen. Visiting the galleries and the historic shrines, Dorothea is increasingly demoralized by art that seems to be making tremendous and urgent utterances, but in some alien tongue. For those who bring adequate knowledge with them on their visit, Eliot says, Rome may reveal itself as the "spiritual centre and interpreter of the world." For Dorothea there was no such possibility: ". . . the gigantic broken revelations of that Imperial and Papal city [were] thrust abruptly on the notions of a girl who had been brought up in English and Swiss Puritanism, fed on meagre Protestant histories and on art chiefly of the hand-screen sort," a girl who was at the same time "plunged in tumultuous preoccupation with her personal lot" (xx.143). Frequently she sought relief by driving out into the Campagna "where she could feel alone with the earth and sky, away from the oppressive masquerade of ages, in which her own life too seemed to become a masque with enigmatical costumes." James's heroine also finds the Campagna a place of solace and respite. Disheartened by the enigmas of her marriage and the heavy aura of Rome, where "in the starved churches, the marble columns . . . seemed to offer a companionship in endurance and the musty incense to be a compound of long-unanswered prayers," Isabel, like Dorothea, seeks the Campagna "to be far away, under the sky, where she could descend from her carriage and tread upon the daisies" (xlix.423). Although I do not, with Mrs. Leavis, consider the James passage "parasitic"[16]—there is less of bafflement and more of resignation in Isabel's mood and Rome is for her both more intelligible and sadder —it does seem likely that James is not unmindful of Dorothea's experience.

The "weight of unintelligible Rome" was to remain with Dorothea through the rest of her life, an oppressive recurrent image of alienation. In a long passage Eliot presents Dorothea's view as her most extended account of Dorothea's inner life in the weeks following her marriage.

> Ruins and basilicas, palaces and colossi, set in the midst of a sordid present, where all that was living and warm-blooded seemed sunk in the deep degeneracy of a superstition divorced from reverence; the dimmer but yet eager Titanic life gazing and struggling on walls and ceilings; the long vistas of white forms whose marble eyes *seemed to hold the monotonous light of an alien world: all this vast wreck of ambitious ideals, sensuous and spiritual,* mixed confusedly with the signs of breathing forgetfulness and degradation, at first jarred her as with an electric shock, and then urged themselves on her with that ache belonging to a glut of confused ideas which check the flow of emotion. Forms both pale and glowing took possession of her young sense, and fixed themselves in her memory even when she was not thinking of them, preparing strange associations which remained through her after-years. (xx.143–144, italics mine)

The passage suggests limitations of Dorothea's mind that will remain with her throughout the novel. In important ways she is the antithesis of Emma Bovary. It is not hard to imagine how Emma would have reveled in feeling the color, the variety, the excitement of Roman life, enjoying it the more for her inability to understand it. But Dorothea's mind was to remain "theoretic" and ardently searching for principles beneath the confusion of day-to-day living. Much later, long after the death of Casaubon, she is to speak of poetry and art as "things that adorn life for us who are well off" and to congratulate Will Ladislaw because he has become interested in politics and thinks "about the rest of the world" (liv.395). Music was associated for her with "practising silly rhythms on the hated piano" (xxviii. 202). Will Ladislaw attempts to lead her out of her "fanatical sympathy" with moral problems and her lack of "sturdy neutral delight in things as they were" (xxx.215). In the end, however, it is Dorothea's view that prevails. Will gives up art and poetry for politics and finally (and somewhat implausibly as Leslie Stephen was to remark) secures a seat in Parliament. One must remember, however, that the problem is not a simple one. Dorothea is always and throughout the paradox of a mind that is not merely theoretic, but *passionately* theoretic, a young girl who has thrown all her youthful vitality into a passion to understand life rather than merely to enjoy life. F. R. Leavis in *The Great Tradition* does not allow at all sufficiently for the amount and quality of irony that George Eliot employs in her presentation of Dorothea; but he has reason to associate George Eliot's own temperament with that of the heroine of *Middlemarch*. Henry James in his review of *Middlemarch*, indeed, observes much the same sort of mentality as Dorothea's at work in Eliot's writing of the novel. It is Eliot's "generalizing instinct," as he sees it, "of *brain*, in a word, behind her observation" that gives such high distinction to her work and makes her stand alone among English novelists.[17] James is, of course, speaking of the mature George Eliot who had found a visit to Rome and its "broken grandeur" in 1860 a source of delight and illumination.[18] Dorothea is to a considerable extent George Eliot in her provincial girlhood, passionately theoretical but as yet unequipped with the sort of education that could render Rome understandable.

It is Dorothea's passion for understanding, turned by her education into strange channels, that has led her to expect to find freedom from a woman's life in Middlemarch by marrying a man whose breadth of vision will lead her toward knowledge and wisdom. All the unconscious cruelty that Dorothea's romantic egoism is capable of by blindly treading upon Casaubon's own tenderly guarded ego comes out in the moment when Dorothea asks Casaubon to start his book, proposing to copy to his dictation, pressing upon him the moment he has dreaded for years. The "drama of incommunicability," as prominent in *Middlemarch* as it is in *Madame Bovary* and to be, if anything, still more a part of the substance of *Portrait of a Lady* and James's later novels, has begun in earnest. "She was as blind to his inward troubles as he to hers: she had not yet learned those hidden conflicts in her husband which claim our pity. She had not yet listened patiently to his heart-beats, but only felt that her own was beating violently" (xx.149). At the same time there is awakened in Casaubon a "sudden terror" that Dorothea's period of worship has ended and that in her youth and presumption she is about to expose him to "the most exasperating of all criticism,—that which sees vaguely a great many fine ends, and has not the least notion what it costs to reach them." The breach between husband and wife is never healed. Dorothea is henceforward to be feared by Casaubon as a personification of the unappreciative world. She has managed to wound him in his most sensitive part. He had hoped to secure in marriage "a soft fence against the cold, shadowy, unapplausive audience of life" but had instead obtained a "cruel outward accuser."

Soon after the scene in which Dorothea wounds Casaubon by asking him to start writing his book, Will Ladislaw, during the course of conversation, intimates to her that Casaubon's work is in any case futile since German scholarship has really superseded much of what Casaubon has planned to achieve by his Key to all Mythologies (xxi. 154). Casaubon has underestimated and misunderstood Dorothea, who is far from desiring to be his cruel accuser. Instead she begins to feel a profound sadness toward him. "To-day she had begun to see that she had been under a wild illusion in expecting a response to her feeling from Mr. Casaubon, and she had felt the waking of a presentiment that there might be a sad consciousness in his life which made as great a need on his side as on her own" (xxi.156). Eliot's figure of the scratched mirror and the candle of the ego seems implied in the sentences that follow. For the first time Dorothea is aware that her husband possesses "an equivalent centre of self, whence the lights and shadows must always fall with a certain difference." Dorothea has now traveled beyond the self-absorbed high drama that preoccupied her girlhood into fuller insight into human struggles and human suffering. She is the only one of the four main protagonists who achieves any real growth in this direction, breaking through the concentric patterns that enclosed her youthful egoism and learning slowly and painfully to achieve the kind of sympathetic understanding that George Eliot herself believed to be the only fulfilling perspective upon the human drama.

Dorothea's life with Casaubon in the months that follow involves further pain of disillusion and a series of defeated efforts to find some means of touching her husband's life as he retreats farther and farther into his private world. In less than three months after her marriage, her girlhood notions of an heroic life have given place to much darker visions: "All existence seemed to beat with a lower pulse than her own, and her religious faith was a solitary cry, the struggle out of a nightmare in which every object was withering and shrinking away from her" (xxviii.202). In her tendency to tread in the wrong places Dorothea manages to wound her husband's ego still more deeply. She does not dream that Casaubon can be jealous of his young cousin Will Ladislaw—and jealous in respects that do not ordinarily play a part in stories of a January–May triangle. He has no question of Dorothea's sexual fidelity to him. He is jealous of her losing what remains of her power of belief, her former faith in him as a scholar, for a sharing of Will Ladislaw's chillingly skeptical view of him, a cruelly personal rendering of the unapplausive world. Thus by trying innocently but blindly to persuade Casaubon to allow Will Ladislaw, as his cousin, some further financial support, Dorothea makes Casaubon's alienation much deeper. From Casaubon's affront and anger Dorothea experiences a sort of terror that represents, for her, a further foreboding but undefined sense of inhabiting a world where the sunlit paths of a few months earlier have given way to blank walls—a motif that was to become more explicit in the Gwendolen Harleth plot of *Daniel Deronda*: "Hearing him breathe quickly after he had spoken, she sat listening, frightened, wretched—*with a dumb inward cry for help to bear this nightmare of a life in which every energy was arrested by dread*" (xxxvii.275, italics mine).

The theme of isolation is profoundly explored in Eliot's treatment of the months during which Casaubon sinks toward his death and Dorothea tries vainly to break through the barriers with which Casaubon surrounds himself. By degrees "she was travelling into the remoteness of pure pity and loyalty towards her husband" (xxxvii.269).

It is not until shortly before Casaubon's death, however, that Dorothea allows herself to confront directly her sense of his complete rejection of her. Casaubon has declined her attempts to offer him compassion and has gone into the library to "shut himself in, alone with
his sorrow."

> She was in the reaction of a rebellious anger stronger than any she
> had felt since her marriage. Instead of tears there came words:—
> "What have I done—*what am I—that he should treat me so? He
> never knows what is in my mind—he never cares.* What is the use of
> anything I do? He wishes he had never married me."
> She began to hear herself, and was checked into stillness. Like one
> who has lost his way and is weary, she sat and saw as in one glance all
> the paths of her young hope which she should never find again. *And
> just as clearly in the miserable light she saw her own and her husband's
> solitude—how they walked apart so that she was obliged to survey him.
> . . .* Was it her fault that she had believed in him—had believed in his
> worthiness?—*And what, exactly, was he?*—She was able enough to
> estimate him—she who waited on his glances with trembling, and
> *shut her best soul in prison, paying it only hidden visits,* that she might
> be petty enough to please him. (xlii.312–313, italics mine)

The "drama of incommunicability" reaches its apex for Dorothea
in the extended passage just quoted in abridgement. Eliot implies
that Dorothea's meditation extends over a period of several hours.
"Dorothea sat motionless in her meditative struggle, while the evening slowly deepened into night." It is worth noting *that the passage
could be placed in Isabel Archer-Osmond's extended meditation of
James's famous chapter 42 with scarcely an alteration.* I am not by
any means suggesting "indebtedness" in any way implying servile
imitation, but rather the length Eliot had already traveled in fiction
along the path James was to extend toward the twentieth-century
psychological novel. Flaubert had also, as we have seen, gone his own
lengths along a similar path; but the differences rather than the
similarities are what strike one most forcibly in what is probably
Emma's moment of completest isolation from her husband—the
moment when Hippolyte's screams reach the Bovary parlor and
Emma looks upon her mate with a contempt rendered nearly absolute: "How could she (she who was so intelligent!) have let herself be
deceived again? Moreover, what deplorable mania had driven her to

ruin her life with continual sacrifices? She recalled all her instincts of luxury, all the privations of her soul, all the sordid details of her marriage, of the household, her dreams falling into the mire like wounded swallows; everything she had longed for, everything she had denied herself, all that she might have had! And for what—for what?" (II.xi.255–256).

Dorothea's scene ends with a moment of shared misery between husband and wife—a suggestion of the differences between Casaubon and James's sinister dilettante Gilbert Osmond for all their considerable similarities in large pretensions and fear of assessment, since no such moment could have been possible with that owner of the mask-like villa whose windows appeared as "heavy lids, but no eyes," seeming "less to offer communication with the world than to defy the world to look in" (xxii.192). Even in Dorothea's and Casaubon's brief moment of mutual sympathy, however, there is only the awareness that both inhabit a troubled world; and Casaubon's kindly meant admonition that she is young "and need not to extend [her] life by watching" is followed by Dorothea's surge of pity across a gulf, a "thankfulness that might well up in us *if we had narrowly escaped hurting a lamed creature*" (xlii.314, italics mine). Earlier, after Casaubon had undergone his initial heart attack, Lydgate, as Casaubon's physician, had been struck by Dorothea's pleading for guidance in the treatment of her husband: "For years after Lydgate remembered the impression produced in him by this involuntary appeal—this cry from soul to soul, without other consciousness than their moving with kindred natures *in the same embroiled medium, the same troublous fitfully-illuminated life*" (xxx.214, italics mine). Such moments of human communication are precious in Eliot's scheme of things, but a brooding consciousness of the embroiled medium, the dark world capable of only fitful moments of illumination, is ordinarily the background against which they occur.

Although Dorothea's efforts to penetrate the barriers her husband sets about his private life are defeated, George Eliot herself, with obvious awareness that she is achieving something new for the English novel, gives the reader an intimate knowledge of what goes on in his inner world. Eliot has chosen the least appealing of bridegrooms and husbands (so far as the expectations of careless and conventional readers of popular English novels are concerned) for her analysis, and she is clearly feeling her own matured powers in creating this unprecedented study in psychological realism. The first such passage occurs after the return from Rome and the honeymoon:

> One morning, some weeks after her arrival at Lowick, Dorothea—
> *but why always Dorothea? Was her point of view the only possible one
> with regard to this marriage?* I protest against all our interest, all our
> effort at understanding being given to the young skins that look bloom-
> ing in spite of trouble; for these too will get faded, and will know the
> older and more eating griefs which we are helping to neglect. In spite
> of the blinking eyes and white moles objectionable to Celia, and the
> want of muscular curve which was morally painful to Sir James,
> *Mr. Casaubon had an intense consciousness within him, and was
> spiritually a-hungered like the rest of us.* (xxix.205, italics mine)

The complacent egoism Casaubon had exhibited earlier in the narrative, in assuming that, in poor health and nearing fifty, he was eligible
for the hand of a blooming young lady possessed of all suitable qualifications, including a good understanding, is elaborated with irony
but not with ridicule. After all, he would offer handsome settlements
and "neglect no arrangement for her happiness" so that he was justly
confident of meeting the requirements of society in such a marriage.
It is his misfortune to marry a young lady whose "good understanding" is of a most exceptional variety in its tendency to take a passionate view of abstractions—she is precisely fitted to be his nemesis as he
is to be hers. For Casaubon is unable to take a passionate view of
anything. Casaubon has assumed that a young lady of good understanding will be happy to subordinate her intelligence to his own and
prove properly "educable and submissive," but this assumption has
had the direst consequences for him. "Providence, in its kindness,"
he had assumed at the time of the courtship, "had supplied him with
the wife he needed. A wife, a modest young lady, with the purely appreciative, unambitious abilities of her sex, is sure to think her husband's mind powerful. Whether Providence had taken equal care of
Miss Brooke in presenting her with Mr. Casaubon was an idea which
could hardly occur to him" (xxix.205–206).

The comic overtones of the situation shade over into something
darker. Casaubon was aware "that the world was getting dimmer and
. . . he felt lonely." It was time to see if he could taste domestic de-

lights *"before they too were left behind by the years"* (italics mine). Casaubon's life has long been characterized by small sufferings such as fail to afford the sufferer a compensating sense of importance in his own eyes or the eyes of others.

He had not had much foretaste of happiness in his previous life. To know intense joy without a strong bodily frame, one must have an enthusiastic soul. Mr. Casaubon had never had a strong bodily frame, and his soul was sensitive without being enthusiastic: it was too languid to thrill out of self-consciousness into passionate delight; it went on fluttering in the swampy ground where it was hatched, thinking of its wings and never flying. His experience was of that pitiable kind which shrinks from pity, and fears most of all that it should be known: it was that proud narrow sensitiveness which has not mass enough to spare for transformation into sympathy, and quivers thread-like in small currents of self-preoccupation or at best of an egoistic scrupulosity.

It is part of Eliot's conception to give Casaubon's "egoistic scrupulosity" larger implications and to defeat any tendency in her reader to simplify her portrait. If small jealousies mar Casaubon's nature—suspicions that other scholars undervalue his pamphlets or that the Archdeacon has not even read them—he is nevertheless "resolute in being a man of honour according to the code; he would be unimpeachable by any recognised opinion."

For such a man, a wife who expects performance for the world deserving a niche near that of Locke or Milton is the unkindest of dispensations. Dorothea's insistence on Casaubon's beginning at once the writing of his Key to all Mythologies is in its way a blinder act of unconscious cruelty than Emma Bovary's requiring Charles to perform a brilliant operation on Hippolyte's club foot. Eliot, in an authorial intrusion of a sort peculiarly her own, insists on viewing Casaubon with a kind of devastating sympathy that is at the one time both defense and conviction:

> *For my own part I am very sorry for him.* It is an uneasy lot at best, to be what we call highly taught *and yet not to enjoy: to be present at this great spectacle of life and never to be liberated from a small hungry shivering self*—never to be fully possessed by the glory we behold, *never to have our consciousness rapturously transformed into the vividness of a thought, the ardour of a passion, the energy of an action, but always*

to be scholarly and uninspired, ambitious and timid, scrupulous and dimsighted. (xxix.206–207, italics mine)

We see much more of Casaubon's inner world as the novel moves toward the time of his death. The story has become to a still greater degree a narrative where, to borrow from D. H. Lawrence, all the action may be said to have moved inside. Casaubon is increasingly soured by his growing suspicions that Dorothea, far from becoming a happiness and support to his own inadequate sense of self-worth, has put further trust in the opinions of Will Ladislaw and become the cruelest part of the world that mocks his pretensions.

> She nursed him, she read to him, she anticipated his wants, and was solicitous about his feelings; but there had entered into the husband's mind the certainty that she judged him, and that her wifely devotedness was like a penitential expiation of unbelieving thoughts—was accompanied by a power of comparison by which himself and his doings were seen too luminously as a part of things in general. His discontent passed vapour-like through all her gentle loving manifestations, and clung to that inappreciative world which she had only brought nearer to him. (xlii.306)

Casaubon's suffering is the greater because he cannot put his suspicions into words without exposing himself in a light his pride cannot allow. "The tenacity with which he strove to hide his inward drama made it the more vivid for him; as we hear with the more keenness what we wish others not to hear." Something of both the similarities and the significant differences between the situation of Dorothea and Casaubon and that of Isabel and Gilbert Osmond may be suggested by eclectic quotation from Isabel's soliloquy in *The Portrait of a Lady*:

> She knew of no wrong he had done; he was not violent, he was not cruel: she simply believed he hated her. That was all she accused him of, and the miserable part of it was precisely that it was not a crime, for against a crime she might have found redress. He had discovered that she was so different, that she was not what he had believed she would prove to be. . . . He was not changed; he had not disguised himself, during the year of his courtship, any more than she. But she had seen only half his nature then, as one saw the disk of the moon when it was

partly masked by the shadow of the earth. . . . Hadn't he all the appearance of a man living in the open air of the world, indifferent to small considerations, caring only for truth and knowledge and believing that two intelligent people ought to look for them together and, whether they found them or not, find at least some happiness in the search? . . . But he expected her intelligence to operate altogether in his favour, and so far from desiring her mind to be a blank he had flattered himself that it would be richly receptive. He had expected his wife to feel with him and for him, to enter into his opinions, his ambitions, his preferences; and Isabel was obliged to confess that this was no great insolence on the part of a man so accomplished and a husband originally at least so tender. . . . It was her scorn of his assumptions, it was this that made him draw himself up. He had plenty of contempt, and it was proper his wife should be as well furnished; but that she should turn the hot light of her disdain upon his own conception of things—this was a danger he had not allowed for. He believed he should have regulated her emotions before she came to it; and Isabel could easily imagine how his ears had scorched on his discovering he had been too confident. When one had a wife who gave one that sensation there was nothing left but to hate her. (xlii.350–356)

In both instances the drama has all gone inside—there is nothing much observable on the surface to betray the conflicts of mind with mind, temperament with temperament, that constitute the real substance of the narrative. The villain of the piece—so far as he may be called by that name—has his own code and scrupulosities and it is no crude infidelity that makes him fear or, for Osmond's part, hate, his wife. He also suffers, and his suffering comes from nothing more easily definable than her refusal to accept him at his own most favorable estimate of himself cultivated with much care and frequent misgivings in the face of an unapplausive world. The wife's sin is being too intelligent to believe in him! If the relation of Osmond to Isabel is more complex and more intricately explored than the relation of Casaubon to Dorothea, the latter is equally a refinement on the relation of Charles to Emma Bovary, though in that also, especially in the final chapters of the novel, the drama has gone largely inward.

Fear that a second heart attack will cut short his now frantic labors on the Key to all Mythologies dominates Casaubon in his final months. Such fear might in itself appear heroic; but Eliot undercuts its nobler aspects by making a large part of it a mere wish for vengeance on the scholars who have doubted him and criticized his pamphlets. Whereas Dorothea has matured in spirit through the disillusionments of their marriage, Casaubon (and Osmond here also suggests kinship with him) has diminished more and more into spitefulness. George Eliot traces in some detail the workings of his mind in rationalizing for himself his specifying in his will that Dorothea is to be disinherited if she marries Will Ladislaw (xlii.308–309). Nothing could emphasize better how Casaubon has shut himself away in isolation, and how unable he is to understand Dorothea's motivations. Nevertheless he believes in her fidelity to a vow sufficiently to attempt to make her swear, as his own time grows short, to complete his Key to all Mythologies after his death. To take such a vow would be for her a form of spiritual and intellectual suttee; yet she delays her answer knowing that ultimately she cannot bear to refuse. "Neither law nor the world's opinion compelled her to this—only her husband's nature and her own compassion . . ." (xlviii.353). She is saved only by her delay, for when she comes to tell Casaubon she will consent, she finds him dead.

With the death of Casaubon, Dorothea yields the center of the stage to Lydgate and Rosamond. Through the painful lessons of her marriage she has given up, Eliot makes clear, the self-dramatizations of her girlhood for a deepening awareness of the world outside the concentric patterns of her own ego. Her blunders from short-sightedness continue in diminished form but do not lead her into cynicism on learning her errors. Indeed Eliot insists that in some areas of importance Dorothea, with her stubborn belief in the potential goodness of others, sees better than more pragmatic natures like her sister Celia. "She was blind, you see, to many things obvious to others—likely to tread in the wrong places, as Celia had warned her; yet her blindness to whatever did not lie in her own pure purpose carried her safely by the side of precipices where vision would have been perilous with fear" (xxxvii.273). The tone here and occasionally elsewhere in the second half of the novel seems overheavily weighted toward the moralistic. A good many critics, including F. R. Leavis and such later appreciative students of *Middlemarch* as W. J. Harvey, who allow for far more irony in Eliot's treatment of Dorothea than does Leavis, have considered the scenes in which Dorothea moves toward her second marriage unsatisfactory.[19] Yet to make Will Ladislaw in any degree an heroic character who would fulfill at least a part of Dorothea's girlhood visions is the very thing Eliot wished to avoid. Dorothea begins the novel rashly absorbed in her drama of heroic selfhood. Like Don Quixote she insists on reading reality according to her own version of romance (fantastically, a romance built from theological tracts including Casaubon's own pamphlet on Biblical cosmology, but nevertheless a romance affording heroic postures in praying on a cottager's floor or declining jewels or giving up—or thinking about giving up—such pleasures of the world as riding). When the vision is shattered by the world of her marriage where "every energy was arrested by dread," Dorothea must come to terms with the harsher aspects of reality. Her girlhood illusions cannot sustain her, and her spirit must grow or perish. Dorothea is, on plan, the single one of Eliot's four main protagonists who survives the breaking of her pattern of illusion without becoming cynical and nursing the wounds and bruises inflicted by the real world (like Lydgate), or ending life still hugging one's conceits and frustrations (like Casaubon), or hardened in a shell of incommunicative self invulnerable in its concentric rigid patterns to the conception that there could be any other sort of vision really possible (like Rosamond). Dorothea alone learns that if life cannot be unalloyedly beautiful it can at least be worth living in earnest pursuit of worthy aims. The conditions of a dark reality deny her the possibility of sainthood, but a vision of significant (more than a little Comtean) sharing in the work of humanity takes its place. It would probably be impossible to avoid a sense of anticlimax given this plan and such a heroine as Dorothea. Will Ladislaw has to figure as something considerably below a conventional hero of fiction if Dorothea is to be shown making her terms with the sort of reality Eliot conceives of. This seems to be Eliot's meaning in the closing paragraphs of the novel.

Dorothea herself had no dreams of being praised above other women, feeling that there was always something better which she might have done, if she had only been better and known better. Still, she never repented that she had given up position and fortune to marry Will

Ladislaw . . . . No life would have been possible to Dorothea which was not filled with emotion, and she had now a life filled also with a beneficent activity which she had not the doubtful pains of discovering and marking out for herself.

Will, having put aside his earlier attempts to find himself in poetry or painting or bohemian living, has become dedicated to furthering the human weal through politics and has (however unconvincingly in the eyes of the reader) won a seat in Parliament.

Dorothea could have liked nothing better, since wrongs existed, than that her husband should be in the thick of a struggle against them, and that she should give him wifely help. *Many who knew her, thought it a pity that so substantive and rare a creature should have been absorbed into the life of another.* . . . *But no one stated exactly what else that was in her power she ought to have done* . . . . (italics mine)

Dorothea has made her adjustment to a Dark Universe in which Saint Theresas can no longer flourish.

Certainly those determining acts of her life were not ideally beautiful. They were the mixed result of young and noble impulse struggling amidst the conditions of an imperfect social state, in which great feelings will often take the aspect of error, and great faith the aspect of illusion. *For there is no creature whose inward being is so strong that it is not greatly determined by what lies outside it.* A new Theresa will hardly have the opportunity of reforming a conventual life, any more than a new Antigone will spend her heroic piety in daring all for the sake of a brother's burial: the medium in which their ardent deeds took shape is for ever gone. But we insignificant people with our daily words and acts are preparing the lives of many Dorotheas, some of which may present a far sadder sacrifice than that of the Dorothea whose story we know.

Her finely-touched spirit had still its fine issues, though they were not widely visible. (italics mine)

The true test of a religion, George Eliot had written Sarah Hennell in 1869, would be "that it should enable the believer to do without the consolations which his egoism would demand."[20] What is rather clearly meant to be the highest point of Dorothea's experience comes after a night of suffering when she believes (wrongly) that Will Ladislaw has proved "a detected illusion" and has been unfaithful to his profession of love for her. Dorothea sobs herself to sleep on the cold floor of her bedroom; but in the early morning she resolves to "clutch her own pain" and, subordinating her personal sense of loss, to do what she can to save the marriage of Rosamond and Lydgate.

> She opened her curtains, and looked out towards the bit of road that lay in view, with fields beyond, outside the entrance-gates. On the road there was a man with a bundle on his back and a woman carrying her baby; in the field she could see figures moving—perhaps the shepherd with his dog. Far off in the bending sky was the pearly light; *and she felt the largeness of the world and the manifold wakings of men to labour and endurance.* She was a part of that involuntary, palpitating life, and could neither look out on it from her luxurious shelter as a mere spectator, nor hide her eyes in selfish complaining. (lxxx.578, italics mine)

All the overtones are of a Comtean vision,[21] of a sharing of duty, a sympathy in fellowship in a world of "labour and endurance," where Dorothea, even following a crisis of intense disillusion, can resolve to reject preoccupations centering in her own ego and find fulfillment in a religion of humanity.

ii. Tertius Lydgate and Rosamond Vincy

There are curious parallels between the Lydgate-Rosamond plot of *Middlemarch* and the plot of *Madame Bovary*, though they seem to be the result of two authors searching independently for a plot that will lend itself to an exploring in double perspective of private lives of illusion that flourish in the midst of provincial realities. In both, a physician in a small town in the provinces marries a wife who desires luxuries beyond the family's means. Debt becomes a mounting peril for the household (with the wife reckless in regard to the meaning of debt) and eventually defeats all the husband's best plans. But Lydgate is no Charles, Rosamond is no Emma, and there is no suicide in *Middlemarch,* unless we count Lydgate as one of a sort specially suited to Eliot's conception of things, in which arsenic can be considered scarcely more fatal to the human being than the loss of generous ambitions and the bitterness of living on in the body after the demise of the spirit.

Tertius Lydgate is often presented as a victim of Middlemarch society; but he is far more the victim of his own romantic egoism. It is his egoism which assures him of much strength of purpose where in fact he has very little, and his ability to judge character and situation where he finds, too late, that he reads the reality around him through the distortion of romantic patterns sometimes as far from fact as those of Emma Bovary. His kind of romantic egoism is, like Dorothea's, Promethean rather than Satanic. In his dramatization of self he dreams of becoming a hero of science who will hold to his purposes in the face of great difficulties, like Vesalius, and make crucial discoveries for mankind regarding the nature of living tissue (xv.110). But, as Eliot remarks at a critical point in his history, this man who intended to dedicate his life to medical science was "very warm-hearted and rash" (xxxi.222). Rosamond thinks of him at times as "an emotional elephant," and the phrase seems to echo itself in situations she is not thinking of. While he was still pursuing his medical studies, Lydgate discovered with some astonishment that he "had two selves within him apparently" (xv.113) which must learn to accommodate each other, though on that occasion the time of accommodation was postponed.

In presenting the character of Lydgate, George Eliot is quite conscious—even, if anything, more so than in presenting Casaubon—that her subject is an innovation of importance. Lydgate is, like Casaubon, a study in failure; but Eliot gives far more space to the portrayal of Lydgate's gradual decline into misfortune. Even his eventual defeat, though it is complete in his own judgment, is paradoxically a failure that both his wife Rosamond and the world at large (the world of earlier novelists in particular) would consider a success. For his failure consists of his becoming a prosperous society doctor with a wealthy clientele. In electing such a subject Eliot is quite consciously breaking through the conventions of the earlier novel where social station and interior well-being are assumed to go hand in hand. We are never tired of love stories, Eliot says—"never weary of listening to the twanging of the old Troubadour strings"—but are comparatively uninterested in the story of man's passion for the pursuit of truth, and perhaps especially when it concerns failure in the pursuit of truth through pursuing love at the same time:

> In the story of this passion, too, the development varies: sometimes it is the glorious marriage, sometimes frustration and final parting. And not seldom the catastrophe is bound up with the other passion, sung by the Troubadours. *For in the multitude of middle-aged men who go about their vocations in a daily course determined for them much in the same way as the tie of their cravats, there is always a good number who once meant to shape their own deeds and alter the world a little. The story of their coming to be shapen after the average and fit to be packed by the gross, is hardly ever told even in their consciousness*; for perhaps their ardour in generous unpaid toil cooled as imperceptibly as the ardour of other youthful loves, till one day their earlier self walked like a ghost in its old home and made the new furniture ghastly. *Nothing in the world more subtle than the process of their gradual change!* In the beginning they inhaled it unknowingly: you and I may have sent some of our breath towards infecting them, when we uttered our conforming falsities or drew our silly conclusions: *or perhaps it came with the vibrations from a woman's glance.* (xv.107, italics mine)

In the fifteenth chapter of *Middlemarch*, when George Eliot begins in earnest upon the Lydgate plot of her novel, we are given an unusually detailed account of Lydgate's past pursuit of his career and his view of his aims and purposes now he has reached twenty-seven and has taken up his medical practice at Middlemarch. Left an orphan while still in public school, Lydgate had asked his guardians to apprentice him to a country doctor. Though of aristocratic birth, the nephew of a baronet and the son of an officer in the army, he had been left only a small inheritance; and so his guardians agreed to the apprenticeship. Lydgate had already formed a passionate desire to study anatomy. From the pages of an old encyclopaedia, he had suddenly envisioned the glory and romance of a scientific career. "But the moment of vocation had come, and before he got down from his chair, the world was made new to him by a presentiment of endless processes . . . . From that hour Lydgate felt the growth of an intellectual passion." (It is worth noting that Eliot's two chief protagonists for her novel of provincial life—Lydgate and Dorothea—are driven by a passion for the abstract or theoretical. There is apparently no such phenomenon in the society of Yonville l'Abbaye unless we count Homais as a burlesque version; but James, in turn, gives Isabel Archer an enthusiasm for knowledge and wisdom and the atmosphere of noble theories akin to Dorothea's, and it is remarkable that both find husbands whose lives are much occupied with professing to an intellectual passion without really possessing it.)

Lydgate, following his apprentice days, had continued his medical studies in London, Edinburgh, and Paris. He was convinced that "the medical profession as it might be was the finest in the world; presenting the most perfect interchange between science and art; offering the most direct alliance between intellectual conquest and social good." Such statements would prepare the reader for a straightforward history of a brilliant and heroic career, if Eliot did not immediately undercut them. From the last sentence she proceeds, however: "Lydgate's nature demanded this combination: he was an emotional creature, with a flesh-and-blood sense of fellowship which withstood all the abstractions of special study. He cared not only for 'cases,' but for John and Elizabeth, *especially Elizabeth*" (xv.108, italics mine). Flesh-and-blood relationships are to be emphasized a few paragraphs later.

It is at this strategic point that Eliot places her often-cited pronouncement on Lydgate's "spots of commonness." The phrase is intentionally paradoxical. Lydgate is not "common" as the public in general regards commonness but designedly the opposite. He is the nephew of a baronet, and his manners and tastes are of a sort society regards as impeccable. It is his unconscious arrogant assumptions— the result of being reared as a gentleman and taught to take for granted privileges and distinctions he does not earn—that Eliot insists upon calling "spots of commonness": "Lydgate's conceit was of the arrogant sort, never simpering, never impertinent, but massive in its claims and benevolently contemptuous. . . . All his faults were marked by kindred traits, and were those of a man who had a fine baritone, whose clothes hung well upon him, and who even in his ordinary gestures had an air of inbred distinction." Eliot is quite conscious of what she is doing; she anticipates a young lady reader's inquiring incredulously how there "can be any commonness in a man so well-bred, so ambitious of social distinction, so generous and unusual in his views of social duty." Presumably the young lady has

expected a novel that will add to the undistinguished sameness of
"favourite love-stories in prose and verse" Eliot speaks of in her
"Prelude" to *Middlemarch* as constituting the reading of women.
Eliot replies: "Lydgate's spots of commonness lay in the complexion
of his prejudices, which, in spite of noble intention and sympathy,
were half of them such as are found in ordinary men of the world:
that distinction of mind which belonged to his intellectual ardour,
did not penetrate his feeling and judgment about furniture, or wom-
en, or the desirability of its being known (without his telling) that
he was better born than other country surgeons." Eliot is providing a
prologue to her tragedy of unpaid butchers' bills. Lydgate "did not
mean to think of furniture at present; but whenever he did so, it was
to be feared that neither biology nor schemes of reform would lift him
above the *vulgarity of feeling* that there would be an incompatibility
in his furniture not being of the best" (xv.112, italics mine). The
theme has more in common with *Madame Bovary* than appears at
first glance. Both Lydgate and Rosamond share with Emma an admiration for luxury, wealth, and beauty of the sentimental "keepsake"
variety. Emma's story is to a significant extent a tragedy of spots of
commonness, false assumptions of superiority based on what is in
reality a vulgarity of feeling. And for that reason tradesmen are to
prove her nemesis as they do Lydgate's. Women, Lydgate reflects
early in the novel, ought to provide "a paradise with sweet laughs
for bird-notes, and blue eyes for a heaven" (xi.70), as Miss Brooke
eminently does not. And he thinks of Rosamond, whom he has already observed with approval: "She is grace itself; she is perfectly
lovely and accomplished. That is what a woman ought to be; she
ought to produce the effect of exquisite music." This is a "keepsake"
theory of life and of a woman's place in it. While Lydgate is later
capable of ridiculing the absurd notions of luxury, distinction, and
beauty in the English *Keepsake* Ned Plymdale has brought Rosamond, he is in process of courting, in Rosamond, a beauty whose
view of distinction is largely that of just such sentimental literature.
Lydgate can laugh at the "ladies and gentlemen with shiny copper-
plate cheeks and copper-plate smiles" that Ned Plymdale admires in
the *Keepsake* and the sort of clothes an engraver has given a bride-
groom coming out of church ("Did any haberdasher ever look so
smirking?") and the verses of Lady Blessington and L.E.L.; but he

confesses to having "used to know Scott's poems by heart," a fact that echoes ironically with his conduct in Paris in an earlier chapter. Rosamond herself, Eliot tells us, "was not without relish" for the *Keepsake* authors (xxvii.200). She is familiar with "the best novels, *and even the second best*" (xvi.124, italics mine), and knows "much poetry by heart"—poetry that is also probably of a second-best variety, for her favorite poem is Tom Moore's *Lalla Rookh*, in which the beautiful princess of that name, daughter of the Emperor Aurengzebe, falls in love with Feramorz, a young poet also of great beauty, but is gratified to learn in the end that she has lost her heart without loss of rank. Feramorz is actually her betrothed, the King of Bucharia himself, who has wooed her in disguise. Under the influence of Lydgate, whose aristocratic lineage, white hands, and unexceptionable manners and dress make him an admirer worth cultivating, Rosamond "diligently attended to that perfection of appearance, behaviour, sentiments, and all other elegancies" of a sort that would appeal to him. Following to the letter a "*Keepsake*" ideal of feminine occupation, she became "more than ever . . . active in sketching her landscapes and market-carts and portraits of friends, in practising her music, and in being from morning till night her own standard of a perfect lady" (xvi.124). Rosamond's theory of distinction, in sum, like Emma Bovary's, has a great deal to do with sentimental literature; and so does Lydgate's.

Lydgate's romantic assumptions about women, coupled with the rashness of his emotional nature, had already, during his student life in Paris, rushed him headlong into a perilous situation. He had fallen in love with an actress in a melodrama. Lydgate did not intend his to be more than an imaginary romance, being in love with her "as a man is in love with a woman whom he never expects to speak to," and contenting himself with frequent visits to see her act her part in the melodrama, in which she was called upon to stab the actor who played her lover. But Lydgate was present on the night of her actually stabbing and killing her stage lover, who was in real life her husband. Though even many of her warmest admirers believed in her guilt, Lydgate found himself rising to her defense. He knew nothing of her except that she was in distress, and that she was beautiful. The young man who had once memorized all of Scott's poems followed "the fitful swerving of passion to which he was prone" and responded with the "chivalrous kindness which helped to make him morally lovable" (xv.112). Laure, the actress, was eventually released, since no case could be made against her. By this time Lydgate, in the course of many interviews, had "found her more and more adorable," though part of her charm consisted of her saying very little. "She was melancholy and seemed grateful; her presence was enough, like that of evening light." When she leaves Paris without warning, Lydgate abandons his scientific study, unable to think of anything except "the unhappy Laure, stricken by ever-wandering sorrow, herself wandering, and finding no faithful comforter." The scene, and Eliot's phrasing as well, would fit easily into one of the many sentimental tales featured in the keepsakes or to be found in the pages of a great many second-best romantic poets and novelists; but for Lydgate it possesses a force of reality that drives him into headlong action. With difficulty he seeks Laure out at Avignon, where she is appearing under the same name, playing "a forsaken wife carrying her child in her arms." When he speaks to her after the play, her "quietude . . . seemed to him beautiful as clear depths of water." He is more than ever determined to propose to her, though a part of him knows his own folly. "He knew that this was like the sudden impulse of a madman—incongruous even with his habitual foibles. No matter! It was the one thing which he was resolved to do. *He had two selves within him apparently, and they must learn to accommodate each other and bear reciprocal impediments*" (xv.113, italics mine). But his proposal is to bring his whole romantic vision collapsing around him.

Again Laure paused a little and then said, slowly, "*I meant to do it.* . . . he wearied me; he was too fond: he would live in Paris, and not in my country; that was not agreeable to me." . . .

Lydgate stood mute, and unconsciously pressed his hat on while he looked at her. He saw this woman—the first to whom he had given his young adoration—amid the throng of stupid criminals.

"You are a good man," she said. "But I do not like husbands. I will never have another."

In three days' time Lydgate was once more at his studies in Paris, "believing that illusions were at an end for him." From now on "he would take a strictly scientific view of woman, entertaining no expectations but such as were justified beforehand."

The ironies of the Laure incident are quite marked because the reader has already learned of Lydgate's strong attraction to a second beauty accomplished in the art of acting though technically an amateur. Rosamond's abilities in that direction have been stressed in a scene played specifically for Lydgate's benefit, a scene in which Mary Garth, plain and brown, is forced to assume a part, maneuvered skillfully by Rosamond for purposes of upstaging. Eliot underlines the meaning of the scene. Rosamond, we are assured, "was by nature an actress of parts that entered into her physique: *she even acted her own character, and so well, that she did not know it to be precisely her own*" (xii.87, italics mine). Lydgate would have been surprised to learn how much of Rosamond's good nature and grace were products of training. She was "a sylph caught young" and educated at Mrs. Lemon's select fashionable school. Here young ladies were taught "refinement" of a sort calculated to attract the admiration of gentlemen with the same conception of what "refinement" meant. Lydgate, for all his aristocratic connections, possesses the requisite vulgarity of feeling regarding "furniture, or women" to figure among them. Rosamond had been the prize pupil at Mrs. Lemon's, "where the teaching included all that was demanded in the accomplished female—even to extras, *such as the getting in and out of a carriage*" (xii.71, italics mine). Eliot's specifying this last extra affords a helpful index of how far Mrs. Lemon's courses could go in pursuing the appearance of elegance (as in acted drama) without much regard to substance. Emma Bovary, studying the keepsakes in her convent school at Rouen, absorbed an ideal of feminine achievement that also put high value on poses connoting leisurely elegance ("English ladies lolled in carriages, or glided through parks in handsome equipages driven by two postilions . . . . Other ladies were pictured dreaming on sofas . . ." [I.vi.52–53]). Rosamond had been taught to sing in such a manner as to appeal to a drawing-room audience. It was, one gathers, indifferent to her whether she was called on for a popular ballad or for Mozart—"she only wanted to know what her audience liked" (xvi.119). She played the piano with deep feeling, but the fact was further evidence of her talent for acting; for the feeling was not her own but that of the unusually gifted music master she had profited from at Mrs. Lemon's: "Rosamond, with the executant's instinct, had seized his manner of playing, and gave forth his large rendering of noble music with the precision of an echo. It was almost startling, heard for the first time. A hidden soul seemed to be flowing forth under Rosamond's fingers; and so indeed it was . . . ." Lydgate leaves the house after his first visit to the Vincys quite unaware that he has again confused a talented performance for a glimpse into the reality of the performer. He is not in a marrying mood, since his plans for a scientific career must bar an early marriage; but he is convinced that Rosamond is a paragon among women: "Certainly, if falling in love had been at all in question, it would have been quite safe with a creature like this Miss Vincy, who had just the kind of intelligence one would desire in a woman—polished, refined, docile, lending itself to finish in all the delicacies of life, *and enshrined in a body which expressed this with a force of demonstration that excluded the need for other evidence*" (xvi.121, italics mine).

Yet Rosamond is herself a victim of the illusion that she helps to promote. She has her own "spots of commonness" that prevent her seeing Lydgate more clearly than as the distinguished male (essentially faceless) who is necessary to the completion of her imagined world, in which "her favourite house with various styles of furniture" figures large (xxvii.197). The prices that realtors or outfitters set on such objects do not concern her: she had "never thought of money except as something necessary which other people would always provide." Her father, a fairly well-to-do ribbon manufacturer, had never denied her anything that she really desired. Lydgate seems a safe prospect for marriage to her on the basis of his appearance and manners and, above all, his being nephew of a baronet. Her reading and her schooling at Mrs. Lemon's had trained her in notions that are approximately as realistic as Emma Bovary's and possess some aspects in common:

In Rosamond's romance *it was not necessary to imagine much about the inward life of the hero, or of his serious business in the world*: of course, he had a profession and was clever, as well as sufficiently handsome; but the piquant fact about Lydgate was his good birth, which distinguished him from all Middlemarch admirers, and presented marriage as a prospect of rising in rank and getting a little nearer to that celestial condition on earth in which she would have nothing to do with vulgar people, and perhaps at last associate with relatives quite equal to the county people who looked down on the Middlemarchers. (xvi.123, italics mine)

It is in speaking of Rosamond that Eliot presents her most elaborate image of the abraded mirror and the candle, where the scratches "seem to arrange themselves in a fine series of concentric circles round that little sun" (xxvii.195). While Lydgate thinks of the pleasures life with Rosamond will offer a lucky male once she is captured within the gravitational field of that man's ego-centered world (not his own, since he must postpone marriage, being dedicated to scientific research), Rosamond thinks of Lydgate as a satellite necessary to her own plans. She was "entirely occupied not exactly with Tertius Lydgate as he was in himself, but with his relation to her" (xvii.124). When her aunt Harriet Bulstrode, having learned the amount of attention Lydgate has been devoting to Rosamond, warns her against becoming engaged to a doctor, unable to support her in her accustomed manner, Rosamond, confident in her ignorance of the "serious business of the world" and the inward life of Lydgate, ignores the warning. "She was not a fiery young lady and had no sharp answers, but she meant to live as she pleased" (xxxi.219). When, however, Lydgate himself is exposed to Mrs. Bulstrode's pointed intimations that he is seeing too much of her niece, he resolves to avoid the Vincy home in the future "except on business." He manages to keep his vow for some time, during which Rosamond begins to study her experience in the light of another scene in what she has read or witnessed at the theater. "She felt that she was beginning to know the pang of disappointed love . . . . Poor Rosamond lost her appetite and felt as forlorn as Ariadne—*as a charming stage Ariadne left behind with all her boxes full of costumes and no hope of a coach*" (xxxi.221, italics mine). "There are many wonderful mixtures in the world which are called love," Eliot observes pointedly, "and claim the privileges of a sublime rage which is an apology for everything (*in literature and the drama*)."

Lydgate stays away for ten days. On the eleventh he uses his need to communicate with Rosamond's father to serve him as an excuse for a visit to the Vincy home. He could have called at the warehouse, or have left a message at the door; but such devices "apparently did not occur to him." Rosamond attempts to act nonchalant but cannot suppress tears, and it is the sight of these that conquers him. George Eliot reminds us that "the ambitious man who was looking at those Forget-me-nots under water [Rosamond's tear-filled eyes] was very warm-

hearted and rash" (xxxi.222). On another memorable moment of his
life that ought to have served him as warning Lydgate, moved by
rash but morally lovable impulses, had risen to the need of beauty in
distress. Now, with a "sudden belief that this sweet young creature
depended on him for her joy," he embraces Rosamond. "In half an
hour he left the house an engaged man, whose soul was not his own,
but the woman's to whom he had bound himself."

Rosamond's unfitness to be the wife of a struggling young physician—even one without aspirations for furthering medical science—
are obvious to nearly everyone except Lydgate and Rosamond. Mrs.
Plymdale makes innuendoes about Rosamond's expensive habits to
Mrs. Bulstrode (xxxi.217). Mrs. Bulstrode flatly tells her niece to give
up thoughts of Lydgate because she is not "fit to marry a poor man"
(xxxi.218) and later, hearing that the engagement has in fact taken
place, wonders what a girl brought up in luxury will do on a small
income (xxxvi.254). Mr. Vincy deplores seeing his daughter's expensive education wasted in marriage to "a poor man" (xxxvi.259).
What such persons are not aware of is that Lydgate is nearly as innocent about the realities of money as Rosamond herself. It is one of
his assumptions as a gentleman and the nephew of a baronet that
money matters take care of themselves. The quicksands of debt—
prosaic realities that announce themselves only after the victim is well
beyond solid ground—occupy much space in the unfolding of the
Lydgate-Rosamond plot as they do in the history of Emma Bovary.
Lydgate leases a large house because Rosamond admires it and "Marriage, of course, must be prepared for in the usual way." He acquires
debts "in an episodic way, very much as he gave orders to his tailor for
every requisite of perfect dress, without any notion of being extrava-
gant" (xxxvi.255). Since he has a dislike for unsightly crockery, Lydgate buys an expensive dinner service he happens to see on display;
and when Rosamond's mother fears servants may break it, Lydgate
assures her that it is important to "hire servants who will not break
things" (xxxvi.258). Meanwhile Rosamond feels she is exercising
foresight and prudence in buying linen, lace, and embroidery of a
sort proper for a bride who on her honeymoon is "going to visit at a
baronet's." Scenes preceding the wedding are strong in "binocular
vision" or pungent counterpointing. When Rosamond declares that
despite her father's disapproval she will go ahead with plans for the

wedding because "I never give up anything that I choose to do," Lydgate murmurs a fervent "God bless you!" It is on the surface a situation a sentimental novelist would find congenial to his hand. Eliot makes it an opportunity for exploring sinister realities underlying the stage or fictional appearance. Lydgate sees it in terms of a cliché which suggests that he, like Rosamond (and like Emma Bovary) has been in his time a devotee of romantic oriental tales: "An unmistakable delight shone forth from the blue eyes that met his, and the radiance seemed to light up all his future with mild sunshine. Ideal happiness (of the kind known in the Arabian Nights, in which you are invited to step from the labour and discord of the street into a paradise where everything is given to you and nothing claimed) seemed to be an affair of a few weeks' waiting, more or less" (xxxvi.257). The role of impetuous lover seems demanded, and Lydgate responds by pressing for an early marriage: " 'Why should we defer it?' he said, with ardent insistence. 'I have taken the house now: everything else can soon be got ready—can it not? You will not mind about new clothes. Those can be bought afterwards.' " Lydgate has no real notion of how importantly the word "clothes" figures literally and with wider implications in Rosamond's plans. She laughs and dimples prettily. She has never heard of "wedding clothes being bought after marriage." But Lydgate pursues his own vision. He is thinking of a future in which he will carry on his scientific research in his serious hours, and Rosamond will relax his mind from such labors in his leisure: " 'Remember, we are looking forward to *a better sort of happiness* even than this—being continually together, *independent of others, and ordering our lives as we will*. Come, dear, tell me how soon you *can be altogether mine*' " (italics mine). The phrases underlined are, of course, expressions of ideas familiar to sentimental literature. They have much irony, even in the light of what the reader already knows of Lydgate and Rosamond and the interconnection of people's lives in Middlemarch, especially the lives of people who are rushing headlong into expenses beyond the size of their income. They will take on added meaning in the rest of the novel. The tone of serious pleading in Lydgate's voice impresses Rosamond. She "became serious too, and slightly meditative; in fact, *she was going through many intricacies of lace-edging and hosiery and petticoat-tucking, in order to give an answer that would at least be approximative*" (italics mine). Lydgate is unaware that his chief attraction in the eyes of Rosamond has nothing to do with his strength of intellect or his scientific ambitions but lies in his aura of aristocracy. Worship of rank will later cause Rosamond to disobey Lydgate's orders and bring on the premature birth, and the death, of their child. In the present scene Rosamond is devoting earnest calculation to the question of clothing because, for her, the great event of the honeymoon will be, of course, their visit with the family of Sir Godwin, Lydgate's uncle. The design and number of evening dresses for this initiation into the life of the aristocracy—she hopes it will extend to at least a quarter of their time—is crucial in her thinking. When Lydgate suggests they take six weeks for their honeymoon, Rosamond protests that a longer period must be taken, thinking to prolong the visit with Sir Godwin. "She looked at her lover with some wondering remonstrance as she spoke, and he readily understood that she might wish to lengthen the sweet time of double solitude." There is a great deal more—the question would be whether there is possibly more than enough—of Eliot's parody of lovers' dialogue. Rosamond "thought that no one could be more in love than she was," and Lydgate was sure that "after all his wild mistakes and absurd credulity, he had found perfect womanhood," while the reader is made fully aware that each is fixed in his own strongly concentric world and beholding the other, for all his sense of the sort of communion promised in romantic literature, across a wide hiatus. It is a drama of incommunicability during courtship played in lighter accents than that of Dorothea and Casaubon, but with equally sinister implications, and consequences.

The first months following the wedding and honeymoon (both of which Eliot passes over without chronicling) carry forward the Lydgate-Rosamond plot chiefly through realistic treatment of the way Lydgate in his arrogance and intentness on medical reform makes enemies of Middlemarch's other practitioners. Rosamond finds an ominous pleasure for her idle life in flirting a little with Will Ladislaw (whose heart is really devoted to Dorothea Casaubon). The death of Rosamond's baby marks a point in Lydgate's disillusion as both fact and symbol. Rosamond's insistence on riding horseback, despite her husband's orders as her physician to discontinue during her pregnancy, comes of her worship of the aristocracy. The temptation to accompany Captain Lydgate, third son of the baronet, on his rides during a visit is too great for her. The satisfaction of having a cousin who is a baronet's son "was enough for the time to melt away some disappointment in the conditions of marriage with a medical man even of good birth: it seemed now that her marriage was visibly floating her above the Middlemarch level." There are no apparent intimations of a liaison, but Captain Lydgate has clearly become Rosamond's image of the ideal man. She practices on the Captain as she had practiced earlier on her husband the charms she had learned at Mrs. Lemon's and from her reading. She takes fresh pains with her music and the "careful selection of her lace." Lydgate is not jealous by nature, and, aside from fearing the danger involved to Rosamond in riding, "preferred leaving a feather-headed young gentleman alone with his wife to bearing him company" (lviii.424). The Captain's qualities are gross but they are also fashionable. He parts his hair in the middle, as elegant society of the time dictated, and he shows "an ignorant security that he knew the proper thing to say on every topic." He has all the spots of commonness that mar Lydgate's nature without any of the compensating virtues. How far Rosamond has gone in rejecting her husband as the center of her imaginative world is underscored. In her sureness that rank and fashion are criteria that are not open to serious question, she lectures Lydgate on his rudeness and urges him to imitate the Captain's manner. " 'The fact is, you would wish me to be a little more like him, Rosy,' " Lydgate replies, "in a sort of resigned murmur, with a smile which was not exactly tender, and certainly not merry. . . ." The words "were like a sad milestone marking how far he had travelled from his old dreamland." During the forbidden ride with the Captain, Rosamond's horse shies, and Rosamond, though not thrown, is frightened sufficiently to cause the premature birth and loss of her child. In all their future conversations, Rosamond insists that her being frightened on the ride had nothing to do with the death of their child. "Lydgate could only say, 'Poor, poor darling!'—but he secretly wondered over the terrible tenacity of this mild creature. There was gathering within him an amazed sense of his powerlessness over Rosamond" (lviii.427).

The "terrible tenacity" that underlies Rosamond's flower-like, fragile, and infantine appearance becomes a persistent motif. Rosamond's avowal of steadfastness in the course of their lovers' dialogue ("I never give up anything that I choose to do") is to reverberate in Lydgate's experience with more and more sinister meaning, threatening to cancel all his finest moments. Even in the time of Captain Lydgate's visit, he is already "conscious of new elements in his life as noxious to him as an inlet of mud to a creature that has been used to breathe and bathe and dart after its illuminated prey in the clearest of waters." With the death of Rosamond's baby, "all the embroidered robes and caps had to be laid by in darkness." It is in the same chapter that many of Lydgate's brightest hopes are also interred, and a "creeping paralysis" seizes on his enthusiasm. When a debt for three hundred and eighty pounds becomes due, there is no way to avoid the humiliation of surrendering part of the household plate, together with some of Rosamond's jewelry, and allowing a man to invade the house to take inventory of the furniture. When Lydgate asks Rosamond to help him think out their predicament together, her reply "fell like a mortal chill" upon him. "It seemed that she had no more identified herself with him than if they had been creatures of different species and opposing interests" (lviii.436), and Lydgate can only look at her with "a despairing acceptance of the distance she was placing between them."

The theme of alienation continues strong in the remaining chapters of the novel. Lydgate tries frantic means of relief from his anxieties; but he is too proud to rely long on opium and too rational to trust beyond the running out of an impulse to his luck at gambling. Meanwhile Rosamond remains aloof and unforgiving. Eliot's theory of an author's obligation to instruct readers in insight and sympathy requires her to present Rosamond's point of view with as much toleration as possible. She makes an attempt, but her conception of Rosamond's almost absolute egocentrism makes such insight as she can manage provide very little sympathy.

> She was convinced of her having acted in every way for the best; and each grating or angry speech of Lydgate's served only as an addition to the register of offences in her mind. Poor Rosamond for months had begun to associate her husband with feelings of disappointment, and the terribly inflexible relation of marriage had lost its charm of en-

couraging delightful dreams. It had freed her from the disagreeables of her father's house, but it had not given her everything that she had wished and hoped. The Lydgate with whom she had been in love had been a group of airy conditions for her, most of which had disappeared, while their place had been taken by everyday details which must be lived slowly from hour to hour, not floated through with a rapid selection of favourable aspects.

Mrs. Lemon's school and her own favorite reading have not prepared Rosamond for life in a world remote alike from luxury and aristocratic pursuits. She had not realized what was implied in marrying a physician.

The habits of Lydgate's profession, his home preoccupation with scientific subjects, which seemed to her almost like a morbid vampire's taste, his peculiar views of things which had never entered into the dialogue of courtship—all these continually-alienating influences, even without the fact of his having placed himself at a disadvantage in the town, and without that first shock of revelation about Dover's debt, would have made his presence dull to her. . . . it seemed to her (perhaps she was right) that an invitation to Quallingham [Sir Godwin's estate], and an opening for Lydgate to settle elsewhere than in Middlemarch—in London, or somewhere likely to be free from unpleasantness—would satisfy her quite well . . . . (lxiv.484)

When Rosamond frustrates Lydgate's hope of obtaining a loan from his uncle (a remote hope at best) by writing a blundering letter that she considers in impeccable taste, he is infuriated, but soon feels the need to give up his anger. "As for him, the need of accommodating himself to her nature, which was inflexible in proportion to its negations, held him as with pincers" (lxv.488). The simile is appropriate; for Lydgate, even in wishing to excuse her conduct, is forced to think of her across a widening gulf as "an animal of another and feebler species." Yet, granted the terms of their struggle, Rosamond is to prove the creature better fitted for survival. The last sentence of the chapter enunciates for a second time the major irony of their two lives: with all the superiorities of his nature over hers, "Nevertheless, she had mastered him."

Several chapters later, after Lydgate's efforts to free himself from debt that involved him, though essentially guiltless, in a scandal concerning Bulstrode and the death of Raffles, Eliot returns to the pattern of Rosamond's and Lydgate's relationship, in which the generous and aspiring nature must accommodate itself and its movements to the narrower and enclosed: "Even this trouble, like the rest, she seemed to regard as if it were hers alone. He was always to her a being apart, doing what she objected to. . . . There was an underlying consciousness all the while that he should have to master this anger, and tell her everything, and convince her of the facts. For he had almost learned the lesson that he must bend himself to her nature, and that because she came short in her sympathy, he must give the more" (lxxv.555).

Dorothea Casaubon "with her ready understanding of high experience" is eager to assure Lydgate of her complete faith in his probity—a faith that is justified despite appearances—though his wife is not. It is a measure of how far Lydgate's pride has been broken by debt and isolation that he can be grateful for Dorothea's declaration and her taking over the most humiliating of his indebtednesses. But though Dorothea's confidence in him can soothe his spirit, there is nothing that can restore his self-trust. He is forced to confess, when she urges him to reconsider his plans for leaving Middlemarch: " 'I am no longer sure of myself—I mean of what it would be possible for me to do under the changed circumstances of my life. . . . I can think of nothing for a long while but getting an income' " (lxxvi.562). Eliot's final sentence devoted to the Lydgate-Rosamond plot, aside from a pungent paragraph in her "Finale," again underlines Lydgate's bondage to the beautiful "infantine" creature that has tamed his spirit and destroyed the world of his splendid ambitions. *He must walk as he could, carrying that burthen pitifully*" (lxxxi.586, italics mine).

> *They, hand in hand, with wandering steps and slow,*
> *Through Eden took their solitary way.*

Lydgate's departure from what had once been the place of his bright hopes reads like a modern variant (as Eliot probably intended it should) on Milton's lines, with the fact of isolation no longer exterior but moved inside the later Adam's consciousness.

In the "Finale," an unnumbered concluding chapter devoted in the tradition of Victorian novels (but with a difference) to brief sketches carrying the lives of the various characters beyond the main action of the narrative, Eliot describes the fortunes of Lydgate and Rosamond in ensuing years. Lydgate is destined to die at fifty. "He had gained an excellent practice, alternating, according to the season, between London and a Continental bathing-place; having written a treatise on Gout, a disease which has a good deal of wealth on its side." The mockery of such a career for a man who had once hoped to "move the world a little" is acute. "His skill was relied on by many paying patients, but he always regarded himself as a failure; he had not done what he once meant to do." It is important to Eliot's plan and meaning that Lydgate's life should, from the public view, appear successful. "His acquaintances thought him enviable to have so charming a wife, and nothing happened to shake their opinion." Like Bella Wilfer-Harmon of Dickens' *Our Mutual Friend*, Rosamond is awarded a life upholstered with every domestic luxury. The implications in the two novels (Dickens' novel had appeared only seven years earlier) are almost diametrically opposed. Dickens is providing his heroine, after a period of trial that has proved her worthy, with the rise in fortune and setting that his public expected. He is writing in the tradition of the English novel from Richardson onward that called (even in the novels of Jane Austen) for inward state to be reflected in outward condition. Eliot is consciously breaking with the tradition. It is Dorothea her heroine (so far as the term is allowable) who is to end in relative poverty, having chosen to give up her fortune. It is Rosamond, a character without any real parallel in the art of Dickens, where intensive concern with psychological realism is scarcely a factor, who prospers to outer view. For Lydgate as well, outward prosperity gives the lie direct to inward condition. "As the years went on he opposed [Rosamond] less and less whence Rosamond concluded that he had learned the value of her opinion; on the other hand, she had a more thorough conviction of his talents now that he gained a good income, and instead of the threatened cage in Bride Street provided one all flowers and gilding, fit for the bird of paradise that she resembled. [No one is likely to accuse Eliot of an excess of sympathy for Rosamond; but the play of images in the last sentence resembles something approaching cruel and inhuman punishment from the author.] *In brief, Lydgate was what is called a successful man*" (italics mine). Lydgate's death, leaving a heavy insurance on his life, does not end Rosamond's good fortune. Like Homais, who flourishes in sciolism and self-assurance while others around him fail the tests for survival, Rosamond lives on in health and good estate. She exchanges widowhood for marriage to "an elderly and wealthy physician, who took kindly to her four children," and she remains as certain as she has been at all stages of her career that her opinions have invariably been judicious and Lydgate's errors have come from not following them. She "often spoke of her happiness as 'a reward'—she did not say for what, but probably she meant that it was a reward for her patience with Tertius, whose temper never became faultless, and to the last occasionally let slip a bitter speech which was more memorable than the signs he made of his repentance."

Lydgate's bitterest speech must have been his calling her his basil plant, with an allusion, which escaped Rosamond, to the story of Isabella and the pot of basil as told by Boccaccio in the *Decameron* and Keats in his poem: "He once called her his basil plant; and when she asked for an explanation, said that basil was a plant which had flourished wonderfully on a murdered man's brains."

iii. Nicholas Bulstrode

Critics have generally considered the Bulstrode-Raffles plot of *Middlemarch* melodramatic and tend to award their praise to the brief but brilliant scenes of his wife's disillusion and readjustment of her worlds after learning the secret her husband has guarded during the many years of their married life. Though Bulstrode plays a part in the lives of nearly all the other characters either directly or indirectly, we see very little of his private world until over half the novel is finished. Then, with the advent of the rascally Raffles, a former accomplice and now his blackmailer, we learn much more of what goes on inside the pious banker and landowner who wields formidable power over the other citizens of Middlemarch. Dickens would have made him into an out-and-out Pecksniff or a Reverend Mr. Chadband with brilliant results in the manner of his quite different idiom. But George Eliot, with her theory of inducing sympathy and insight in her reader, has other purposes in mind and is not given to painting in primary colors. To secure the reader's sympathy for Bulstrode is perhaps more than

Eliot assumed, but providing insight, at least, into the life of this inner world she could undertake with greater confidence. It is evident at times from her tone that in presenting the private experience of this morally unlovable character she is conscious of accepting a challenge and deliberately essaying a subject no predecessor had seriously attempted. Young Henry James, in his critique of 1873, pointed out her portrayal of Bulstrode as a singular failure in the novel, despite evidence of the great care the author had expended upon her subject: "To but one of these accessory episodes—that of Mr. Bulstrode, with its multiplex ramifications—do we take exception. It has a slightly artificial cast, a melodramatic tinge, unfriendly to the richly natural coloring of the whole. Bulstrode himself—with the history of whose troubled conscience the author has taken great pains—is, to our sense, too diffusely treated; he never grasps the readers' attention." James admired, on the other hand, the swift and consummate moment of insight Eliot provides us into the mind of Harriet Bulstrode: "But the touch of genius is never idle or vain. The obscure figure of Bulstrode's comely wife emerges at the needful moment, under a few light strokes, into the happiest reality."[22]

Even before Raffles enters the scene (though in the same chapter), Eliot suggests the way Bulstrode, for all the pious assured front with which he faces Middlemarch society, habitually pleads his case in his own conscience, never securing a full acquittal but more than half convincing himself that his success in the outer world has come to him, despite the devious channels by which it had chosen to make its way in his earlier years, from a source in divine dispensation. He would earnestly like to convince himself that his acquisition of Stone Court, the handsome estate he has just purchased, fits into such a pattern: ". . . he had bought the excellent farm and fine homestead simply as a retreat which he might gradually enlarge as to the land and beautify as to the dwelling, until it should be conducive to the divine glory that he should enter on it as a residence, partially withdrawing from his present exertions in the administration of business, and throwing more conspicuously on the side of Gospel truth the weight of local landed proprietorship, which Providence might increase by unforeseen occasions of purchase" (liii.381). In Joshua Rigg's willingness to part with this splendid estate, the hand of Providence has again been made manifest. But Eliot warns us that thus associating thoughts (and diction) of Gospel truth and Providence with thoughts (and diction) of commerce is simply Bulstrode's variant of a very common habit among human beings. Eliot's image of the candle of the ego and the mirror of circumstance, whose surface abrasions seem always concentric to it, seems again implied: "This was not what Mr. Bulstrode said to any man for the sake of deceiving him: it was what he said to himself—it was as genuinely his mode of explaining events as any theory of yours may be, if you happen to disagree with him. *For the egoism which enters into our theories does not affect their sincerity; rather, the more our egoism is satisfied, the more robust is our belief*" (italics mine). The appearance of John Raffles with his sadistic pleasure in taunting Bulstrode—a pleasure that Eliot assures us is even stronger than his desire for money to be extorted by hinted threats of exposure—ushers in a period of acute mental anguish: "Five minutes before, the expanse of his life had been submerged in its evening sunshine which shone backward to its remembered morning: sin seemed to be a question of doctrine and inward penitence, humiliation an exercise of the closet, the bearing of his deeds a matter of private vision adjusted solely by spiritual relations and conceptions of the divine purposes. And now, as if by some hideous magic, this loud red figure had risen before him in unmanageable solidity—an incorporate past which had not entered into his imagination or chastisements" (liii.384).

Bulstrode, to repeat, is not by any means a simple hypocrite, nor have his misdeeds of the past been of a directly criminal nature. He is in no danger of being turned over to the law. An orphan educated at a commercial charity-school, Bulstrode had begun his career as a banker's clerk. He had been an enthusiastic member of a "Calvinistic dissenting church" during his youth and still treasured memories of his speaking in prayer meetings and in private homes during those years as the happiest time of his life, "the spot he would have chosen now to awake in and find the rest a dream" (lxi.450). An acquaintance formed at church, however, had led him to become confidential accountant to a pawnbroker's firm. When he soon discovered that the house made most of its enormous profits from receiving goods "without strict inquiry as to where they came from," he struggled to justify his continuing: "He remembered his first moments of shrinking. They were private, and were filled with arguments; some of these taking the form of prayer. . . . The profits made out of lost souls—where can the line be drawn at which they begin in human transactions? Was it not even God's way of saving His chosen? 'Thou knowest,'—the young Bulstrode had said then, as the older Bulstrode was saying now—'Thou knowest how loose my soul sits from these things —how I view them all as implements for tilling Thy garden rescued here and there from the wilderness.' " (lxi.451). The process of convincing himself that Providence required him to serve (euphemisms aside) as a fence for thieves was long and intricate; but he managed to discover by degrees that he was justified: "Metaphors and precedents were not wanting; peculiar spiritual experiences were not wanting which at last made the retention of his position seem a service demanded of him." Thus Bulstrode began "carrying on two distinct lives; his religious activity could not be incompatible with his business as soon as he had argued himself into not feeling it incompatible." When the proprietor of the business died, Bulstrode after a time married the widow, who had been left much wealth. There was danger, however, that the property would not be left to him if a daughter, who had run away from the family some years earlier in shame at her parent's manner of business (to join the stage) could be found. The daughter was indeed found, but beside Bulstrode only one man, Raffles, knew that this was so. Raffles, paid for remaining silent, left the country for America. More than Casaubon, Bulstrode enmeshed himself in the tangles of his own metaphors: "There were hours in which Bulstrode felt that his action was unrighteous; but how could he go back? He had mental exercises, called himself nought, laid hold on redemption, and went on in his course of instrumentality." Even after the death of his first wife, Bulstrode continued in the business for thirteen years. Then, having amassed a fortune of a hundred thousand pounds, he left London for Middlemarch and there became a citizen of importance, "a banker, a Churchman, a public benefactor" as well as a silent partner in other trading concerns. He married in time a handsome second wife from a substantial manufacturing family, the Vincys. For nearly thirty years, with his past "benumbed in the consciousness," he had led a life of respectability and pious works.

Eliot insists once again (as if she were not quite as sure of the effect of her subject as in other parts of her novel) that she is not presenting a study in simple religious hypocrisy. Bulstrode's illusion of a special relation to Providence is not a mask to parade before others but an active and earnest element in his life—the result of a special form of romantic egoism acting in this particular personality: "There may be coarse hypocrites, who consciously affect beliefs and emotions for the sake of gulling the world, but Bulstrode was not one of them. He was simply a man whose desires had been stronger than his theoretic beliefs, and who had gradually explained the gratification of his desires into satisfactory agreement with those beliefs. *If this be hypocrisy, it is a process which shows itself occasionally in us all, to whatever confession we belong ...*" (italics mine). During the weeks after Raffles has found him, Bulstrode's mental turmoil is very great; but it is intensified when at last Raffles returns to Stone Court in a condition so much worsened by heavy drinking that his death seems imminent. Bulstrode cannot help hoping in an unchristian way for a Providential escape by that means: "If it should turn out that he was freed from all danger of disgrace—if he could breathe in perfect liberty—his life should be more consecrated than it had ever been before. He mentally lifted up this vow as if it would urge the result he longed for—he tried to believe in the potency of that prayerful resolution—its potency to determine death. He knew that he ought to say, 'Thy will be done;' and he said it often. But the intense desire remained that the will of God might be the death of that hated man" (lxix.511).

Lydgate, as the physician called in, provides the unwelcome information that Raffles may even yet survive his attack if he is denied alcohol and kept on extremely moderate doses of opium should sleeplessness continue after several hours. "He insisted on the risk of not ceasing; and repeated that no alcohol should be given." The process by which Bulstrode, whose image of himself as an instrument of Providence is no pretence but an essential part of his life and thought, becomes a murderer is swiftly traced. It is in the main a matter of omissions. In giving up his post by Raffles' bedside to Mrs. Abel the housekeeper, Bulstrode forgets to tell her when the doses of opium have to be discontinued. He remembers his omission some time later, but persuades himself that inasmuch as Raffles is still moaning, Lydgate's prescription may be "better disobeyed than followed, since there was still no sleep" (lxx.520). A little later still, when the housekeeper taps at his door demanding brandy for the man she believes is dying, Bulstrode finds the temptation to let matters take their course more than he can resist. He gives her the key to the wine-cellar. Bulstrode rises early the next morning for a period of especially earnest prayer— a fact on which Eliot comments: "Does any one suppose that private prayer is necessarily candid—necessarily goes to the roots of action? Private prayer is inaudible speech, and speech is representative: who can represent himself just as he is, even in his own reflections?" Raffles is in a deep coma, well advanced on his road to death, as Bulstrode finds with a sense of vast relief: "As he sat there and beheld the enemy of his peace going irrevocably into silence, he felt more at rest than he had done for many months. His conscience was soothed by the enfolding wing of secrecy, which seemed just then like an angel sent down for his relief." It was nevertheless urgent for Bulstrode to insist to himself that he had not positively aided in the process: "And who could say that the death of Raffles had been hastened? Who knew what would have saved him?"

The incident plays an important part in the lives of other characters. Raffles has talked of Bulstrode's past in public places before returning to Stone Court for the last time. There are therefore strong suspicions, upon the death of Raffles, that Bulstrode, in connivance with Lydgate as physician, has in some way assisted fate. Nothing can be proved, but Bulstrode, and Lydgate as well, find themselves dishonored in the eyes of Middlemarch. At a meeting of an important town committee, the members ask Bulstrode to defend himself against the suspicions that have grown up around him. It is profoundly important for Eliot's conception of Bulstrode's character and the special nature of his illusion of himself as an instrument of Providence that he can have no such protection as a Pecksniff, a Uriah Heep, a Volpone, or a Tartuffe can summon to his defense. Bulstrode cannot hide behind a cleverly contrived mask and boldly defy the public that accuses him. To admit to himself that the face with which he has fronted the public is not legitimately his own would be to renounce a vital part of his own reality. Bulstrode, facing his accusers, has a terrible sense that God has in fact disowned him. Lydgate, who is another member of the board, seeing the livid face of Bulstrode at this moment, fears for his suffering a stroke. At first Bulstrode is unable to answer at all.

*The quick vision that his life was after all a failure, that he was a dishonoured man, and must quail before the glance of those towards whom he had habitually assumed the attitude of a reprover—that God had disowned him before men and left him unscreened to the triumphant scorn of those who were glad to have their hatred justified—*the sense of utter futility in that equivocation with his conscience in dealing with the life of his accomplice, an equivocation which now turned venomously upon him with the full-grown fang of a discovered lie:—all this rushed through him like the agony of terror which fails to kill, and leaves the ears still open to the returning wave of execration. *The sudden sense of exposure after the re-established sense of safety came—not to the coarse organisation of a criminal but—to the susceptible nerve of a man whose intensest being lay in such mastery and predominance as the conditions of his life had shaped for him.* (lxxi.533–534, italics mine)

Though Bulstrode's immediate sense of disillusion, isolation, and exposure is so strong that for a time he cannot speak, his powerful egoistic will is soon at work struggling to adjust itself to his altered world.

But in that intense being lay the strength of reaction. Through all his bodily infirmity there ran a tenacious nerve of ambitious self-preserving will, which had continually leaped out like a flame, scattering all doctrinal fears, and which, even while he sat an object of compassion for the merciful, was beginning to stir and glow under his ashy paleness. Before the last words were out of Mr. Hawley's mouth, Bulstrode felt that he should answer, and that his answer would be a retort. He dared not get up and say, 'I am not guilty, the whole story is false'—*even if he had dared this, it would have seemed to him, under his present keen sense of betrayal,* as vain as to pull, for covering to his nakedness, a frail rag which would rend at every little strain. (italics mine)

Finally he is able to speak, though he has not the strength to rise from his chair. His words, however, seem directed much more to his own inner consciousness than to the members of the board. The speech is not of a sort to convince the members of the board of his innocence of the charges that have been raised against him; it is much more like a confession of guilt so far as their perspective is concerned. *Bulstrode is essentially striving to re-establish in his own consciousness his right to view himself as superior to other men in his devotion to Providence, even if Providence has deserted him!* " 'Say that the evil-speaking of which I am to be made the victim accuses me of mal-practices—' here Bulstrode's voice rose and took on a more biting accent, till it seemed a low cry—'*who shall be my accuser? Not men whose own lives are unchristian, nay, scandalous—not men who themselves use low instruments to carry out their ends*—whose profession is a tissue of chicanery—who have been spending their income on their own sensual enjoyments, while I have been devoting mine to advance the best objects with regard to this life and the next' " (italics mine). The phrases italicized suggest how far he is occupied with defending himself not to his exterior audience but to himself. He is employing words that will offend and alienate those that hear (or overhear) him. He is interrupted with hisses and murmurs, and his life of influence and honor in Middlemarch is at an end.

Bulstrode still must face the effect of the disclosures upon his wife. He cannot bear to tell her himself; and it is her brother (Rosamond's father) who finally informs her "very inartificially, in slow fragments, making her aware that the scandal went much beyond proof, especially as to the end of Raffles" (lxxiv.549). Her life with Bulstrode has been colored by conscious pride in her husband and in the joint influence their pious example exerts upon the community. Harriet Bulstrode has entertained complete faith in her husband. In something of a parallel to his own adjustments of two worlds, exposed daily to his metaphors and trains of thought though not to his secret, she has managed, Eliot tells us earlier, to conciliate piety and worldliness, "the nothingness of this life" with "the desirability of cut glass, the consciousness at once of filthy rags and the best damask" (xxvii.198). We learn little of her private world until her brother's revelations of the scandals of Bulstrode's past that he has kept from her through the years of their marriage. Eliot presents her moment of disillusion, as James was to observe, with "a few light strokes" that have the touch of genius in them.

> She locked herself in her room. She needed time to get used to her maimed consciousness, her poor lopped life, before she could walk steadily to the place allotted her. A very searching light had fallen on her husband's character, and she could not judge him leniently: the twenty years in which she had believed in him and venerated him by virtue of his concealments came back with particulars that made them seem an odious deceit. He had married her with that bad past life hidden be-

hind him and she had no faith left to protest his innocence of the worst that was imputed to him. Her honest ostentatious nature made the sharing of a merited dishonour as bitter as it could be to any mortal. (lxxiv.549–550)

Many of her values—regarding lace and large houses and cut glass and furniture—are of a Vincy sort she shares with her niece Rosamond; but her time of disgrace reveals a nature that throws into sharper relief the appalling study of the extreme of egocentricity Eliot provides in the younger woman.

The man whose prosperity she had shared through nearly half a life, and who had unvaryingly cherished her—now that punishment had befallen him it was not possible to her in any sense to forsake him. There is a forsaking which still sits at the same board and lies on the same couch with the forsaken soul, withering it the more by unloving proximity. She knew, when she locked her door, that she should unlock it ready to go down to her unhappy husband and espouse his sorrow, and say of his guilt, I will mourn and not reproach. But she needed time to gather up her strength; she needed to sob out her farewell to all the gladness and pride of her life.

The ritual she chooses to announce to herself the alteration in status on which she must now enter is, as Barbara Hardy observes,[23] one peculiarly in keeping with her perspective on her world: "When she had resolved to go down, she prepared herself by some little acts which might seem mere folly to a hard onlooker; they were her way of expressing to all spectators visible and invisible that she had begun a new life in which she embraced humiliation. She took off all her ornaments and put on a plain black gown, and instead of wearing her much-adorned cap and large bows of hair, she brushed her hair down and put on a plain bonnet-cap, which made her look suddenly like an early Methodist" (lxxiv.550).

Bulstrode had awaited her coming "perishing slowly in unpitied misery. Perhaps he would never see his wife's face with affection in it again." When she does enter the room, he dares not look at her.

He sat with his eyes bent down, and as she went towards him she thought he looked smaller—he seemed so withered and shrunken. A movement of new compassion and old tenderness went through her

183

like a great wave, and putting one hand on his which rested on the arm of the chair, and the other on his shoulder, she said, solemnly but kindly—

'Look up, Nicholas.'

He raised his eyes with a little start and looked at her half amazed for a moment: her pale face, her changed, mourning dress, the trembling about her mouth, all said, 'I know;' and her hands and eyes rested gently on him. He burst out crying and they cried together, she sitting at his side.

The Bulstrodes, like the Lydgates, are to go out from the regions of Middlemarch under a shadow; but they will leave like Milton's couple hand in hand. Virginia Woolf called *Middlemarch* one of the few novels designed for "grown-up people." It is a part of Eliot's devotion to psychological realism and her break with the conventional ending bestowing rewards and punishments according to merit that causes her to award what is possibly the happiest of her marriages to the least lovable of her principal characters. Failure in marriage among the better-intentioned constitutes, as we have seen in some detail, a major subject in *Middlemarch*, occupying the primary focus in both the Dorothea-Casaubon and the Lydgate-Rosamond plots that dominate the novel.

This chapter has not been aimed at providing a balanced view of Eliot's masterpiece as seen from a broad perspective. Large parts of the novel—there are critics who would say the parts of it that matter most—have been all but ignored to concentrate upon the particular forms that illusion and inner as opposed to public reality take in the lives of the five protagonists Eliot marks out for intensive analysis. Chapters and portions of chapters devoted to the Mary Garth-Fred Vincy plot and pages presenting the Reverend Camden Farebrother add valuably to the scope of Eliot's very large novel. So do the episodes involving the life and death of Peter Featherstone. Chapters dealing with the business of Middlemarch to the near exclusion of other threads of the novel contribute strongly to the remarkable sense of realism that pervades the novel—the rich impression of a community and its environs beheld in vital motion. Few critics would, however, question the fact that the private experience of Dorothea and Casaubon, Lydgate and Rosamond, constitutes an essential focus of the novel or that the portrayal of Bulstrode, though perhaps less central, represents an integral part of Eliot's plan. These are the parts of the novel that especially distinguish it as a work of major importance in the progress of psychological narrative. It is not hard to see why Henry James, reading *Middlemarch* not long after it was published, found himself marking "innumerable passages for quotation and comment" and pronouncing the two "histories of matrimonial infelicity" full of "that supreme sense of the vastness and variety of human life ... which it belongs only to the greatest novels to produce."[24]

NOTES

1. "Middlemarch," in *Henry James: The Future of the Novel*, ed. Leon Edel (New York, 1956). See *ibid.*, pages 82, 85–86 for quotations from James's critique of *Middlemarch* in this paragraph and page 75 for the quotation from his critique of Dickens (originally published in *The Nation* in 1865).

2. *Henry James: The Conquest of London* (New York, 1962), II, 433–434. James's likeness or indebtedness to George Eliot is, as intimated in my chapter I, a prominent theme in F. R. Leavis's *The Great Tradition*. The most extended study of the relationship is the unpublished doctorate dissertation of Philip Leon Greene—"Henry James and George Eliot" (New York University, 1962). See also W. J. Harvey's brief but concentrated observations in *The Art of George Eliot* (London, 1963), pp. 19–24, *et passim*, and George Levine's important essay, "Isabel, Gwendolen, and Dorothea," *ELH*, XXX (1963), 244–257. Leon Edel in his introduction to the Riverside edition of *The Portrait of a Lady* (pp. xv–xvii—see below, note 6) protests against overemphasis on James's indebtedness in his portrait to George Eliot, and his brief itemization of fairy-tale and melodramatic aspects of the plot (p. ix)—"a rich uncle, a poor niece, an ugly sick cousin who worship her from a distance, three suitors, a fairy-godmother who converts the niece into an heiress, and finally her betrayal by a couple of her cosmopolite compatriots into a marriage as sinister as the backdrop of a Brontë novel"— suggests how widely divergent some features of Isabel's story are from Dorothea's.

3. Harvey, pp. 24–25.

4. "Gustave Flaubert," in *Henry James: The Future of the Novel*, p. 137. James had written the essay as a preface to an edition of *Madame Bovary* published in 1902.

5. *Ibid.*, p. 138.

6. James's notebook entry, given as an appendix in *The Portrait of a Lady*, ed. Leon Edel (Boston, 1956), p. 485. Quotations from the novel will hereafter be identified by chapter and page numbers of this edition supplied in parentheses.

7. Leavis, p. 97.

8. See especially Barbara Hardy's excellent chapter, "The Ironical Image," *The Novels of George Eliot* (New York, 1967), pp. 215–232.

9. *Middlemarch*, ed. Gordon S. Haight (Boston, 1956), "Prelude," p. 3, italics mine. Quotations from the novel will hereafter be identified by chapter and page number of this edition supplied in parentheses.

10. *Madame Bovary, Oeuvres complètes*, ed. Louis Conard, (1910; Paris, 1930), VIII, part I, chapter vi, page 49. Quotations from *Madame Bovary* will hereafter be identified by part, chapter, and page numbers of this edition supplied in parentheses. For my aims in translating from the French, see my Foreword.

11. For further interesting parallels between Dorothea and Isabel, see especially F. R. Leavis and George Levine as well as my chapter VI. See also Philip Leon Greene, "Henry James and George Eliot," diss. New York University, 1962, especially pages 143–167.

12. Haight's introduction to *Middlemarch*, p. xviii.

13. See, for example, ii.13; iv.26, 30; v.33; vii.48.

14. See especially ii.15; vii.49; xxx.211; xxxvii.270.

15. "Henry James and the Trapped Spectator," *Explorations* (1947; New York, 1964), p. 179.

16. Q. D. Leavis, "A Note on Literary Indebtedness: Dickens, George Eliot, Henry James," *Hudson Review*, VIII (1955), 423–428.

17. "Middlemarch," p. 88.

18. *The George Eliot Letters*, ed. Gordon S. Haight (New Haven, 1954–55), III, 284–285 (to John Blackwood, April 3, 1860).

19. Leavis, pp. 196 ff. For Will Ladislaw as an Orpheus who is too weak to sustain the considerable mythic overtones Eliot surrounds him with, so that they function as unintentional satire, see Harvey, pp. 186 ff. Harvey sees a part of Will's "dwindling down" as intentional on Eliot's part. "Yet when all is said and done, he remains a radically unsatisfactory character, the weakest thing in the novel, and Dorothea, in so far as she is involved with him, shares that weakness" (p. 195). Ian Milner, in *The Structure of Values in George Eliot* (Prague, 1968), pp. 81 ff., argues for the structural necessity of Dorothea's marriage to Will and inclines to see Will as a fancy portrait of George Henry Lewes.

20. *Letters*, V, 68–69.

21. Gordon Haight in *George Eliot: A Biography* (New York, 1968), pp. 301 ff., warns us that Eliot's concern for Comtean doctrine "has been greatly exaggerated." By 1867 (p. 390) Lewes himself was no longer a thoroughgoing disciple. On the other hand, the overtones of Comtean doctrine are pretty clearly audible in the passage just quoted.

22. "Middlemarch," p. 88.

23. *The Appropriate Form: An Essay on the Novel* (London, 1964), p. 199.

24. "Middlemarch," pp. 86–87.

V

FROM HETTY SORREL TO GWENDOLEN HARLETH: THE MIRROR AND THE FACE OF DEATH

HETTY SORREL, GWENDOLEN HARLETH, AND EMMA BOVARY ARE HERO-ines with more in common than is at once apparent. Hetty's "Journey in Despair" requires dealing with at some length, and Gwendolen's story will dominate this chapter. It may be well, however, to start with a larger view of the range of Eliot's novels.

i. FROM *Adam Bede* TO *Felix Holt*

Like Flaubert, George Eliot was loath to settle down in territory once she had explored it. *Adam Bede* (1859), Eliot's first full-length work of fiction, is a brilliantly achieved idyll of rural life, redolent of the author's fondest memories of the Midlands countryside. Her general good will toward her characters is a distinguishing mark of this excellent novel. Darker tones anticipating later elements in her writing are evident, it is true, in the remarkable Hetty Sorrel plot; yet it is notable that even here Eliot feels impelled to save Hetty with a last-minute reprieve. A golden haze dominates Eliot's landscape in *Adam Bede* and all save a memorable but relatively small portion of her episodes. Even her closing with an implausible marriage between Adam Bede and Dinah Morris, both in their quite separate ways idealizations of originals she had loved, though it is generally con-

187

sidered a flaw, is one in keeping with the tone of benevolent nostalgia that colors her canvas.

With *The Mill on the Floss* (1860), Eliot turns as the work progresses from simple idyll to searching realism, following with less benevolent distance the experience of a single character and moving toward a more somber reading of life. This is especially so in the late chapters and the finale. The richly symbolic (and richly ambiguous) scene in which Maggie Tulliver, together with her brother, drowns in the floods of the river that has played a unifying force in her experience throughout the tale presents more questions than it answers and continues a subject for lively debate among critics. In some respects, Maggie Tulliver is George Eliot's most ambitious exploration of the emotional life of any of her successive heroines. Marcel Proust was to wax enthusiastic over her portrayal of Maggie's early years[1] and one can see why this would be so; for a major part of the novel is occupied with Eliot's invoking, as her heroine's, her own bittersweet experience of childhood, a recapturing of times past with a greater clarity of backward vision than she had employed in *Adam Bede*. But Maggie Tulliver is a portrait in a markedly different manner from that Eliot was to adopt in her later years. In her quiet acceptance of adversity, Maggie is in fact closer to Mary Garth of *Middlemarch* than she is to Dorothea Brooke. She is not to a significant degree a study in romantic egoism. Like Frédéric Moreau of Flaubert's *Sentimental Education*, Maggie is characteristically acted upon by circumstance rather than interacting with it, a fact figuring strongly in the river imagery that plays so large a part in this tale. She has, indeed, her moments of challenge; but renunciation—sometimes enforced, more often sternly self-imposed—becomes the pattern of her life. For all its numerous excellences, despite its splendid delineation of English provincial life, *The Mill on the Floss* is for many readers a less than completely satisfying narrative. One can hardly quarrel with F. R. Leavis's judgment that Eliot's presentation of Maggie Tulliver's inner life, though indeed "done from the inside," is limited in effectiveness: "One's criticism is that it is done too purely from the inside. Maggie's emotional and spiritual stresses, her exaltations and renunciations, exhibit, naturally, all the marks of immaturity. . . . There is nothing against George Eliot's presenting this immaturity with tender sympathy; but we ask, and ought to ask, of a great novel something more."[2] The consummate playing of ironic counterpoint between inner vision and outer reality is not yet in Eliot's scope; and her personal involvement with her character here places her in significant contrast to Flaubert in *Madame Bovary* with his concept of "impersonality." She was not to develop her own method of ironic presentation for another dozen years.

With *Romola* (1863)[3] George Eliot turned from her own century to the Renaissance and from the English Midlands that she knew to the Florence of Savonarola and the Medicis that she had worked up by arduous research, amassing notes of a magnitude all but worthy of Casaubon. The virtues of Eliot's ambitious and heavily detailed historical novel have been much debated, but from nearly any perspective her portrayal of Tito Melema must be judged a memorable study in moral attrition and one of her major achievements. It is not, however, an ambitious study of Tito's inner reality; indeed, it is hard to believe that any very active life of the imagination goes on inside him. For Tito, though often viewed intimately, is viewed primarily from the outside. He is eminently a character whose desires are, like Bulstrode's, stronger than his moral impulses; but no theory of an austere Providence to bargain with impedes him. He is a clever and unscrupulous hedonist willing to exploit his closest friends and loved ones along with his enemies. The scene in which Tito declines to aid or recognize Baldassare among the prisoners being led past is a powerful one. Baldassare, his foster father, had been for him the kindest and most generous of fathers; by this single refusal to make a disagreeable choice Tito is cutting all his deepest ties to normal morality. But Tito's egoism is not romantic by nature, nor given to vivid internal drama. He sees an exterior reality only too graphically (even as, it is implied, a number of other intellectuals in Eliot's Florence are in the habit of seeing it) as a problem, uncomplicated by metaphysics, in getting the greatest good in terms of temporal power and the world's luxuries at the least expense in personal inconvenience. He is a memorable figure, worthy at least of the qualified praise Henry James allowed him[4] and second only to Gwendolen Harleth's husband Grandcourt in *Daniel Deronda* among George Eliot's villains, though mention of Grandcourt suggests what a great distance Eliot was still to travel in the power of portraying evil.

Romola herself fails of becoming one of Eliot's happiest creations.

Indeed, she represents a distinct falling away from Maggie Tulliver although she shares traits in common. There is in Romola, as W. J. Harvey observes, a crippling imbalance, with "too much of the sanctity and too little of the human."[5] The author has not yet learned to avoid the dangers inherent in idealizing her heroine's nature. Romola has Maggie Tulliver's penchant for "giving up" without the sort of ironic coloration Eliot was later to impart to that trait in Dorothea Brooke. There is no real intensity to Romola's inner life, despite all the progressive disillusions of marriage to Tito Melema— a subject Eliot might have found much more to her hand a few years later in her career.

It is curiously symptomatic of Eliot's problems with her heroines in the two early novels that in both *The Mill on the Floss* and *Romola* the young maiden reaches a critical turn in the narrative by simply letting the currents carry her in an open boat—and both the situation and its implications are a good deal richer in the earlier of the two. We learn enough of Maggie's nature to make it safe to say she would not have been content (as is Romola) to give her later years to helping tend the children of a deceased husband's mistress. To imagine Gwendolen Harleth settling down in the family of Mrs. Glasher is to conjure up a scene that invokes dramatically the many degrees by which George Eliot's art is to deepen and darken in the dozen years between *Romola* and *Daniel Deronda*.

In *Felix Holt* (1866), George Eliot creates a remarkable though briefly sketched portrait in romantic egoism. It is the scenes dealing specifically with Mrs. Transome that impel F. R. Leavis to designate this novel as the point at which Eliot "becomes one of the great creative artists."[6] Viewed as a whole, *Felix Holt* is not, however, a satisfying novel. Felix himself remains throughout a talkative abstraction, George Eliot's idealization of the working man who reads and thinks. Mrs. Transome is not the only romantic egoist in the plan of the novel. Esther Lyon, whom Felix by means of long perorations converts to his own way of thinking and ultimately the acceptance of his hand in marriage, is intended to be another. Like Emma Bovary (Esther is indeed half French by birth), Esther has self-destructive predilections for luxuries she cannot afford; but Esther's inner world is not presented with any real intensity. Eliot's heroine with her mild vices and antisocial habits of vision is all too obviously made to order.

She will, the reader soon realizes, have no deeply passionate moments in renouncing her temptations and becoming a convert to Felix.

In Mrs. Transome of Transome Court, on the other hand, we have George Eliot's first intensive study of romantic egoism (unless one counts Hetty Sorrel, with all her limitations) and one of her most memorable characters, though done in rapid fashion. Mrs. Transome has an arrogance of station that is stronger than Lydgate's and a dissatisfaction with her confined life nearly equal to Emma Bovary's. "She had the high-born imperious air which would have marked her as an object of hatred and reviling by a revolutionary mob. Her person was too typical of social distinctions to be passed by with indifference by any one; it would have fitted an empress." It was her destiny "to be defiant in desperate circumstances, and to feel a woman's hunger of the heart forever unsatisfied."[7] With her life confined by monotonous limits, she had turned for escape to romantic novels and poems. The sort of education allowed young women had proved quite inadequate for meeting the problems of her actual life (as it had done with Emma Bovary and was to do with Dorothea Brooke and with Rosamond Vincy and Gwendolen Harleth). Such knowledge and accomplishments as she had been taught became in time "as valueless as old-fashioned stucco-ornaments, of which the substance was never worth anything." Her life as she grew older became increasingly filled with anxieties compounded by her possession of an especially "hungry, much-exacting self" that did not suffer money cares gladly, or the disapproval of neighbors, or the grim awareness of advancing age. What remained as a satisfaction for her above all else was the exerting of power over others:

Mrs. Transome, whose imperious will had availed little to ward off the great evils of her life, found the opiate for her discontent in the exertion of her will about smaller things. She was not cruel, and could not enjoy thoroughly what she called the old woman's pleasure of tormenting; but she liked every little sign of power her lot had left her. She liked that a tenant should stand bareheaded below her as she sat on horseback. She liked to insist that work done without her orders should be undone from beginning to end. She liked to be courtesied and bowed to by all the congregation as she walked up to the little barn of a church. She liked to change a labourer's medicine fetched from the doctor, and substitute a prescription of her own. If she had only been more haggard or less majestic, those who had glimpses of her outward life might have said she was a tyrannical, griping harridan, with a tongue like a razor. No one said exactly that; but they never said anything like the full truth about her, or divined what was hidden under that outward life,—a woman's keen sensibility and dread, which lay screened behind all the petty habits and narrow notions, as some quivering thing with eyes and throbbing heart may lie crouching behind withered rubbish. (i.42–43)

Eliot supplies by far the greater part of Mrs. Transome's life only in brief retrospect. By the time of the action she is already an old woman, with her youthful period of illusion long past and the early pain of disillusion that came with confronting the hard facts of her outer reality also well behind her. In the "Introduction" that opens the novel, preceding the first chapter, we are told that, forty years earlier, as a handsome and spirited girl of high family but severely straitened means, she had chosen marriage to "as poor, half-witted a fellow as you'd wish to see" (a coachman is speaking) for his estate, and given birth to an eldest son who "had been just such another as his father, only worse,—a wild sort of half-natural, who got into bad company." Later we learn that her second son, born ten years after-ward, is the result of the humiliating sin of her life—a liaison with the lawyer of the estate, an undistinguished and vulgar-mannered man who still exerts influence over her because of the secret they share. The plot is essentially melodramatic. The elder son, feeble-minded and vicious, has died; the younger son, the result of the liaison with the lawyer Matthew Jermyn, eventually returns from the Near-East as the heir of the estate. Resembling his mother too well, he peremptorily takes away her power over the lives of her tenants— the one pleasure of her aging years. Events lead inevitably to the recognition scene in which Jermyn declares himself to Harold Tran-some as his real father and, following that, the resultant scene (pre-sented with a compressed force *not* suggesting melodrama) in which Harold confronts his mother with the secret of his birth:

She had taken off her walking-dress and wrapped herself in a soft dressing-gown. She was neither more nor less empty of joy than usual. But when she saw Harold, a dreadful certainty took possession of her. It was as if a long-expected letter, with a black seal, had come at last.

Harold's face told her what to fear the more decisively, because she had never before seen it express a man's deep agitation. Since the time of its pouting childhood and careless youth she had seen only the confident strength and good-humoured imperiousness of maturity. The last five hours had made a change as great as illness makes. Harold looked as if he had been wrestling, and had had some terrible blow. His eyes had that sunken look which, because it is unusual, seems to intensify expression. . . .

He looked still at his mother. She seemed as if age were striking her with a sudden wand,—as if her trembling face were getting haggard before him. She was mute. But her eyes had not fallen; they looked up in helpless misery at her son.

Her son turned away his eyes from her, and left her. In that moment Harold felt hard; he could show no pity. All the pride of his nature rebelled against his sonship. (xlvii.212–213)

Writing *Romola*, Walter Allen maintains, had made important new demands upon George Eliot's creative imagination; it had taken her out of her former dependence upon nostalgic memories of life in provincial England, so that when she returned to write of the Midlands in *Felix Holt* and then in *Middlemarch*, the scope of her artistic sympathy had been greatly extended.[8] Certainly in the six years between *The Mill on the Floss* and *Felix Holt* Eliot's power for handling character had greatly increased. Nevertheless F. R. Leavis seems to be overgenerous in finding in such scenes as the one just quoted evidence that Eliot has already reached the maturity of her powers.[9] *Middlemarch*, which was to come at the end of another six-year span, represents still another impressive advance over its predecessor in the portrayal of characters as seen from the inside.

It is in *Middlemarch*, as I have tried to show at length in chapter four, that Eliot discovers her full powers for dealing with the inward life of her characters. Above all, it is through her superb manipulation of tone in the voice of the narrator that she contrives to combine intimacy with clarity of vision, sympathy with ironic distancing. There is also, however, a fresh power in Eliot's way of managing frequent glimpses of the protagonist's exterior reality as it is mirrored, each time according to the particular concentric curvatures involved, in the minds of other members of the community—in her allowing us to view Dorothea Brooke's future husband, for example, as he is seen from the point of sight of Sir James Chettam or Mrs.

Cadwallader or Mr. Brooke ("He is pretty certain to be a bishop, is Casaubon. . . . —a deanery at least. They owe him a deanery" [vii.49]), or to see Dorothea herself as she is reflected in the assessing eye of the artist Naumann or in Rosamond Lydgate's angle of vision. In *Middlemarch* as in *Madame Bovary*, the pattern of illusion, the protagonist's special distortion of reality, becomes a major subject for fiction, and with Eliot's own equivalent for Flaubert's manner of "binocular vision." In *Middlemarch*, as W. J. Harvey says, Eliot's "steadiness and clarity of ironic contemplation" reaches full maturity.[10] It is characteristic of George Eliot, however, that after the splendid success of this novel with both the critics and the public, and in spite of her own obvious sense in the writing of it (despite periods of depression and self-doubt) of mastery in the handling of her narrative, she should in her last novel enter on fresh experiments in both her subject and her manner of treating it.

ii. EMMA, HETTY, GWENDOLEN, AND THE BANEFUL MIRROR

With *Daniel Deronda* (published in instalments during 1874–76 and as a completed novel in 1876), an abrupt shift takes place toward absorption with profounder shades of the malign than had penetrated Eliot's earlier novels. As Jerome Thale observes: "It is not just a darkening of the world—which had been somber enough even in *Adam Bede*—but a new and direct confrontation of certain kinds of evil, of perversity, hitherto unacknowledged."[11] The delightful counterpoint of inner vision with genre pictures of provincial life that gave special charm to *Middlemarch* has been discarded. The world of *Daniel Deronda* is predominantly, and especially in the Gwendolen Harleth part, the world of upper-class society. Daniel Deronda, like Felix Holt, remains an arbitrary creation, and the movement of the novel devoted to his interests fails of carrying real conviction. Gwendolen Harleth's inner life is less complex than that of the major characters in *Middlemarch*, but it is colored by exposure to depths in the nature of evil that have not entered into that novel. The Dark Universe that takes such dramatic forms in *Madame Bovary* is evident in *Middlemarch*, as we have seen, mainly in moments of acute awareness of isolation and frustration. When Dorothea feels her profoundest sense of alienation, her voice momentarily becomes like "a low cry from some suffering creature in the darkness" (lxxxi.582). The Gwendolen Harleth part of *Daniel Deronda* presents more overtly sinister enactments of the motif in correlatives nearer Flaubert's in their dramatic coloring.

It is notable that the theme plays a somewhat similar part in Eliot's first novel, *Adam Bede* (1859), published within two years of *Madame Bovary*. Passionate absorption in selfhood, passionate preoccupation with one's own image and identity (the identity so full of living reality in the private moment and so certain to end, from the larger perspective, in inescapable nothingness) is a major theme common to these three novels. Employing sentimental literature as her magic mirror, Emma Bovary studies her reflection in a succession of roles— seated at an Erard piano playing for admiring audiences, writing elegant poetry about a mother's grave, performing Lucia di Lammermoor in the operatic tenor Edgar Lagardy's tender embraces. Hetty Sorrel, less facile of imagination and without Emma's resources in literature, performs rites of self-adoration before an antique mirror with lighted candles, adorning herself in bits of cheap finery and pursuing fantasies of a life of wealth and luxury in the caresses of a faceless but aristocratic lover.[12] Gwendolen Harleth, like Hetty Sorrel, finds a fascination in the reflections of an actual mirror and, like Emma, projects her own identity into a series of roles drawn from literature. All three are so much absorbed in the dramas of their own personalities that the masculine personalities that figure in their lives remain enigmas and essentially unreal (except that in a limited sense Grandcourt ultimately becomes for Gwendolen the most terrible of realities), and it is significant that the children that figure in their respective situations remain for them unreal and unloved. Hetty Sorrel has no maternal fondness for the Poyser children she tends daily; Emma sees Berthe as an unattractive facsimile of Charles, no extension of her own beauty or personality; Gwendolen Harleth finds in her half-sisters little more than inconveniences and vexations that have to be tolerated. For all three, absorbed adoration of self leads to disastrous consequences in a sinister outer reality.

Hetty Sorrel and Gwendolen Harleth are the two characters in all of Eliot's novels who are made to confront most directly the chill sense of the emptiness lying outside the human world. Some critics, to be sure, have judged Hetty so constricted in moral life as hardly to

be considered to exist as a moral entity.[13] Barbara Hardy seems closer
to the mark when she treats Hetty and her fate as a generalized human action, a "tragedy of the little soul."[14] Hetty Sorrel in her time
of suffering is Everyman (or, to be more precise, Everywoman) and
though her narrow egoism and self-absorption are extreme, her acute
sense of alienation is in its implications universal. Eliot takes care, as
Hetty adjusts her earrings before the antique mirror, to underline
the larger meaning of Hetty's coming fate: ". . . it is too painful to
think that she is a woman, *with a woman's destiny before her,—a*
woman spinning in young ignorance a light web of folly and vain
hopes which may one day close round her and press upon her a
rancorous poisoned garment, changing all at once her fluttering,
trivial butterfly sensations into a life of deep human anguish."[15] Critics
have a habit of complaining—and with justice—against Eliot's austere
moralizing over this unfortunate girl. In part, Eliot's heavy-handed
presentation, however, comes from her own acute awareness of the
larger meaning of her scenes, her feeling more sharply than the reader,
especially in the earlier portions, the stark contrast between Hetty's
complacent fantasies before the mirror and the moment in which the
"shattering of all her little dream-world" must come, crushing her
"pleasure-craving nature with overpowering pain" (xxxi.340). The
scenes mean overdeeply to their creator as correlatives for her own
dark sense of cosmic eventualities, and she invests them as narrator
with more emotion than they can assimilate.

Knowledge that she is carrying Arthur Donnithorne's child brings
Hetty to thoughts of suicide. Earlier in her sheer animal beauty and
her indifference to the human interests of others, Hetty has often, as
Knoepflmacher observes, been "made to stand for all that is inhuman
in 'Nature.' "[16] Now "Nature" becomes awesomely alien, and Hetty
is painfully aware of her human vulnerability. "Her great dark eyes
wander blankly over the fields like the eyes of one who is desolate and
homeless, unloved . . ." (xxxv.372). She searches for a certain "dark
shrouded pool." Whether Eliot is conscious of her parallels to the
myth of Narcissus is an open question, but at least the place Hetty
seeks has powerfully symbolic suggestions of the dark, blotched
mirror in which she had formerly worshiped her image. "She sits
down on the grassy bank, against the stooping stem of the great oak
that hangs over the dark pool. She has thought of this pool often in

196

the nights of the month that has just gone by, and now at last she is come to see it. She clasps her hands round her knees and leans forward, and looks earnestly at it, as if trying to guess what sort of bed it would make for her young round limbs" (xxxv.372).

Life, even under humiliating conditions, still seems preferable to death, however, and Hetty undertakes her "Journey in Hope" (to quote Eliot's chapter heading) to find Arthur and confront him with his fatherhood. Learning at Windsor that his regiment has left for Ireland, Hetty enters on her "Journey in Despair," an aimless wandering, with further thoughts of ending her own life and that of her unborn baby by drowning. She searches half-unconsciously beneath a hostile sky for a pool where, sinking beneath the reflecting surface, she can escape from a life that has lost all its attractions. It is characteristic of Eliot's manner at the time of *Adam Bede* that she must make quite specific the import of her images. Hetty's face was by now "sadly different from that which had smiled at itself in the old specked glass or smiled at others when they glanced at it admiringly." Desperation has given it a "hard and even fierce look" and the eyes have lost their brightness. The pool she finally comes upon seems to possess traces of the sort of magic fascination the antique mirror had once held for her. It "was as if the thing were come in spite of herself, instead of being the object of her search. There it was, black under the darkening sky,—no motion, no sound near. . . . The pool had its wintry depth now . . ." (xxxvii.393). But though her hope in life is gone, Hetty is reluctant to face the moment of death. "There was no need to hurry,—there was all the night to drown herself in." She falls asleep and wakens chilled in deep night. "She was frightened at this darkness,—frightened at the long night before her." This night of Hetty's beside the dark pool, her mind alternating between impulses to end her misery and memories of simple joys—("The bright hearth and the warmth and the voices of home,—the secure uprising and lying down, . . . all the sweets of her young life")—constitutes perhaps the most memorable embodiment in all Eliot's novels of the human situation in a darkly impersonal cosmos. "The horror of this cold and darkness and solitude—out of all human reach—became greater every long minute; it was almost as if she were dead already, and knew that she was dead, and longed to get back to life again. But no: she was alive still; she had not taken the dreadful leap. She felt a strange contradictory wretchedness and exultation,—wretchedness, that she did not dare to face death; exultation, that she was still in life, that she might yet know light and warmth again" (xxxvii.394).

Groping her way in the dark fields to a sheepfold, Hetty gives way to "tears and sobs of hysterical joy that she had still hold of life, that she was still on the familiar earth, with the sheep near her. The very consciousness of her own limbs was a delight to her; she turned up her sleeves, and kissed her arms with the passionate love of life." A scene with the coming of morning stresses still further Hetty's isolation in her experience of suffering. Confronted in the doorway of the fold by a peasant who tends the sheep, Hetty feels a new depth of humiliation when he treats her like a beggar or madwoman. Hetty has by now, as Reva Stump observes, "taken on the appearance of a 'wild' woman outside the pale of even the lowest level of society" and "has become an alien even to an isolated shepherd."[17]

George Eliot leaves her detailed narrative of Hetty's "Journey in Despair" at this point. Much later, when Hetty in prison confides in Dinah Morris, we learn that after further aimless wandering and the birth of her baby Hetty had thought of drowning the child so that she could return once more to the Poyser family: "I couldn't bear being so lonely, and coming to beg for want. . . . I thought I'd find a pool, if I could, like that other, in the corner of the field, in the dark" (xlv.462–463). Failing to find such a pool, she had dug a shallow grave for the infant and left it in a wood, covered with grass and chips. At the last moment Hetty is saved from hanging for her crime by the melodramatic appearance of Arthur Donnithorne waving a pardon. The conclusion is much less memorable than the chapters that deal with Hetty's wanderings in despair. It is the journey that embodies with remarkable power the themes of isolation and the indifference of a darkened universe in this first extended narrative of Eliot's, published two years after *Madame Bovary*, in the year of Darwin's *Origin of Species*.

iii. GWENDOLEN HARLETH AND THE FACE OF DEATH

Self-worship, absorption with one's own identity, and the consequences of such idolatry in the world of outer circumstance is a theme that figures to a greater or lesser extent in every one of Eliot's novels;

but it is in the first and the last that it is treated most directly and dramatized with special prominence. Though Gwendolen Harleth of *Daniel Deronda* is a more intricate personality than Hetty Sorrel of *Adam Bede*, and far more active of imagination, parallels between the two in situation and in habits of thought go deeper than the many contrasts between the two young women would suggest. Self-adoration is if anything stronger in Gwendolen than in Hetty; and in a scene not unlike Hetty's before the antique mirror we have the impression underlined:

[Gwendolen] had a naïve delight in her fortunate self, which any but the harshest saintliness will have some indulgence for in a girl who had every day seen a pleasant reflection of that self in her friends' flattery as well as in the looking-glass. And even in this beginning of troubles, while for lack of anything else to do she sat gazing at her image in the growing light, her face gathered a complacency gradual as the cheerfulness of the morning. Her beautiful lips curled into a more and more decided smile, till at last she took off her hat, leaned forward and kissed the cold glass which had looked so warm.[18]

The consultation of mirrors becomes a recurrent symbol for Gwendolen's extreme absorption with self. Later in the novel, trying to assess realistically her chances for coping with her family's financial troubles, she is drawn automatically toward her mirror: "Then catching the reflection of her movements in the glass panel, she was diverted to the contemplation of the image there and walked toward it. . . . Seeing her image slowly advancing, she thought, 'I *am* beautiful'—not exultingly, but with grave decision" (xxiii.187). The mirror is, like Hetty's antique glass, conveying a delusive sense of powers over circumstance and flattering Gwendolen with false hopes, as she is soon to learn from Herr Klesmer. For Gwendolen confuses her gifts in physical beauty with potentialities for a career in singing or in acting. Herr Klesmer, himself a musician who has won his way to prominence by prolonged years of arduous dedication, will soon send such hopes crashing to ground. Hetty has played roles before her mirror in an uncomplicated way, but with Gwendolen the themes of self-adoration and role-playing become intricately and profoundly intermingled. The first notion that Gwendolen seizes upon when with her mother and sisters she enters the house they are to inhabit for

199

some time is the fresh opportunity for assuming a flattering role (with her weak and overindulgent mother serving as so frequently for her audience): " 'Here is an organ. I will be Saint Cecilia: some one shall paint me as Saint Cecilia. Jocosa (this was her name for Miss Merry [the governess]), let down my hair. See, mamma!' " Eliot makes it plain in the context, as one critic has remarked, that "other activities might be rather more to the purpose on entering a new house."[19] The notion of her beauty as Saint Cecilia is still much in Gwendolen's mind when later she and her mother enter for the first time the room they are to share and she promises to help unpack:

> But her first movement was to go to the tall mirror between the windows, which reflected herself and the room completely, while her mamma sat down and also looked at the reflection. 'That is a becoming glass, Gwendolen; or is it the black and gold colour that sets you off?' said Mrs. Davilow, as Gwendolen stood obliquely with her three-quarter face turned towards the mirror, and her left hand brushing back the stream of hair.
>
> 'I should make a tolerable Saint Cecilia with some white roses on my head,' said Gwendolen,—'only, how about my nose, mamma? I think saints' noses never in the least turn up. I wish you had given me your perfectly straight nose; it would have done for any sort of character . . . .'
> (iii.17)

Though Gwendolen complains charmingly that her nose with its upward tilt would limit her possibilities for acting ("Mine is only a happy nose; it would not do so well for tragedy"), sinister tones have already, in the first chapters of the novel, entered into Eliot's portrayal. The "healthy young lady" who possesses the delightful countenance and who declares she is determined to be happy despite some tendency of other people to interfere with her (iii.18), a remark that wounds her mother, has demonstrated an unusual capacity for terror only a short time earlier during the initial exploration of the downstairs rooms. Her small half-sister had opened a hinged panel in the wainscoting and exclaimed with surprise at the picture revealed behind it.

> Every one, Gwendolen first, went to look. The opened panel had disclosed the picture of *an upturned dead face, from which an obscure*

figure seemed to be fleeing with outstretched arms. 'How horrible!' said Mrs. Davilow, with a look of mere disgust; *but Gwendolen shuddered silently,* and Isabel, a plain and altogether inconvenient child with an alarming memory, said—

'*You will never stay in this room by yourself, Gwendolen.*'

'*How dare you open things which were meant to be shut up,* you perverse little creature?' said Gwendolen, in her angriest tone. Then snatching the panel out of the hand of the culprit, she closed it hastily, saying, '*There is a lock—where is the key?* Let the key be found, or else let one be made, and *let nobody open it again*; or, rather, let the key be brought to me.' (iii.16, italics mine)

Certain moments of sinister awareness and certain unpleasant memories Gwendolen also attempts to keep locked behind the wainscoting. Though never of a deliberately cruel nature, she holds "a disagreeable silent remembrance of her having strangled her sister's canary-bird in a final fit of exasperation at its shrill singing *which had again and again interrupted her own*" (iii.15, italics mine). She remembered at times also with "some filial compunction" the night when her mother, in pain, had asked her to fetch a bottle of pain-alleviating medicine, only to have the request refused with a grumble by the "healthy young lady, snug and warm as a rosy infant in her little couch" who preferred not to expose herself to the cold. As with Eliot's less complex treatment of Hetty Sorrel, cosmic implications are not far below the surface of homely details; for Gwendolen is susceptible to "fits of spiritual dread"—"occasional experiences, which seemed like a brief remembered madness, an unexplained exception from her normal life" (vi.44). Sudden frights could afflict her when with an abrupt sense of alienation, as when walking without a companion, she would observe "some rapid change in the light. Solitude in any wide scene impressed her with an undefined feeling of immeasurable existence aloof from her, in the midst of which she was helplessly incapable of asserting herself." Eliot enters upon the novel with an inscription (probably of her own making) as motto, in which man's brief moment in Time is contrasted with the infinite nature of sidereal time, an expanse so incalculable that Science itself though dividing its unit into billions, must set an arbitrary beginning where even a billionth part of that "all-presupposing fact" must lie outside human calculation. As for Gwendolen, the "little astronomy taught her at school

201

used sometimes to set her imagination at work in a way that made her tremble: but always when some one joined her *she recovered her indifference to the vastness in which she seemed an exile*; she found again *her usual world in which her will was of some avail . . ."* (vi.45, italics mine).

A memorable seizure of terror, involving once more the picture of the dead face and fleeing figure, strikes Gwendolen while she is following in larger terms than usual her passion for acting her own beauty in roles calculated to reflect it flatteringly in the admiration of others. She has been the dominant force in planning an evening's entertainment for an audience drawn from neighboring estates, and she has cleverly arranged matters so that the central focus of the evening will be upon her appearance in a tableau as Hermione of *A Winter's Tale.*

> Herr Klesmer, who had been good-natured enough to seat himself at the piano, struck a thunderous chord—but in the same instant, and before Hermione had put forth her foot, the movable panel, which was on a line with the piano, flew open on the right opposite the stage and *disclosed the picture of the dead face and the fleeing figure, brought out in pale definiteness* by the position of the wax-lights. Every one was startled, but all eyes in the act of turning towards the opened panel were recalled by a piercing cry from Gwendolen, who stood without change of attitude, but with *a change of expression that was terrifying in its terror. She looked like a statue into which a soul of Fear had entered*: her pallid lips were parted; her eyes, usually narrowed under their long lashes, were dilated and fixed. (vi.42, italics mine)

Eliot devotes a considerable amount of care to making this sudden appearance of the dark picture in Gwendolen's line of vision at the critical moment seem plausible: The small half-sister who had originally uncovered the painting in Gwendolen's presence had been unable to deny her curiosity, we are told, and had purloined the key for a second look only to be frightened away before she could relock the panel. The heavy chord that Herr Klesmer had struck on the piano had been enough to jar the panel loose at the precise instant of Hermione's stepping from her pedestal (a moment Gwendolen had "counted on as a means of showing her pretty foot and instep"). There is nothing comparable to this scene, bordering on melodrama in its bizarre contrasts, in all of *Middlemarch*—even Raffles' death is presented by means of a succession of less sensational incidents. But Eliot is much concerned with epitomizing at this early stage in her novel the divided character of Gwendolen's experience—her habitual brilliant, complacent enjoyment of her own extreme beauty on the one hand, and the ominous undercurrent already on rare but memorable occasions breaking the surface—an undercurrent of prophetic fear that the universe will refuse to shape itself to her desires, will not allow her to act the destiny she intends. Barbara Bodichon had seen in Dorothea Brooke, even in the early chapters of *Middlemarch*, "a child dancing into a quick sand on a sunny morning" and felt with "a sort of horror" being a witness to the process as if it were all going on before her at the moment.[20] In the Gwendolen Harleth part of *Daniel Deronda*, Eliot has portrayed the twofold nature of the child herself in far darker colors and made both the dancing progress and the composition of the perilous sands in which she must struggle for survival part of a morality play with "horror" taking a decidedly more prominent part in the script. Dorothea Brooke's maladjustments in marriage involve moments of bleak introspection and alarm at the frustrations of her own best intentions; Gwendolen's "swift travel from her bright rash girlhood into [an] agony of remorse" (lvi.522) is to involve horrifying fantasies of murdering her husband: " 'And I fought against them—I was terrified at them—*I saw his dead face*'—here her voice sank almost to a whisper close to Deronda's ear—*'ever so long ago I saw it*; and I wished him to be dead. And yet it terrified me. *I was like two creatures*. I could not speak—I wanted to kill—it was as strong as thirst—and then directly—I felt beforehand I had done something dreadful, unalterable—that would make me like an evil spirit' " (lvi.520, italics mine).

It is the pronouncedly dual nature of Gwendolen, with emphasis on the darker part, that Deronda (in the opening paragraph of the novel) sees on first viewing her at a continental gambling salon, long before she chooses him as her father confessor. Gwendolen is, characteristically, absorbed in acting herself in a flattering role: "She had begun to believe in her luck, others had begun to believe in it; she had visions of being followed by a *cortège* who would worship her as a goddess of luck and watch her play as a directing augury." And when her luck at the table turns bad, she is unwilling to give up her hold on her audience: "Since she was not winning strikingly, the next best thing was to lose strikingly. She controlled her muscles, and showed no tremor of mouth or hands. Each time her stake was swept off she doubled it." A sense of an active element of evil in Gwendolen's arresting beauty impresses onlookers other than Deronda. Her unusual sea-green robes and silver ornaments cause one man to call her a "striking girl," and his male companion replies, " 'Yes; she has got herself up as a sort of serpent now, all green and silver, and winds her neck about a little more than usual.' " The first speaks a moment later of her "*ensemble du serpent*" but then adds that hers is "a sort of Lamia beauty." Considering the part Gwendolen is to play in the novel, it is a prescient remark, for the mythological lamia is a creature divided against itself—with the body of a serpent and the head of a woman. Eliot fortifies the image a few paragraphs later. Gwendolen's robes when she walks fall in "gentle curves attractive to all eyes except those which discerned in them too close a resemblance to the serpent, and objected to the revival of serpent-worship." Both the image and the idea behind it Eliot is intent on keeping alive in the reader's mind. Gwendolen's cousin Rex, Eliot assures us a few chapters later, had in his handsome face "nothing corresponding to the undefinable stinging quality—as it were a trace of demon ancestry—which made some beholders hesitate in their admiration of Gwendolen" (vii.48). Yet, Eliot continues, part of the goodness that Rex was sure existed unalloyed in his beautiful cousin was not a mere young lover's hallucination. Goodness "is a large, often a prospective word; like harvest, which at one stage when we talk of it lies all underground, with an indeterminate future . . . ." The ensuing pages do not suggest, however, that Gwendolen is growing in the direction of goodness. She rides roughshod over the sensitivities of this twenty-year-old cousin, accepting his adoration merely as a convenient relief from boredom and rebuffing his proposal, when it comes, with an abrupt rudeness touching ferocity. "I shall never love anybody," Gwendolen afterward sobs to her mother. "I can't love people. I hate them" (vii.59).

Like Hetty Sorrel at her antique glass and like Emma Bovary in her early imaginary romance with the Viscount of Vaubyessard, Gwendolen prefers reveries that, reflecting her own identity heightened in coloring in the center of the mirror, leave the hero relatively faceless. Gwendolen's "thoughts never dwelt on marriage as the ful-filment of her ambition; the dramas in which she imagined herself a heroine were not wrought up to that close." For "this delicate-limbed sylph of twenty meant to lead. . . . She meant to do what was pleasant to herself in a striking manner; or rather, whatever she could do so as to strike others with admiration and get in that reflected way a more ardent sense of living, seemed pleasant to her fancy." Meantime her dominance over her mother and her half-sisters is almost absolute. She was their "princess in exile, who in time of famine was to have her breakfast-roll made of the finest-bolted flour from the seven thin ears of wheat, and in a general decampment was to have her silver fork kept out of the baggage." She was one of those persons who claim without question their right to rule those surrounding them, Eliot tells us, all of whom have possessed in common "a strong de-termination to have what was pleasant, with a total fearlessness in making themselves disagreeable or dangerous when they did not get it" (iv.26–28).

A major movement of the novel, however, concerns what happens when two such natures, each fully intent on having his unimpeded way at the cost of others, come into conflict. Though Gwendolen feels she cannot love people, she is aware that "she could not look forward to a single life" (iv.26), social pressures and the meager opportunities of women being constituted against such a future. She is, indeed, open to the attractions in wealth and distinction promised by a brilliant marriage. Henleigh Grandcourt seems to those about her to offer such a chance, and Gwendolen herself finds in him a pleasant contrast to her cousin Rex. For Grandcourt pursues courtship with the apparent coolness and detachment that characterize his dancing: "No man could have walked through the quadrille with more irreproachable ease than Grandcourt; and the absence of all eagerness in his attention to her suited his partner's taste." The war of wills between these two destined for marriage has already begun: "She was now convinced that he meant to distinguish her, to mark his admiration of her in a noticeable way; and it began to appear probable that she would have it in her power to reject him, whence there was a pleasure in reckon-ing up the advantages which would make her rejection splendid, and in giving Mr. Grandcourt his utmost value" (xi.87). But she con-siders acceptance rather than rejection of him an alternate possibility.

He is "the most aristocratic man she had ever seen"; and the coldness of his manners is in her eyes an important part of his distinction. Despite her own passion for acting roles, Gwendolen entertains no suspicion that Grandcourt may be himself performing a personality that is only superficially related to his own. The central question about him is for her "how far his character and ways might answer her wishes; and unless she were satisfied about that, she had said to herself that she would not accept his offer" (xi.89).

A few pages later the reader is given a clearer view of Grandcourt than any Gwendolen will have before the terrible revelations following their marriage. Grandcourt's pleasure, while he leisurely takes his coffee and cigar, in witnessing the jealous suffering of his spaniel bitch suggests habits of sadism that will figure in larger events later. Petting a tiny Maltese rival, Grandcourt watches in leisurely amusement the anguish of the spaniel until it suits him better to have the bellowing animal thrown out. He treats Lush, his confidant and informal secretary, with only somewhat more consideration than he shows for his spaniel. His want of respect for Lush, Eliot tells us, had been absolute from the beginning of their companionship fifteen years earlier; but habit had "confirmed his sense that he might kick Lush if he chose—only he never did choose to kick any animal, because the act of kicking is a compromising attitude, and a gentleman's dogs should be kicked *for* him. He only said things which might have exposed himself to be kicked if his confidant had been a man of independent spirit" (xii.93). The amalgam suggested of arrogance, venom, cold sloth, and mental violence ("for Grandcourt is before all things brutal," Constantius says in James's review[21]) is a fair sample of the man Gwendolen is to marry.

The initial period of courtship, however, comes to an abrupt end. Confronted by Grandcourt's former mistress, who still expects marriage of him and the legitimizing of their four children, Gwendolen experiences a spasm of fear with a more direct relation to her life than those that had beset her in the past; ". . . it was as if some ghastly vision had come to her in a dream and said, 'I am a woman's life.' " "Gwendolen's uncontrolled reading," Eliot remarks a few paragraphs later, "though consisting chiefly in what are called pictures of life, had somehow not prepared her for this encounter with reality" (xiv.114). In the chronology of the action (as opposed to its place in the narrative structure) the opening scene of the novel, in which Gwendolen gambles at the Leubronn casino, having fled from Grandcourt's imminent proposal of marriage, occurs at this juncture. Brought back to England by the family's loss of all finances, Gwendolen is forced to weigh her stakes and chances for a more desperate wager. The only alternative to taking a place as a governess—a humiliation all but unthinkable to her imperious nature—is to consent to Grandcourt's resumption of his courtship in the face of her knowledge of his dingy history and her belief, heavy on her conscience, that she will deprive Grandcourt's children by Lydia Glasher of their birthright.

Gwendolen's hopes for a third choice founded on her talent for acting have been deflated once and for all by the redoubtable Herr Klesmer—almost certainly a character drawn from Eliot's earlier acquaintance with the pianist-composer Anton Rubinstein[22]—who renders it clear that her notions of a professional career "have no more resemblance to reality than a pantomime" (xxiii.192). Klesmer's words force Gwendolen to a moment of depressing insight into her situation viewed outside her habitual tightly ego-centered vision. "You have exercised your talents—you recite—you sing—from the drawing-room *standpunkt*." Before the interview with Klesmer she had found grave assurance of her beauty and her chances for success in the theater by consulting her mirror. Now all things, including the "very reflection of herself in the glass," had become "no better than the packed-up shows of a departing fair."

The prospect of wronging Mrs. Glasher and her children makes the encouraging of Grandcourt's renewal of his suit painful; for despite her serpentine tendencies, Eliot assures us, Gwendolen shrank with "mingled pride and terror" from deliberate harm to others. Moreover her feeling of repulsion at being "expected to unite herself with an outworn life, full of backward secrets" is also acute. The stages of her coming to accept Grandcourt have much to do with his skill at performing in the role of suitor a part that fitted his coldness of nature but revealed to her nothing whatever of its pleasure in brutality. She experienced no sense of panic at awareness of "a silent man seated at an agreeable distance, with the subtlest atmosphere of attar of roses and an attention bent wholly on her" (xxvii.222). Though night terrors from thoughts of Mrs. Glasher occasionally possess her, the terrors of poverty are still stronger in her consciousness. Grandcourt improves his position by openly showing his pleasure when Gwendolen assumes the role of princess. A little play in which Grandcourt willingly takes the identity of ready and unquestioning servitor becomes the accepted mode of the courtship. "The scene was pleasant on both sides. A cruder lover would have lost the view of her pretty ways and attitudes, and spoiled all by stupid attempts at caresses, utterly destructive of drama. Grandcourt preferred the drama; and Gwendolen, left at ease, found her spirits rising continually as she played at reigning. Perhaps if Klesmer had seen more of her in this unconscious kind of acting, instead of when she was trying to be theatrical, he might have rated her chance higher." Mistaking the playing at command for the reality of command itself can be, however, an irretrievable error. She was already "*thinking of him, whatever he might be,* as a man over whom she was going to have indefinite power; and her loving him having never been a question with her, any agreeableness he had was so much gain" (xxviii.233, italics mine).

The dread fact beneath his ready acquiescence to playing servitor in their mutual drama is that Grandcourt is already relishing a masterdom over her—a pleasure not unlike his pleasure in the amusing anguish of his bellowing spaniel or his daily abasement of Lush. He is fully aware that Gwendolen, in the very moment of their play-acting at affection, feels not the slightest attraction toward him but is driven to the game by her family's poverty. "From the very first there had been an exasperating fascination in the tricksiness with which she had—not met his advances, but—wheeled away from them. She had been brought to accept him in spite of everything—brought to kneel down like a horse under training for the arena, though she might have an objection to it all the while. . . . He meant to be master of a woman who would have liked to master him, and who perhaps would have been capable of mastering another man" (xxviii.237).

The recurrent imagery of horsemanship in *Daniel Deronda* sets up ironies of its own. Gwendolen during the early days of his courting had seen in the apparently unassertive Grandcourt a nearly flawless chance for power. She had "wished to mount the chariot and drive the plunging horses herself, with a spouse by her side who would fold his arms and give her his countenance without looking ridiculous" (xiii.99–100). But Gwendolen's image of mastering horses, as Barbara Hardy observes, "turns into Grandcourt's vision of her as a mastered horse."[23] A scene near the outset of Gwendolen's wedded life sets the tone for much that is to follow. She had gone through the wedding itself in a show of buoyant recklessness pointedly phrased to remind the reader of her performance at the gaming tables of Leubronn—with Gwendolen "standing at the game of life" as she had stood at the roulette table, "with many eyes upon her, daring everything to win much—or if to lose, still with *éclat* and a sense of importance"; and following the wedding she had gaily informed her mother that she would now have everything for merely beckoning— "enjoying everything gloriously—splendid houses—and horses—and diamonds, I shall have diamonds . . . ." But a few hours later at the Grandcourt estate she receives a box from Lydia Glasher containing the Grandcourt family diamonds and a carefully worded curse for the new bride. It is enough to throw Gwendolen into a more violent spasm of terror than she had ever experienced. As so often earlier in the novel, reflections of mirrors figure in her fresh moment of crisis. On entering her new boudoir she had studied her image in one of several glass panels in the room. With the reading of Mrs. Glasher's note, she "could not see the reflections of herself" now giving back her image as so many identical women, all of them afflicted with tremors of their lips and hands, their faces "petrified white." It is a fantastic detail—as if the many identities Gwendolen has formerly played at being have reappeared as so many ghostly simulacra to assist at the visitation of a terribly excessive vengeance upon her. The entrance of Grandcourt into the room "brought a new nervous shock, and Gwendolen screamed again and again with hysterical violence. . . . He saw her pallid, shrieking as it seemed with terror, the jewels scattered around her on the floor" (xxxi.268).

How far Gwendolen's spasm of terror is induced simply by Lydia Glasher's note invoking disaster for her marriage or how far the note is rather a culminating spark for igniting the accumulation of shadowy moments of terror, both the conscious and the unacknowledged, that have been building in Gwendolen in the weeks preceding the marriage it is hard to say. The first weeks of married life, in any event, soon obliterate her belief in her power to dominate. The "beautiful, healthy young creature . . . no longer felt inclined to kiss her fortunate image in the glass." The man who had obligingly played her servitor in courtship has turned instead into an enigmatic force best imaged as a form of lower animal life—as a torpedo (an electric eel) with its power of paralyzing its victim,[24] or as a species given to destroying its prey by unhurried constriction. "Already, in seven short weeks, which seemed half her life, her husband had gained a mastery which she could no more resist than she could have resisted the benumbing effect from the touch of a torpedo. Gwendolen's will had seemed imperious in its small girlish sway; but it was the will of a creature with a large discourse of imaginative fears: a shadow would have been enough to relax its hold. And she had found a will like that of a crab or a boa-constrictor which goes on pinching or crushing without alarm at thunder" (xxxv.317). Grandcourt displays great ingenuity in finding her vulnerabilities and making the most of them for rendering her "proud and rebellious spirit dumb and helpless before him." He is proficient in playing in its most pronounced forms the drama of incommunicability. Grandcourt had become to her "a blank uncertainty . . . in everything but this, that he would do just what he willed, and that she had neither devices at her command to determine his will, nor any rational means of escaping it." Gwendolen, who had formerly felt a terror of space in observing stars with their implications of illimitable aloofness, now finds in marriage a nearer and more frightening embodiment of a universe oppressing her with sensations of helplessness and isolation.

What Grandcourt himself is not aware of, however, is that Gwendolen is rebelling far more fiercely under his domination than he could find it possible to believe. The prevalence of evil, so much stronger in *Daniel Deronda* than in any of Eliot's previous novels, is at work not only in her sadistic husband but in Gwendolen herself. The lamia or serpent aspect of Gwendolen, sensed by the gentlemen at the Leubronn casino and suggested earlier in her history by such domestic details as her strangling her sister's canary and her refusal to leave her warm bed to fetch her mother's pain-relieving medicine, is now driven into feverish activity.[25] She must struggle with a growing fantasy of murdering her husband. The two major plots of the novel link when Gwendolen asks the grave young Daniel Deronda to serve as her father confessor. She has need of one, for though a "root of conscience" remains alive in her, her fantasies become increasingly vivid, linking themselves to the dark painting behind the panel that had once sent her into a paralysis of fear. The vision that she dreaded "took more decidedly than ever the form of some fiercely impulsive deed, committed as in a dream that she would instantaneously wake from to find the effects real though the images had been false: to find death under her hands, but instead of darkness, daylight; instead of satisfied hatred, the dismay of guilt; instead of freedom, the palsy of a new terror—*a white dead face from which she was for ever trying to flee* and for ever held back" (liv.507, italics mine).

In *Middlemarch* Eliot had made it her concern and pride to work with gradual causes, presenting the lives of characters falling within the realm of the normal, offering their experiences with strong implications and occasional statements of their representativeness. In the Gwendolen-Grandcourt plot of *Daniel Deronda*, and especially in the later chapters, Eliot undertakes a narrative of a different sort— dealing with the pronouncedly abnormal, often with language to suit: It is a "white-lipped, fierce-eyed temptation with murdering fingers" that obsesses Gwendolen in demon-visits (liv.507). When the incident of Grandcourt's drowning comes, it is apparently no act of Gwendolen's that is responsible. In her deeply disturbed mind, however, she has already projected such an event with a terrible concentration: "She was not afraid of any outward dangers—she was afraid of her own wishes, which were taking shapes possible and impossible, like a cloud of demon-faces. She was afraid of her own hatred, which under the cold iron touch that had compelled her to-day had gathered a fierce intensity. . . . She clung to the thought of Deronda . . . . And yet quick, quick, came images, plans of evil that would come again and seize her in the night, like furies preparing the deed that they would straightway avenge" (liv.513).

The actual death of Grandcourt occurs under conditions that convince her she has played a part in it. Falling from his yacht, he had suffered a cramp in the water and cried to her to throw him a rope.

'I saw him sink, and my heart gave a leap as if it were going out of me. I think I did not move. I kept my hands tight. It was long enough for me to be glad, and yet to think it was no use—he could come up again. And he *was* come—farther off—the boat had moved. It was all like lightning. . . . But he was gone down again, and I had the rope in my hand, no, there he was again—his face above the water—and he cried again—and I held my hand, and my heart said, "Die!"—and he sank;

and I felt "It is done—I am wicked, I am lost!"—And I had the rope in my hand—I don't know what I thought—I was leaping away from myself—I would have saved him then. I was leaping from my crime, and there it was—close to me as I fell—there was the dead face—dead, dead. It can never be altered. That was what happened. That was what I did. You know it all. It can never be altered.' (lvi.524)

This is, to repeat, a long distance from the sort of human experience Eliot had chosen for exploring in the quieter life of the town of Middlemarch. Daniel Deronda sees a representative moral to be drawn from Gwendolen's murderous impulses—"Within ourselves our evil will is momentous and sooner or later it works its way outside us"— but it is a most unrepresentative reader who will find himself struggling with so virulent a demon as Gwendolen discovers in her nature or be exposed to such extreme and colorful alternatives as she is driven to consider. Any outline such as I have given here of the conflict of illusion and reality in Gwendolen's experience—of the shattering of her illusions of special destiny and right to happiness upon the terrible realities of her marriage—gives a very imperfect idea of the subtlety and power with which Eliot develops the Gwendolen-Grandcourt part of *Daniel Deronda*. Richard Holt Hutton writing in *The Spectator* when the novel first appeared suggests perhaps more of Eliot's intended scope and meaning for Gwendolen's story in a single expansive Victorian sentence:

> The struggle between evil and good for Gwendolen, her fear of the loneliness and vastness of the universe over which she can exert no influence, and the selfish plunge which she makes, against all her instincts of right and purity, into a marriage in which she fancies she can get her own way, only to find that she has riveted on herself the grasp of an evil nature which she cannot influence at all, though every day makes her fear and hate that nature more; the counteracting influence for good which Deronda gains with her by venturing,—as a mere stranger,—to warn her and help her against her gambling caprice, and thus identifying himself in her mind with those agencies of the universe beyond the control of her will which 'make for righteousness,' to use Mr. Arnold's phrase; and lastly, that disposal of events which always brings her within reach of Deronda's influence when she most needs it, till good has gained the victory in her, and that influence, too, is withdrawn, to make room for a more spiritual guidance,—all this is told with a power

and a confidence in the overshadowing of human lives by a higher control which is of the essence of the art of the story, and essentially religious.[26]

It must be added, however, that the Gwendolen Harleth plot is "essentially religious" only in a very unorthodox way that does not allow for an assumption of personality in the universe outside the human—any idea of a deity whom Gwendolen can at the end look to for help in her "fear of the loneliness and vastness of the universe over which she can exert no influence." Deronda offers her only the possibility of conquering the terrors bred by her own egoism. His advice is general and undoctrinaire. His own preoccupation with the Zionist movement and his love for Mirah, a girl notably in contrast to Gwendolen in gifts and temperament, keep him from any close relationship to Gwendolen after the death of Grandcourt. Even toward the close of the novel—for all the cataclysmic shocks she has undergone since in the opening chapter she had kissed her image in the mirror with so much complacency—Gwendolen is still absorbed with seeing life in markedly narrow patterns centering in herself. Daniel's revelations about his own new dedication to the Zionist movement serve for the moment to jar her into contemplating with some discomfort a larger view: ". . . she was for the first time feeling the pressure of a vast mysterious movement, for the first time being dislodged from her supremacy in her own world, and getting a sense that her horizon was but a dipping onward of an existence with which her own was revolving" (lxix, 607). But the sensation is quite novel for her: "All the troubles of her wifehood and widowhood had still left her with the implicit impression which had accompanied her from childhood, that whatever surrounded her was somehow specially for her . . . ." It is, to be sure, a good omen that in the last few pages of the book, while her sense of personal disaster still all but overwhelms her, even though she "fell continuously into fits of shrieking," she can assure her mother, "Don't be unhappy. I shall live. I shall be better" (lxix.609).

The story of Gwendolen Harleth contains Eliot's most ambitious rendering of her own deeply disturbed consciousness of inhabiting two worlds—the personal world of human light and warmth and the expansive outer universe in whose blank nothingness the human sphere must eventually be engulfed and canceled. Gwendolen's terror of stars and open space is with her long before her first encounter with Grandcourt. The picture of the dead face and fleeing figure had already spoken dread meanings to her. An unexpected sight of it, a sudden revelation in the midst of an especially self-admiring moment, acting her own youth and beauty before the waxlights for an appreciative audience, transforms her into a pallid "statue into which a soul of Fear had entered." Later the dead face haunts her fevered visions as the face of Grandcourt in the act of dying, and the fleeing figure becomes her own in frantic efforts to escape its special destiny. Her fantasies culminate in the actual sight of Grandcourt's features in the moment of his drowning (he is an excellent swimmer but he has been seized by cramp on this worst of occasions). Eliot's grotesque allegory of dead face and fleeing figure is her closest approach to the sort of "madness" Flaubert achieves in Emma's death scene. It is her starkest (and least plausible, least convincingly woven into the texture of her story) allegory of human life and darkened universe since the appearance of "The Lifted Veil" in the year of Darwin's *Origin of Species* and Hetty Sorrel's "Journey in Despair." The face of death was apparently more prominent than usual in Eliot's personal thoughts during the period of writing *Daniel Deronda*. She suffered acutely from bodily infirmities and was racked by the pain of kidney stone.[27] "Death is the only physician," she wrote Barbara Bodichon in a moment of despondent confiding shortly after completing the novel, "the shadow of his valley the only journeying that will cure us of age and the gathering fatigue of years."[28]

Grandcourt is a more effective embodiment of the darker side of reality than the gruesome painting behind the locked panel that anticipates his advent and blends with him in Gwendolen's fantasies. George Eliot's power in enacting the stages of the relationship, the compelling "specificity" of her treatment and the special dramatic quality of her best scenes are brilliantly analyzed by F. R. Leavis in *The Great Tradition*. The impact of Grandcourt as the prince of darkness owes its great force to the fact that he is so convincingly, so concretely, presented as a type of ordinary human brutality. James as "Constantius" was to describe him admiringly in an ambitious review of *Daniel Deronda* (to be treated at some length in the next chapter) as "a consummate picture of English brutality refined and distilled," a "consummate representation of the most detestable kind of Englishman—the Englishman who thinks it low to articulate," a portrayal in whom "the type and the individual" were splendidly combined. Eliot had created a convincing villain of such unspectacular materials that he could be called, for all his evil force, the "apotheosis of dryness."[29]

The powerful hold that Grandcourt exerts over Gwendolen derives its strength, as F. R. Leavis has pointed out, from her "moral similarity" to him.[30] Gwendolen's darkest propensities, the lamia or serpent tendencies foretold in the imagery of the opening chapter of the novel, are reflected back at her later in Grandcourt. Above all, her passion for acting her own identity for admiring beholders, superficially so unlike Grandcourt's habitual role of cold contempt for an audience, has strong underground roots in common with his hidden nature. Both are ruthless egoists whose vanity, for all its morbid self-absorption, requires for regular sustenance the envious admiration of others. Grandcourt, though he "went about with the sense that he did not care a languid curse for any one's admiration," was in continual need of "a world of admiring or envying spectators." If you "are fond of looking stonily at smiling persons," Eliot assures us, "the persons must be there and they must smile" (xlviii.440). Gilbert Osmond of *The Portrait of a Lady*, James's own "most self-conscious of men,"[31] whose "egotism lay hidden like a serpent in a bank of flowers," whose life was absorbed in fulfilling the role of disdainful "first gentleman of Europe," a part he could maintain only through an enormous expenditure of calculation and ingenuity, seems to have traits in common with both Grandcourt and Gwendolen. For Osmond tries like Grandcourt (if less successfully, being possessed of a cleverer but more mercurial disposition and far less substantial claims on the world's deference) to display "a sovereign contempt for every one but some three or four very exalted people whom he envied, and for everything in the world but half a dozen ideas of his own." As Gwendolen enacts the role of "princess in exile," so Osmond is intent on playing "a prince who has abdicated in a fit of fastidiousness." He keeps a watchful "eye to effect, and his effects were deeply calculated." Osmond strives "to surround his interior with a sort of invidious sanctity . . . to impart to the face that he presented to the world a cold originality." The cultivated attitude of cold aloofness, the conscious enacting of the "drama of incommunicability," suggests Grandcourt; but the energy and the cleverness of the acting suggest Gwendolen. And like both of them, "Osmond *lived exclusively for the world*. Far from being its master as he pretended to be, he was its very humble servant, and the degree of its attention was his only measure of success" (italics mine).

"Drama," W. J. Harvey observes, "is nearly always in George Eliot's novels a metaphor for the self-deluding, dream-spinning, narcissistic type of egoism of which Rosamond is an example."[32] Drama as metaphor figures as a motif of importance in *Middlemarch*, as has been suggested at some length in chapter four. Rosamond is, of course, more than any other inhabitant of *Middlemarch*, an anticipation of the prominence that dramatizing one's identity is to take as a theme in *Daniel Deronda*. She is "by nature an actress of parts that entered into her *physique*; she even acted her own character, and so well, that she did not know it to be precisely her own" (xii.87). The sentence could apply with equal or greater force to Gwendolen. Indeed, Gwendolen, as a critic has already remarked, is "a Rosamond Vincy expanded into a fuller creation, but a Rosamond Vincy still."[33] That is, she is less remarkable for the range and complexity of her own intense but limited inner experience than she is for the part she plays in the lives of others and for the interest of the forces that impinge upon her self-absorbed nature. As "Constantius" sees the matter in James's review, "The very chance to embrace what the author is so fond of calling a 'larger life' seems refused to her. She is punished for being narrow and she is not allowed a chance to expand." James's view of Gwendolen is, however, more complicated than the quotation might suggest, as will be seen in the next chapter.

NOTES

1. See chapter I, p. 9.
2. F. R. Leavis, *The Great Tradition* (1948; New York, 1954), pp. 57–58.
3. I omit *Silas Marner* (1861) as a work of less than novel length. It is not to any marked degree a study in illusion. Silas himself is, like Romola (discussed in the next pages) essentially acted upon rather than engaged in any very active imaginative life.

We learn relatively little of his inward experience though that little is made much of, in a way, as he becomes gradually reconciled to the world in which he has suffered the worst sort of betrayal by a friend and then, after long years of hoarding money, has undergone a second betrayal by fate in having his hoard stolen. James in 1866 considered *Silas Marner* Eliot's achievement to that date in terms of unity of form (an aspect of her art in which he considered her woefully deficient elsewhere) but has little to say about the "poor, dull-witted, disappointed Methodist cloth-weaver" around whom the story is built. See his "The Novels of George Eliot," *Views and Reviews* (Boston, 1908), p. 8. The essay originally appeared in *The Atlantic Monthly* for October, 1866.

4. "The Novels of George Eliot," pp. 29, 34–35. Young James's praise of Tito is quite moderate—a long remove from the sort of enthusiasm he was later to award such personages as Dorothea Brooke, Tertius Lydgate, Gwendolen Harleth, or Henleigh Grandcourt.

5. *The Art of George Eliot* (London, 1963), pp. 182–183.

6. Leavis, p. 73.

7. *Felix Holt, Radical, The Works of George Eliot* (New York, 1910), V, chapter I, pp. 39–40. Further quotations from *Felix Holt* will be identified by chapter and page number of this edition in parentheses.

8. *George Eliot* (London, 1964), p. 137.

9. Leavis, p. 75.

10. Harvey, p. 88.

11. *The Novels of George Eliot* (New York, 1959), p. 125.

12. See my discussion of Hetty Sorrel in chapter I, pp. 22–23.

13. See especially Harvey, p. 44, and U. C. Knoepflmacher, *George Eliot's Early Novels: The Limits of Reason* (Berkeley, Cal., 1968), pp. 122 ff.

14. *The Novels of George Eliot* (1959; New York, 1963), p. 26.

15. *Adam Bede*, ed. Gordon S. Haight (New York, 1959), chapter xxii, p. 256, italics mine. Further quotations from *Adam Bede* will be identified by chapter and page number of this edition in parentheses.

16. *George Eliot's Early Novels*, p. 122.

17. *Movement and Vision in George Eliot's Novels* (Seattle, Washington, 1959), p. 33.

18. *Daniel Deronda*, with an introduction by F. R. Leavis (New York, 1960), chapter ii, p. 10, italics mine, except for *naïve*. Chapter and page numbers in parentheses following further quotations refer to this edition.

19. R. T. Jones, *George Eliot* (Cambridge, 1970), p. 99.

20. Gordon S. Haight, *George Eliot: A Biography* (New York, 1968), p. 446.

21. "*Daniel Deronda*: A Conversation," in *A Century of George Eliot Criticism*, ed. Gordon S. Haight (Boston, 1965), p. 101.

22. Gordon S. Haight, "George Eliot's Klesmer," in *Imagined Worlds: Essays in Honour of John Butt*, ed. Maynard Mack and Ian Gregor (London, 1968), pp. 205–214. The young Rubinstein frequently shared meals in the fall of 1854 with the Leweses at the Hotel Erbprinz at Weimar, where he was about to produce his opera *The Siberian Huntsman*. I offer as a speculation of very little importance: Rubinstein may well have discussed Tom Moore's *Lalla Rookh*, later to become Rosamond Vincy's favorite poem, with George Eliot and possibly have imprinted it better in her creative memory. He was to make *Lalla Rookh* the basis of his opera *Feramors*, and he would likely take his opportunity for discussing the work with a talented Englishwoman.

23. *The Novels of George Eliot*, p. 229.

24. Eliot had used the same image for Lydgate's appalled impression of Rosamond

217

in chapter lxv of *Middlemarch*. For an excellent fuller discussion of Eliot's subtleties in discoursing in images, see chapters 9–11 of Barbara Hardy's *The Novels of George Eliot*.

25. "What had George Eliot to learn from psycho-analysis?" Laurence Lerner inquires. "As a novelist, surely little or nothing." For an analysis at some length of Gwendolen's frightened discovery of "destructive powers in herself," see his "The Education of Gwendolen Harleth," *The Critical Quarterly*, VII (1965), 355–364.

26. "Daniel Deronda," *The Spectator*, XLIX (9 September 1876), 1131–32.

27. Haight, *George Eliot: A Biography*, p. 477.

28. *The George Eliot Letters*, ed. Gordon S. Haight (New Haven, 1954–55), VI, 280.

29. "*Daniel Deronda*: A Conversation," pp. 101, 110.

30. *The Great Tradition* (1948; Garden City, N. Y., 1954), p. 135.

31. *The Portrait of a Lady*, ed. Leon Edel (Boston, 1956), chapter xxxv, p. 289. Further quotations from *Portrait* in this paragraph occur at xxiii.210, xxxix.324–325, and xlix, 353–354.

32. *The Art of George Eliot*, p. 59.

33. U. C. Knoepflmacher, *Religious Humanism and the Victorian Novel: George Eliot, Walter Pater, and Samuel Butler* (Princeton, N. J., 1965), p. 124.

VI

CONCLUSION: THREE VERSIONS OF INTERNALIZED DRAMA

i. Gwendolen, Dorothea, and James's "young person of many theories"

HENRY JAMES, ON READING THE FIRST OF THE EIGHT MONTHLY INstalments in which *Daniel Deronda* initially appeared, was moved to welcome George Eliot's new novel in print without waiting for the rest. Already he was seized with an impression of vast universal import, of "messages from mysterious regions," as by some new sort of cosmic telegraphy. He was nevertheless puzzled as to the direction Gwendolen Harleth's story was to take, whether she was perhaps destined to remain "unexpectedly narrow," as she had struck him as being thus far—"whether, as we may say in speaking of a companion work to *Middlemarch*, the Dorothea element or the Rosamond element is to prevail."[1]

His impression of Gwendolen's tendency toward the Rosamond element was to be confirmed. His reactions by the time of his ambitious review of the completed novel had become curiously mixed, so that he resorted to the unusual and interesting form of a "Conversation" in which three different persons pronounce their opinions.[2] Constantius is the central figure and the most authoritative voice of the three. He is a regular writer of critiques, and he has published a novel of his own (James had within the year brought out his first novel, *Roderick Hudson*). When Theodora—both her outlook and the elements of her name suggest Dorothea—on whom Constantius is paying a call, suggests that he is turning severe in his judgment of Eliot, he is quick to deny the charge: "I defy any one to admire her more, but one must discriminate. Speaking brutally, I consider *Daniel Deronda* the weakest of her books. It strikes me as very inferior to *Middlemarch*. I have an immense opinion of *Middlemarch*." But Constantius, for all his feeling that as a responsible reviewer he must make careful discriminations, is in peril throughout the conversation of lapsing into overenthusiastic judgments upon Eliot, as he is well aware: "I can read nothing of George Eliot's without enjoyment. I even enjoy her poetry, though I don't approve of it. . . . The intellectual brilliancy of *Daniel Deronda* strikes me as very great, in excess of anything the author had [sic] done."

It is apparently as a charming and whimsical kind of caveat for his reader against his own tendency toward uncritical enthusiasms for Eliot that James has devised Pulcheria as a third voice. She is a young lady of precise opinions who has little respect for Eliot's novels. Pulcheria compels Constantius to concede that her strictures are often fully understandable and sometimes entirely justified—especially her finding absurdity in many moments of the Daniel Deronda part of the novel, the part that Constantius himself considers "the cold half of the book": "All the Jewish part is at bottom cold; that is my only objection. *I have enjoyed it because my fancy often warms cold things*; but beside Gwendolen's history it is like the full half of the lunar disk beside the empty one. It is admirably studied, it is imagined, it is understood; but it is not realized" (italics mine). As for the Gwendolen half, Constantius if more careful in framing his statements is nearly as enthusiastic as Theodora: "Gwendolen and Grandcourt are admirable. Gwendolen is a masterpiece. She is known, felt, and presented, psychologically, altogether in the grand manner." And later on, when Pulcheria wishes to dismiss Gwendolen as "a second-rate English girl who spoke of her mother as 'my mamma,' and got into a flutter about a lord," Constantius again insists that her entire history is "superbly told . . . it holds such a wealth of psychological detail, it is more than masterly."

Pulcheria is not intimidated. It is the "narrowness" that James had spoken of in his first review that constitutes Pulcheria's chief objection to Gwendolen, and it is one that she maintains with point and vigor: "The portrait may be admirable, but it has one little fault. *You don't care a straw for the original. Gwendolen is not an interesting girl,* and when the author tries to invest her with a deep tragic interest she does so at the expense of consistency. She has made her at the outset too light, too flimsy; tragedy has no hold on such a girl" (italics mine). Theodora, whose delight in Eliot's novels is so extreme that she would wish *Daniel Deronda* to start up once again and keep coming out in monthly instalments forever, "to be one of the regular things of life," complains that Pulcheria is "hard to satisfy. You said this morning that Dorothea was too heavy, and now you find Gwendolen too light." A few further exchanges lead to Theodora's most judicious speech of the conversation: "Gwendolen is a perfect picture of youthfulness—its eagerness, its presumption, its preoccupation with itself, its vanity and silliness, its sense of its own absoluteness. But she is extremely clever, and therefore tragedy *can* have a hold upon her."

What seems to be taking place in the "Conversation" is that James, whose tendency to make the criticized thing his own—particularly when George Eliot is in question—is finely analyzed by W. J. Harvey,[3] is despite all the warnings of Pulcheria viewing Gwendolen from a highly selective point of sight as a "typical" George Eliot heroine. In the speech Constantius adds in assent to Theodora's—his own most ambitious statement of the "Conversation"—Gwendolen's uniquely serpentine characteristics, her conscious choice in a gamble for wealth and prestige of marriage to a man she cannot possibly consider morally acceptable, her terrible discovery of her own demonic inclinations for murdering him, are outside his selective focus, and in a memorable pronouncement Gwendolen becomes one of Eliot's representative young women, rather than the lamia-inclined and most darkly sinister of all Eliot's portrayals of women: "That is perfectly true. Gwendolen's history is admirably typical—as most things are with George Eliot; it is the very stuff that human life is made of. What is it made of but the discovery by each of us that we are at the best but a rather ridiculous fifth wheel to the coach, after we have sat cracking our whip and believing that we are at least the coachman in person? We think we are the main hoop to the barrel, and we turn out to be but a very incidental splinter in one of the staves."

Gwendolen might well complain that she had had to learn her

lesson in cruel and unusual instalments bordering on melodrama rather than through typical experience. She had learned a part of it in a fit of screaming, strewing diamonds about the floor, and another part beholding the dead face of her private fantasies materialize as her husband's drowning countenance. In any event, Constantius's pronouncement as he continues it seems in important ways more prophetic of James's own heroine of a novel not yet written than it does of Gwendolen's particular history: "The universe, forcing itself with a slow, inexorable pressure into a narrow, complacent, and yet after all extremely sensitive mind, and making it ache with the pain of the process—that is Gwendolen's story."

It is the general story of Emma Bovary and of Hetty Sorrel as well. And it is the story of Dorothea Brooke-Casaubon, except that *narrow* must be omitted or applied with a different meaning and the special nature of her complacency taken into account. These are the limitations one must also make for fitting the description to the story of James's own Isabel Archer of *The Portrait of a Lady*. For Dorothea, to a much greater extent than has been generally recognized, is the real spiritual progenitor of Isabel Archer. Neither Dorothea nor Isabel is narrow in outlook but quite the contrary. Isabel, like Dorothea, possesses in the very essentials of her temperament a passion for idealities that Hetty and Gwendolen do not share and that Emma entertains only when she can invest them with a paradoxical sensuous palpability, as in her erotic visions of deity. Dorothea's nature, Eliot makes explicit, is "altogether ardent, theoretic, and intellectually consequent" (iii.21). Her passionate idealism, her pursuing theories about living that to her are not mere theories but channels for consequent action, leads her, in an excess of faith and a blindness to obvious pitfalls, into a marriage that a less ardently theoretical nature would have found it ludicrous even to consider. "All Dorothea's passion was transfused through a mind struggling towards an ideal life; the radiance of her transfigured girlhood fell on the first object that came within its level" (v.32). Casaubon's talk, full of pretensions to standing on the threshold of vast scholarly achievement, opened to Dorothea's mind a sense of wide vistas, the promise of a life filled with "action at once rational and ardent" (x.64).

As for Isabel Archer, "The idea of the whole thing," James records in his notebook regarding his plans for the novel, "is that the poor girl, who has dreamed of freedom and nobleness, who has done, as she believes, a generous, natural, clear-sighted thing, finds herself in reality ground in the very mill of the conventional."[4] (The central subject of *Middlemarch*, James had written in his review of that novel, the subject central "doubtless in intention" though "not distinctly enough in fact," was the portrayal of an "ardent young girl framed for a larger moral life than circumstance often affords, yearning for a motive for sustained spiritual effort and only wasting her ardor and soiling her wings against the meanness of opportunity."[5]) Isabel Archer, James writes in the completed novel, was "a young person of many theories; her imagination was remarkably active" so that "among her contemporaries she passed for a young woman of extraordinary profundity."[6] Isabel "spent half her time in thinking of beauty and bravery and magnanimity" and was determined to believe the world a "place of brightness, of free expansion, of irresistible action." Her "deepest enjoyment," James remarks in a tone strongly reminiscent of Eliot's in describing Miss Brooke's expansive outlook on life in the opening chapters of *Middlemarch*, "was to feel the continuity between the movements of her own soul and the agitations of the world" (iv.41).

Isabel's distortions of vision are essentially Dorothea's, and Isabel's misconceptions regarding Osmond are in important respects quite similar to Dorothea's regarding Casaubon despite the wide divergences in character between the two husbands. Isabel is betrayed, as she comes to see by the time of her long internal monologue, by her "ardent good faith. She was wrong, *but she believed*; she was deluded, *but she was dismally consistent*. It was wonderfully characteristic of her that, *having invented a fine theory about Gilbert Osmond, she loved him not for what he really possessed, but for his very poverties dressed out as honours*" (xxxiv.288, italics mine).

ii. Eliot and James: the Novel of Gradual Action and Motionless Seeing

Dorothea and Isabel—unlike Hetty or Emma Bovary or Gwendolen—want when they consult their mirrors to see themselves occupying less than the full glass and reflected in the process of carrying out expansive actions consequentially related to noble theories. It is a large difference and one that goes far toward determining the character of the two stories in which they serve as heroines. There may be serious doubts, as Pulcheria suggests, about tragedy's taking a convincing hold on Gwendolen, but there can be no doubt about its working actively in the far more generous inward experience of Dorothea and Isabel. The inexorable pressure of the universe works upon them more slowly and with less trace in external action.

George Eliot wrote John Blackwood that her intention in *Middlemarch* was "to show the gradual action of ordinary causes rather than exceptional." She was attempting to present such gradual action in fresh ways rather than along the timeworn paths—"the Cremorne walks and shows"—of traditional fiction.[7] Her special consciousness of pioneering in tracing the slow attrition of lofty but illusory aspirations in *Middlemarch,* and especially in the careers of Dorothea, Casaubon, and Lydgate, has been considered at length in chapter four. James recorded in his notebook a similar intention of working with gradual causes largely to the exclusion of exciting overt incident. It would, he felt, require all his best resources to present his "opposition of a noble character and a narrow one" in a way that would make Isabel's delusion regarding Osmond command the reader's full interest.

In his "Preface" for *The Portrait of a Lady,* written a quarter-century later for the revised collected edition of his works, James recalls the pride he had taken in making his slight heroine—"the mere slim shade of an intelligent but presumptuous girl"—the sole center of interest. Shakespeare and George Eliot, he says, had been content to enhance the appeal of their "frail vessels," their slender heroines,[8] with underplots and additional centers of interest. But he had in his novel braved the "difficulty of making George Eliot's 'frail vessel,' if not the all-in-all for our attention, at least the clearest of the call." His special pride with Isabel had been what Eliot's had been with Dorothea; he had proposed to avoid sensational exterior incident and to demonstrate "what an 'exciting' inward life may do for the person leading it even while it remains perfectly normal." Isabel's long internal monologue was designed as a "representation simply of her motionlessly *seeing,* and an attempt withal to make the mere still lucidity of her act as 'interesting' as the surprise of a caravan or the identification of a pirate."

Such exercises in motionless seeing are, as was suggested in some detail in chapter four, a prominent feature of Dorothea's story. They are treated at less length in *Middlemarch* but with a greater frequency. Already in *Middlemarch* there is a pronounced tendency of the novelist to relegate to extended passages of analysis the moments of revelation that come to the characters. The action that matters most in the forward movement of the Dorothea-Casaubon story or the story of Lydgate and Rosamond occurs predominantly in passages in which the narrator, opening to view the inward life of the character and speaking for him in the clarity of her own controlling vision, enlarges on his patterns of thought and reverie. Notable among such passages but suggestive of many more are Casaubon's baffled growing awareness that courtship, like patient scholarly endeavor, has failed to warm his life, or later his growing impression that marriage to Dorothea has provided him a cruel accuser rather than a fence against the unapplausive world; Lydgate's progressive demoralization in the tentacles of debt and his gradually accumulating awareness that he must abandon the upper world of his fine aspirations to walk uninspired paths carrying the heavy burden of his wife;—above all, Dorothea's dream of a life freed from petty courses through a liberating marriage and her subsequent struggles to define for herself the chilling realities of a marriage that had become "a perpetual struggle of energy with fear" (xxxix.285).

This is not the method of Henry James, who in *The Portrait of a Lady* is already working his way toward the sort of Flaubertian ideal of "impersonality" for the narrator that would characterize his later fiction; but it is George Eliot's own way of escaping the constrictions of the traditional novel with its heavy reliance on scenes like those of acted drama, limited to dialogue and a single time and setting, for its excitement. In *Middlemarch* she has perfected her way of rendering exciting what takes place in the interior life of her characters, centering the important action, as James was to do to a still larger extent, in the moral and psychological action of her narrative. *Middlemarch* has no dearth of traditional scenes; but, as Quentin Anderson observes, it is in the "fine and satisfying analytic passages"[9] presented in Eliot's own superb voice as narrator that the great preponderance of memorable passages occur. *Daniel Deronda* had been in this respect a retreat on Eliot's part, especially in the Deronda story. It is probably the much greater resort to isolated scene and dialogue in *Daniel Deronda* that impelled James to make Pulcheria complain, "I never read a story with less current. It is not a river; it is a series of lakes." Constantius is inclined to agree: "I know what you mean by Daniel Deronda lacking current. *It has almost as little as Romola*" (italics mine).

Stephen Spender credits James rather than George Eliot with the important discovery—it is in Spender's view "James's great contribution to the novel"—that "passionate activity is intellectual activity." In James as later in Joyce and Proust, the major revelations that come to the protagonists tend to occur not in traditional scenes but in passages of intensive solitary vision. Though scenes involving dialogue that are highly dramatic still occur, their emphasis in James's fiction is in the main "not revelatory; they are the climax of what has already been revealed" in moments of inward experience.[10] Such emphasis on passionate intellectual activity on the part of fine intelligences had already been presented, as we have seen, in George Eliot's *Middlemarch* and especially in her portrayal of the inward experience of Dorothea Brooke-Casaubon. For Dorothea, like Isabel Archer and so many of James's later protagonists of fine intelligence engaged in the drama of inward vision, already demonstrates the sort of excitement a novelist can achieve by placing his emphasis on moments of still lucidity rather than the adventures of pirates or desert caravans. In novels to come much later than *The Portrait of a Lady*, James, it is true, takes to making dialogue itself a vehicle for conveying the excitement of pursuing lucidity. Such periods of co-operation between people engaged in a search for relatively abstract meanings of situation or motive occur with some frequency in *The Wings of the Dove* and in *The Ambassadors*. But the emphasis is still, as with Dorothea Brooke and Isabel Archer, on persons of fine intelligence, persons tending to be passionately theoretical (their "passion," as Austin Warren says, "goes into their seeing"[11]), and James in such scenes was to contrive a highly effective fresh way (anticipated after a fashion in the dialogues of Will Ladislaw and Dorothea) of lending psychological narrative dealing with fine intelligences its particular kind of excitement.

If George Eliot can with some justice be awarded primacy as "the novelist of the idolatries of the super-ego,"[12] so can Henry James in his turn and time be singled out as the "historian of fine consciences." It is Joseph Conrad's term for him, based on James's so often making central to his fiction characters working toward some fine act of renunciation to be performed in a manner "energetic, not violent." The difference, Conrad says, is "wide, enormous, like that between substance and shadow." James has typically dispensed with the older method of solving plots "with rewards and punishments,"[13] Conrad had, of course, by 1905 done not a little work along similar lines himself; but George Eliot in *Middlemarch*, in both the Dorothea and Lydgate movements of her novel, had anticipated James's practice by a good many years. In James's earlier novels, notably in *Roderick Hudson* and *The American*, moments of something very like melodrama had figured in ways James was to reject with rare exceptions beginning with *The Portrait of a Lady*. His determination with that novel to write in such a manner as to render the nonviolent inward life exciting had proved rewarding. He had obviously hit upon his proper subject. The characters surrounding Isabel Archer, he tells us in his "Preface," seemed to arrange themselves about her almost without effort ("I seem to myself to have waked up one morning in possession of them"). The parallels of subject and treatment in George Eliot's own great novel of gradual nonviolent causes at work in the activity of consciences both coarse and fine (from Bulstrode to Dorothea), all of them areas of passionate intellectual activity, have been examined at length in chapter four. It is in *Middlemarch* that Eliot most clearly anticipates James and, to a lesser degree, the psychological novelists of the twentieth century. However much James found to his hand in other writers, the great and obvious fact of his career—obvious enough, perhaps, as to make comment superfluous—is nevertheless his own splendid originality. Isabel Archer possesses in her outlook and situation significant points in common with George Eliot's frail vessels of experience that had preceded her, but *The Portrait of a Lady* is fresh creative work entitled, as Leon Edel says, to claim without apology consideration among the best novels of the century. James had created an American heroine who could take her place (with Dorothea Brooke and Emma Bovary among others) "in the great gallery of the world's fiction."[14]

iii. FLAUBERT AND JAMES: THE NOVEL OF CENTRAL CONSCIOUSNESS AND TOTAL RELEVANCE

In *The Portrait of a Lady* James is exploring territories that Eliot in the manner of her own idiom had already explored with brilliant success, but he is also in important respects following paths already taken by Flaubert in *Madame Bovary*. Though Emma Bovary is not a fine intelligence in a Jamesian sense, her agile imagination dominates Flaubert's novel as a central focus for his tightly unified plan. Her felt presence determines the subject throughout the novel, and perhaps more intensely so than ever in the scenes that occur after her death. There is no accurate calculating in such matters, but it is probable that Joyce[15] and Proust, especially Proust, owed more to Flaubert than they did to James, the essential fineness of whose vessels of experience rendered them remote from the kind of sensuous and biological perceptual data often figuring large in their novels. In playing the game of art in his particular way, however, James was already with *The Portrait of a Lady* meeting a part of the challenges Flaubert had set for himself as artist in *Madame Bovary*. " 'Place the centre of the subject in the young woman's own consciousness,' " James tells us in his "Preface" that he had said to himself, " 'and you get as interesting and as beautiful a difficulty as you could wish. Stick to *that*—for the centre; put the heaviest weight into *that* scale, which will be so largely the scale of her relation to herself. Make her only interested enough, at the same time, in the things that are not herself, and this relation needn't fear to be too limited. Place meanwhile in the other scale the lighter weight . . . press least hard, in short, on the consciousnesses of your heroine's satellites, especially the male; make it an interest contributive only to the greater one.' " James had recorded in his notebook his fear that the whole story would be considered "too exclusively psychological," a fear that had beset Flaubert in regard to *Madame Bovary*.[16] Like Flaubert, however, James had determined to risk putting all his stress on his heroine's relation to herself, making Isabel's extended monologue the high point of the novel. The scheme worked splendidly. The chapter of Isabel's motionless and solitary seeing became "obviously the best thing in the book" and at the same time "only a supreme illustration of the general plan."

228

Looking back from the perspective of his "Preface," James could pronounce *The Portrait of a Lady* "the most proportioned" of all his works with the single exception of *The Ambassadors*.

James functions as an omniscient narrator in *The Portrait of a Lady*, albeit a relatively self-effacing one. He has not yet developed his full resources, and it could easily be argued that Flaubert's *Madame Bovary* of 1857, with its objective method and its poetic power of rendering the ugly and the commonplace vivid and memorable, represents a more modern novel than James's novel of 1881. A central intelligence already dominates James's story, however, and Isabel's pivotal extended internal monologue anticipates the method of such later works as *The Ambassadors*, with the novelist's own felt presence characteristically refined from his scene. This is what Percy Lubbock would call James's fully "dramatizing" his material.[17] It is *The Ambassadors* (1903) that Lubbock elects to analyze at greatest length along with *Madame Bovary* in his widely influential *The Craft of Fiction* (1921), presenting Flaubert and James as the twin luminaries of the internalized narrative. Flaubert, focusing his center of interest in the inward experience of Emma Bovary, had removed the bulk of his action to "the reverberating theatre" of Emma's imagination. In theory, the reader looks directly into the inner experience of Flaubert's heroine as if he were witnessing live action or live thought. James was to perfect this process of permitting the reader to dispense with the intervention of the narrator until there was "no further to go." Neither Flaubert nor James, despite his refinements in the technique, actually attains, of course, anything like full withdrawal, as Lubbock himself is careful to state (and as my analyses of Flaubert's method in chapter two bear witness). "Impersonality" is a tendency and not an absolute; it concerns the author's working with greater tact in the way he conveys his own feelings, "embodying them in living form, instead of stating them directly."

The immense influence of both Flaubert and James upon novelists, still more upon critics, through the first half of the twentieth century tended strongly to transform their theory of the novel as autonomous aesthetic form, fashioned to an "impersonal" method of narration and unified around a central intelligence, into dogma. So much so that defenses of the expansive novel of multiple plots and shifting perspectives or able analyses of the authorial intrusion as an expressive instrument capable (as with George Eliot) of highly sophisticated uses acquired much point and value. Such ambitious statements as those of Barbara Hardy and Wayne Booth[18] have helped to balance matters and make abundantly evident that there are many methods rather than one of laboring with good results in the house of fiction. To what extent James's intimate acquaintance with *Madame Bovary* influenced him in the formulating of his own doctrine of a central intelligence to be "dramatized" as his subject is not at all clear, nor likely to become so. Of greater importance, at least for the present study, is the fact that in *Madame Bovary* Flaubert had already taken the theory and practice of the novel a long distance in the direction of James and Proust and Joyce. From the monologues of Jane Austen's Emma (essentially brilliant dialogues between two or more of Emma's delightful social selves) to the monologues of Flaubert's Emma (or Eliot's Dorothea) is a long distance, for good or for otherwise, depending on one's predilections, toward the interior monologues of Strether, Marcel, Mrs. Ramsay, or even Molly Bloom.

iv. GEORGE ELIOT, FLAUBERT, JAMES, AND THE MODERN NOVEL

Jane Austen was the last great English novelist who could assume that the inner worlds of herself and her characters corresponded in all essential respects and provided a fairly reliable version of the outer world they had in common. She could take "a stable and hierarchic society absolutely for granted" and enjoy a confidence that her readers shared with only shadings of difference her own main beliefs and values.[19] Small wonder that Virginia Woolf, speaking from the distance of a century, colored her intense admiration of her great predecessor with an approach to envy, observing wistfully that to "believe that your impressions hold good for others is to be released from the cramp and confinement of personality." It was a belief that even by the mid-nineteenth century Flaubert and George Eliot had been obliged to do without. Belief in the validity of heroic versions of the inner life as extolled by the Romantics was denied them also. For by mid-century, science had borne in upon them an inescapable sense of void outer space that made the heroic postures of Werther or Manfred or Chateaubriand's René something that must be viewed with irony, and the reveries of more prosaic figures bent on pursuing their own heroic visions a subject of irony as well. For "we all of us, grave or light," Eliot tells us in *Middlemarch*, "get our thoughts entangled in metaphors, and act fatally on the strength of them" (x.63). Dorothea Brooke aspires to be light-bearer to a scholar-hero, and Casaubon's deep-set eyes and grave pedantries are enough to sanction her plunge into a Quixotic marriage; Lydgate dreams of becoming another Vesalius and meanwhile rushes valiantly (as Lochinvar might have done) to the rescue of a beautiful actress who has in fact—though beauty in romantic literature is always innocent—murdered her husband; Casaubon will settle for no less a labor than the production of a synthetic Key to all Mythologies, a task for an intellectual Hercules; Bulstrode, in some ways the most heroic of them all, insists on intimate bargains with Providence; Rosamond, though the least aspiring of Eliot's main characters, fosters romantic notions of an aristocratic marriage and a honeymoon at Quallingham, her own version of Vaubyessard. Theological tracts are the literature on which Dorothea Brooke founds her illusion, and a largely oral and debased version of them is strong in Bulstrode's private reality.

It is the lyrical poets that betray Casaubon with false promises of the joys awaiting him in courtship; but it is Scott and Tom Moore and the keepsakes that foster the visions of Lydgate and Rosamond regarding marriage, even as Scott and Lamartine and the French keepsakes nourish Emma Bovary's visions. For Flaubert's heroine and for Eliot's protagonists in *Middlemarch*, the assurances they find in literature of an exterior reality conforming to their romantic and egoistic inward visions play them false. Whatever the particular form heroic aspiration takes in their experience, it is presented as a pattern of illusion; and the emphasis in *Middlemarch*, as in *Madame Bovary*, is placed upon the contrast of the warmly lighted and flattering world of imaginative vision and the plain and often ugly facts of the outer world with which the human being, whatever goes on in his private experience, must come to terms.

The counterpointing of inner and outer realities, typically in ironic contrast, is a prominent feature, as we have seen, of both novels. It involves the narrator's assuming, whether he makes his ironic commentary mainly by the "impersonal" juxtaposition of scene with scene or object with object as Flaubert so often does, or whether he supplies his commentary in his own controlling voice, as with George

Eliot, that he himself has a solid grip on the character's environment and can work as a realist even while he works as well as an explorer of the inner life of his characters. James was in this regard, even in his last novels, a nineteenth-century writer rather than of the twentieth century. For though his settings do not possess the full vital particularity of Flaubert's or Eliot's, they are still firmly anchored in time and space. Strether's Paris is less substantial than Flaubert's Yonville or Eliot's Middlemarch; but it is solidity itself compared to the myth countries of Marcel's past or Stephen Telemachus's exploded present. Maupassant, Flaubert's disciple, with his own best art to all appearances so firmly grounded in Norman reality, could by 1888 declare his unbelief in any stability of his outer world. The Realist was at best only an Illusionist merely pretending that his impressions could hold good for others: "How childish it is, indeed, to believe in such reality, since for each of us his reality is in his own mind, his own organs. Our eyes, our ears, our powers of taste and smell, create as many different realities as there are human beings on earth. And our brains, informed by those organs, apprehend, analyze, and judge as differently as if each of us belonged to a different race. Each of us . . . has simply his own illusion of the world—an illusion poetical, sentimental, joyous, melancholy, foul, or gloomy in accordance with his own nature."[20] In England by the eighteen-nineties role-playing had ceased to be, as with Rodolphe Boulanger or Rosamond Vincy, a matter of preferring to project a self other than one's own and had become instead a desperately serious matter of finding any sort of self whatever to inhabit.[21] Arthur Symons, said Oscar Wilde (and the phrase could easily be directed back upon him) was a "sad example of an Egoist who had no Ego." The outer world was turning progressively alien, and the mind of the artist was already feeling a resignation beyond that of Flaubert, despite his temperamental fascination with chaos, or Eliot, for all her determination to "do without opium" and face clear-eyed and unblenching all the implications of outer darkness that the scientists could reveal to her. The artist was to retreat much farther inward, and the novel in the twentieth century was to tend to "live permanently inside the minds of its characters."[22]

Eliot's parable of the polished pier glass (borrowed, it seems, appropriately from observations of the philosopher of science Herbert Spencer[23] and played in variations throughout *Middlemarch*) suggests the degree to which, in anticipation of later novelists, she saw each person viewing the world as an isolated individual, shaping his reading of experience concentric to his own minuscule area of outer reality. The drama of incommunicability is written large in *Middlemarch*, even as it is in *Madame Bovary*. The scene at the Comices agricoles, Flaubert's brilliant epitome, is echoed throughout the novel, not only in Emma's frantic searches for someone who can speak her own language but in such sensational failures in communication as Homais' letters to the *Fanal de Rouen* or his dialogues over Emma's corpse with the Abbé Bournisien. The lovers' dialogue between Rosamond and Lydgate is a less brilliant but no less pointed enactment of the illusion of sharing where there is in fact no meeting of minds; and it leads to an inexorably real drama of protracted incommunicability, disillusionment, and the failure of high purposes—a tragedy of unpaid butcher's bills, as Henry James called it, with a heroine that terrified T. S. Eliot more than Goneril or Regan.[24] George Eliot's correlatives for her own sense of human isolation in a darkened universe are less vivid and less violent than the scene of Emma's death by arsenic, though outside *Middlemarch*, at the beginning of her career, in her story of "The Lifted Veil" and in Hetty Sorrel's "Journey in Despair," and at the end with Gwendolen Harleth's obsessions with the dead face and fleeing figure, she embodies it with something approaching the darkness and drama of Emma's final moments. It is George Eliot's characteristic preference for keeping to the action of gradual causes, however, that is paralleled in the powerful enactment of human incommunicability that is central to James's *The Portrait of a Lady*. The theme of isolation and betrayal in a universe that has turned alien is for many readers more poignantly rendered there than in either *Madame Bovary* or any of George Eliot's novels. James, like Flaubert and George Eliot, is facing toward the twentieth century in his preoccupation with the isolated self and its experience of the gradual pressures that force it to surrender its romantic illusions and ache with the process.

Whether less or greater proximity to the twentieth century is for the novelist a good thing or a bad thing is, of course, a question without an answer. Where the high point in psychological narrative occurs, whether with Jane Austen or with James Joyce, is again a question that rewards the asking only if there is no expectation of much agreement in the replies. It is possible to maintain that Flaubert and George Eliot are not psychological narrators in any significant sense —that even James keeps to the surface of the mind rather than exploring the psyche at any depth that greatly matters. D. H. Lawrence felt, on the other hand, that with Joyce and Proust self-consciousness had been "picked into such fine bits that the bits are most of them invisible." The novel, he felt, was dying or already dead.[25] Ortega y Gassett also considered Proust's gigantic novel evidence that the novel was moribund, proof that themes feasible for exploration in fiction had already been exhausted, and the novelist had turned to the elaboration of incidental embellishments, slowing the movement of his work to a point where it seemed "more like a sequence of ecstatic stillnesses" than an action in progress. Perhaps Graham Hough's somewhat more optimistic view of the novel's future and the value of near-hermetic or overelaborate explorations of consciousness is better warranted: "If the novel were to continue on the lines of *Finnegan's Wake* and *The Waves* it would soon cease to exist: if it were to refuse to learn what can be learnt from them it might as well cease." Whatever comes next, or is already arriving, the novel has shown itself capable of immense and welcome variety. Fortunately one does not have to hold to any firm choice, whether he declares for the expansive novels like George Eliot's, where multiple plots and a freer principle of selection permit the novelist to keep "greater faith with the complexities, uncertainties, and changes" of his raw data, enabling his characters to create an impression of "acting from a complete existence,"[26] or whether he prefers the novel of total relevance, intensive focus, and (in some of its advanced versions) microscopic analysis. In what has seemed an inevitable resort to such terms as *pioneering, anticipating,* or *facing forward,* I have not, I trust, conveyed an impression of viewing the art of Flaubert or George Eliot or Henry James as in any way incomplete in itself. All three are secure of their positions among the world's great novelists. Rendering the fact clearer by seeing it from a fresh perspective has been the purpose of this book.

Conclusion

NOTES

1. *The Nation*, February 24, 1876, p. 31.
2. *"Daniel Deronda*: A Conversation," in *A Century of George Eliot Criticism*, ed. Gordon S. Haight (Boston, 1965), pp. 97–112.
3. *The Art of George Eliot* (London, 1963), pp. 14 ff.
4. "James's Notebook Entry," an appendix to *The Portrait of a Lady*, ed. Leon Edel (Boston, 1956), p. 485.
5. "George Eliot's *Middlemarch*," in *Henry James: The Future of the Novel*, ed. Leon Edel (New York, 1956), p. 82. The review was originally published in *The Galaxy* for March, 1873.
6. *The Portrait of a Lady*, ed. Leon Edel (Boston, 1956), ch. vi, p. 52. Further quotations from the novel will be keyed to this edition by chapter and page number in parentheses.
7. *The George Eliot Letters*, ed. Gordon S. Haight (New Haven, 1954–55) V, 168–169.
8. At the end of the eleventh chapter of *Daniel Deronda*, George Eliot generalizes regarding Gwendolen: "Could there be a slenderer, more insignificant thread in human history than this consciousness of a girl, busy with her small inferences of the way in which she could make her life pleasant? . . . In these delicate vessels is borne onward through the ages the treasure of human affections." James quotes the second of the two sentences in his "Preface" verbatim, except for replacing *delicate* with *frail* (possibly from the initial reading of the novel in instalments?). It is curious (though it is not at all likely that he was simply reluctant to invite the comparison) that James speaks of Eliot's "Hettys and Maggies and Rosamonds and Gwendolens" but does not mention Dorothea, the frail vessel of Eliot's by all odds closest in temperament and career to his own.
9. "George Eliot in *Middlemarch*," in *George Eliot: A Collection of Critical Essays*, ed. George R. Creeger (Englewood Cliffs, N. J., 1970), pp. 154–157. Anderson's statements are interestingly corroborated by Karl Kroeber's analyses in *Styles in Fictional Structure: The Art of Jane Austen, Charlotte Bronte, George Eliot* (Princeton, N. J., 1971). See especially his "Evaluations," pp. 181–196.
10. "The Contemporary Subject," in *Henry James: A Collection of Critical Essays*, ed. Leon Edel (Englewood Cliffs, N. J., 1963), pp. 104–105.
11. "Symbolic Imagery," in *Henry James: A Collection of Critical Essays*, p. 126.
12. V. S. Pritchett, "George Eliot," *The Living Novel* (London, 1946), p. 89.
13. "An Appreciation," in *Henry James: A Collection of Critical Essays*, pp. 15, 16.
14. *Henry James, The Conquest of London* (New York, 1962), p. 433.
15. For a highly interesting close analysis of Flaubert's fictional technique in relation to the fictional technique of James Joyce, see Richard K. Cross, *Flaubert and Joyce: The Rite of Fiction* (Princeton, N. J., 1971).
16. See my Chapter I, pp. 19–21.
17. *The Craft of Fiction* (1921; New York, 1957), p. 174. The "picture" of Strether's mind is "transformed into an enacted play" although for chapters together his story "is bare of action in the literal sense" and occupied with data that *"in the plain meaning of the word* is entirely undramatic" (italics mine). Quotations from Lubbock in the remainder of the paragraph occur at pages 189, 172, and 68 respectively.

18. Wayne Booth's *The Rhetoric of Fiction* (Chicago, 1961) and Barbara Hardy's *The Appropriate Form* (London, 1964). F. R. Leavis's *The Great Tradition* (1948) with its emphasis on the primacy of moral import over aesthetic form represents, of course, an earlier statement of the first importance. R. J. Sherrington in his interesting and challenging *Three Novels by Flaubert* (London, 1970), has devoted his book to showing in what ways Flaubert, despite his efforts at impersonality and unity of structure, worked in *Madame Bovary* and in his later novels essentially as a moralist.

19. David Daiches, *The Novel and the Modern World* (1938; Chicago, rev. ed., 1965), pp. 2–3. The quotation of Virginia Woolf that follows appears in Daiches, page 3.

20. Preface to *Pierre et Jean, Oeuvres complètes*, ed. Louis Conard (Paris, 1909), XVIII, xiv–xv.

21. Masao Miyoshi, *The Divided Self: A Perspective on the Literature of the Victorians* (New York, 1969), pp. 320 ff. Wilde's remark is quoted on page 321.

22. J. Isaacs, *An Assessment of Twentieth-Century Literature* (London, 1951), p. 82.

23. N. N. Feltes, "George Eliot's 'Pier-Glass': The Development of a Metaphor," *Modern Philology*, LXVII (1969), 69–71.

24. "George Eliot's *Middlemarch*," p. 86; T. S. Eliot's *The Three Voices of Poetry* (New York, 1954), p. 18.

25. "Surgery for the Novel—or a Bomb," *D. H. Lawrence: Selected Literary Criticism*, ed. Anthony Beal (New York, 1966), p. 115. For Ortega y Gassett, quoted later in the paragraph, see his *The Dehumanization of Art* (1948; Garden City, N. Y., n.d.), p. 74 *et passim*. For Graham Hough, see his *Image and Experience: Reflections on a Literary Revolution* (Lincoln, Nebraska, 1960), p. 78.

26. Barbara Hardy, *The Appropriate Form*, pp. 11, 12, 15.

INDEX

237

Darwin, Charles, *Origin of Species,*
15, 24, 198, 214.
Delacroix, Ferdinand, 106 n. 12.
Dickens, Charles, *Little Dorrit,* 125,
Our Mutual Friend, 125, 174.
Du Camp, Maxime, Letter to, 99.
Dumesnil, René, 48 n. 48.

Edel, Leon, 8, 46 n. 21, 123, 125–26,
185 n. 2, 218 n. 31, 227, 235 n. 4,
n. 6, n. 10.
ELH, 46 n. 21, 185 n. 2.
Eliot, George, v–vii, 1, 8–12, 21–28,
38–43, 98, 187–216 *passim,* 228, 230–
234; letter to, 28; translation, *Das
Leben Jesu,* see Strauss, D. F.
Works: *Adam Bede,* 22–23, 31,
32, 187, 188, 194, 195–199, 201, 204,
214, 222; *Daniel Deronda,* 6, 10, 97,
143, 147, 173–175, 187–198 *passim,*
212, 219–222, 235 n. 8; *Felix Holt,*
6, 190–193; "The Lifted Veil," 23–
24, 95, 214, 233; *Middlemarch,* v–
vii, 1–11 *passim,* 27, 28, 30, 32–35,
36–44 *passim,* 53, 80, 88, 97, 125–
185, 188, 193–195, 203, 211–216,
219, 223, 224, 226, 227, 231, 232–
233; *The Mill on the Floss,* 9, 188–
189, 190, 193; *Romola,* 6, 189–190,
193; *Silas Marner,* 6, 217 n. 3.
Eliot, T. S., 5, 233, 236 n. 24.

Fanger, Donald, 10, 73.
Feltes, N. N., 236 n. 23.
Flaubert, Gustave, v–vii, 1, 2–5, 6–8,
11–12, 16–21, 28, 31, 32–38, 44, 108–
123 *passim,* 128, 140, 148, 187, 195,
214, 225, 230, 231, 232, 234.
Works: *Bouvard et Pecuchet,* 114,
115; *Madame Bovary,* v–vii, 1–10
passim, 17–21, 28–30, 36, 43, 51–105
passim, 108–123 *passim,* 126–129,
135–136, 146, 157, 194, 228–231, 233;
Salammbô, 18–19, 78, 108–110; *Sentimental Education,* 108–114, 188;
A Simple Heart, 115–123; *The*

Temptation of Saint Anthony, 18,
31, 78, 79, 109, 110; *Three Tales,*
115.
Forster, E. M., 27, 42, 49 n. 76.

Galaxy, 45 n. 9, 125, 235 n. 5.
Garrett, Peter K., 46 n. 15.
Gibbon, Edward, 12.
Giraud, Raymond, 110, 124 n. 7.
Goncourt, Edmond de, 7.
Goncourt, Jules de, 7.
Greene, Philip Leon, 46 n. 21, 185 n. 2,
186 n. 11.

Haight, Gordon S., 28, 43, 45 n. 10,
48 n. 66, 135, 186 n. 12, 207, 217 n.
20, n. 21, n. 22, 218 n. 27, 235 n. 2,
n. 7.
Hardy, Barbara, 45 n. 4, 106 n. 9, 183,
186 n. 8, 208–209, 218, n. 24, 230,
236 n. 18, n. 26.
Harrison, Frederic, 26.
Harvey, W. J., 7, 45 n. 4, 46 n. 19, 185
n. 2, 186 n. 19, 190, 194, 216, 217 n.
10, n. 13, 221.
Hennell, Sara, letters to, 26, 156.
Holbach, Paul, 13.
Hölderlin, Johann, 13.
Hough, Graham, 234, 236 n. 25.
Hudson Review, 186 n. 16.
Hulme, Hilda M., 47 n. 32.
Hutton, Richard Holt, 212.
Huysmans, Camille, 30, 69.

Isaacs, J., 37, 52, 232, 236 n. 22.

Jaloux, Edmond, 9.
James, Henry, vi, 2, 3, 23, 30, 43 46,
51, 52, 146, 148, 149, 206, 217 n. 3,
n. 4, 222, 226, 227, 228, 230–234 *passim*; critiques, 2–8, of George Eliot,
5–6, 7–8, 25, 27, 32, 125–126, 140,
145, 176, 185, 189, 206, 217, 223–227;
of Flaubert, 4–5, 7, 45, 52, 105, 109,
126, 228–230.
Works: *The Ambassadors,* 226,